Fear Is Fuel

Fear Is Fuel

The Power to Help You Find Purpose, Passion, and Performance

Patrick J. Sweeney II

ROWMAN & LITTLEFIELD
Lanham • Boulder • New York • London

Published by Rowman & Littlefield
An imprint of The Rowman & Littlefield Publishing Group, Inc.
4501 Forbes Boulevard, Suite 200, Lanham, Maryland 20706
www.rowman.com

6 Tinworth Street, London SE11 5AL, United Kingdom

Distributed by NATIONAL BOOK NETWORK

British Library Cataloguing in Publication Information Available

Library of Congress Cataloging-in-Publication Data

Library of Congress Control Number: 2019953036
ISBN: 978-1-5381-3441-2 (cloth : alk. paper)
ISBN: 978-1-5381-3442-9 (electronic)

♾™ The paper used in this publication meets the minimum requirements
of American National Standard for Information Sciences—Permanence of
Paper for Printed Library Materials, ANSI/NISO Z39.48-1992.

To Christen, who has been there through fear and courage, in good times and bad. Thank you. I love you tons.

For Shannon, P.J., and Declan—My greatest hope for each of you is that you grow into (even more) courageous and happy individuals who make the world a better place. Always search out those things that make you uncomfortable, always set your motivation on something greater than yourself, and always know I'll forever be there to push you along or hold you up whenever you need it, no matter what.

Contents

Introduction

Aerial flight by man is simply a class of problems man is not capable of solving. The flying machine will remain but a myth.

—Professor Simon Newcomb
US Naval Academy and Johns Hopkins University Faculty

1.

A stuffed condor, a full ten feet of wings spread, glassy eyes transfixed on nothing, spun frantically on a big round table as if it had landed on an overpowered record player. Samuel Pierpont Langley watched intently as speed built up. He was a physics and astronomy professor of the highest regard, and almost one of the most famous men in history, but you've probably never heard of him.

He sat watching the bird spin and spin. In 1887 he started a set of unusual experiments at the University of Pennsylvania's Allegheny Observatory, where he worked. He built a spinning table capable of generating tremendous speed. His clever platform enabled him to observe the wind's effect on various objects and shapes. His goal was to define general theories of aerodynamics. His dream was to create a machine so man could fly.

This burning passion drove him to work long hours and develop creative solutions. He went so far as to commission taxidermists to create stuffed condors and albatrosses with their wings spread. He'd mount these birds, frozen in time, to the spinning table and try to replicate their flight. The year was 1887—the same year that Orville Wright strolled into an imposing brick building for his first day at Dayton Central High School. Orville would have never guessed at the time that this man would become his chief rival in an effort to change history.

Langley's keen mind and work ethic were soon noticed in the nation's capital, and he was recruited away from the University of Pennsylvania to become the assistant secretary at the Smithsonian Institute. There, he could garner even more funding and resources for his flying research. In 1894, Langley had a big breakthrough; he mounted a device he called "Aerodrome #4" on top of a houseboat on the Potomac River. He adapted a steam engine onto an unmanned flying machine, powering it 130 feet across the river. This first flying model gave him more incentive to move forward with his aeronautic experiments. But high expectations started to lead to high anxiety.

A flying model was far short of manned flight. It wasn't long before frustration gnawed at Langley. The difficulty and slow speed of his own progress haunted his dreams, while his own predictions set high hopes around the world. For the first time in his career, he allowed the ridicule from the press to get under his skin. Soon he started to avoid the press and was developing anxiety over events where people could question him about his efforts; nonetheless he persisted. Despite problems sleeping and an increasing use of alcohol to take the edge off, he failed to notice the destructive changes taking place within him.

Langley was a success in everything he tried. He pioneered the design and construction of astronomy telescopes; he created a plan for universal time and convinced the railroads to adopt his clock-synchronization system. He was fluent in French and in 1898 received the French Aeronautical Society's highest honor, the Prix Jules-Janssen. As he crested the peak of scientific excellence, his reputation and outward image became as valuable to him as any new innovations he might pioneer. The fearless innovator, who once paid for stuffed albatrosses, started cherry-picking only projects with a high probability of success. He began avoiding projects where he might fail. He became so protective of his reputation that fear of failure started to erode his confidence; his anxiety snowballed to create a hidden fear of the unknown, fear of trying something new.

Two years later, in the fall of 1896, his Aerodrome #6, the same design as the earlier flying glider but with a more powerful engine, was ready to launch. Living up to the weighty anticipation, the unmanned craft flew 4,200 feet and stayed aloft for over a minute. His triumph dished out just the right portion of success to convince dreamers and aviation enthusiasts that manned flight just might be possible. Not everyone was drinking the Kool-Aid, however; the chief engineer of the navy, Admiral George Melville, opined that "a calm survey of natural phenomena leads the engineer to pronounce all confident prophecies for future success as wholly unwarranted, if not absurd."[1] Langley likely took this criticism hard since the government was funding most of his research and the military was certainly going to be one of the earliest possible adopters of his invention.

Langley didn't agree with Admiral Melville. The scientist was convinced that the same design for Aerodrome #6 could work for manned flight. The problem was he didn't want to face the possibility that he would need to completely redesign his vessel to carry a man. He also didn't want to ask for help and look like a fraud. Fired with the fuel of his success and the connections he had built over the past fifteen years, Langley went to Congress and the adventurous former secretary of the navy (now vice president) Teddy Roosevelt and convinced them to fund his efforts. Getting more government money meant more pressure on Langley to succeed. The US government provided $50,000 of funding to Langley based on his ability to sell the dream with his powered glider designs like Aerodrome #6.

Newspapers around the world exploded with headlines of a changing world. Such a well-funded project with so much attention attracted the interest of high-profile scientists and leaders. Langley was more than happy to give interviews and bask in the limelight. He was summering in Europe with his family and hobnobbing with the European elite. Alexander Graham Bell and Andrew Carnegie were among the enthusiasts who provided Langley with yet an additional $50,000 in funding. In today's currency that is equivalent to three million dollars to build the first machine capable of sending a man through the air. Yet it seemed that raising money and garnering press coverage were his primary missions, distracting him tragically from the ultimate goal. As the stakes and his profile grew so did the hidden fear Langley was unknowingly cultivating; it would ultimately prove fatal to both the project and Langley.

2.

Orville and Wilbur Wright opened the Wright Cycle Company, a bicycle repair and manufacturing shop in Dayton, Ohio, in 1892, the year after the younger Orville left high school. Many people have said that the boys had no special background or head start as barely high-school-educated sons of a preacher. The boys disagreed. Orville wrote, "It isn't true to say we had no special advantages. The greatest thing in our favor was growing up in a family where there was always much encouragement to intellectual curiosity."[2] In fact, their father often preached at home the importance of growing up with "mettle"—a combination of courage, persistence, and faith.

In August 1897 when Orville was deathly ill with typhoid fever, he read the news of a famed German aeronautical engineer, Otto Lilienthal, dying after crashing one of his advanced gliders. That sparked a curiosity that, when combined with one other critical ingredient, would change the world.

Orville and Wilbur agreed that human flight was possible and that they should give serious attention to aeronautics. In May 1899 the brothers wrote to the Smithsonian Institute (where Langley was working) asking for any and all publications on aeronautical subjects. Soon the brothers were writing to everyone from the US Weather Bureau secretary to Octave Chanute (a celebrated French-born aeronautical pioneer living in Illinois). Their curiosity with what others had tried and learned was bottomless. They were resolute when asking for help. When others might have been afraid of being a pest, or fearful of rejection, the Wrights persisted until they got answers. Asking for help was likely as scary for them as the test flights, but they knew they could never succeed by themselves.

As their research led to action, the brothers soon discovered that launching a glider in the frying-pan fields of Dayton, Ohio, would be an expensive and time-consuming proposition. To actually launch a glider in Ohio, they would have to build elevated platforms and catapults. They needed to go where nature provided an advantage. They searched for a location that would have natural height and predictable, steady winds. Kitty Hawk, North Carolina, proved to be the perfect solution; they planned their first trip there in 1900. They waited until the busy summer season in the bike shop (their sole source of funding) ended and left in October. News travels quickly around a small community like Dayton; the boys' father and sister were soon attacked with arrows of ridicule and embarrassment over the "insane" efforts of the local bike repairmen gone crazy. The brothers were not doing much to disprove that ridicule down in Kitty Hawk. The two endured a lengthy search to find a suitable workshop and housing. The extra time searching had them behind schedule and when they finally did get to testing, the results were not what they expected.

The brothers were undaunted, however; their faith, in themselves and in God, helped them cultivate an amazing level of courage. Crash after crash reminded them that they were continually putting their lives at risk. Thankfully, they learned the secret of using fear as fuel. The men committed to facing everything with an absolute resolution to succeed. As author David McCullough wrote in *The Wright Brothers*, "To Wilbur and Orville it seemed fear was a stranger."[3] It's more accurate to say that fear was a friend.

After several successful glider flights, the Wrights returned to Dayton to quickly ramp up the bike shop in anticipation of a busy spring season. They were balancing on a pin head between the pursuit of their dream and the demise of their bike business, which kept the cash coming in. Most people would have been fearful of going broke or wasting away their savings on a crazy pursuit, but the Wright brothers were relentless in the face of such an audacious challenge. In characteristic fashion, the brothers asked for help wherever they could find it, evidence that they had few hidden fears driven by ego or appearance. They even invited Chanute, the esteemed engineer, to their home to learn from him. Soon the brothers had built their own makeshift wind tunnel to test new designs. They constantly displayed a willingness to ask for and accept help, a curiosity for others' input, and, of course, that one key ingredient that really led them to success, using fear as fuel. They knew their greatest success was on the other side of their fears, and reveled in the passion and challenge of doing what many thought impossible.

The following year they returned to Kitty Hawk to the most miserable conditions they had ever experienced. Orville wrote home that the mosquitoes appeared "in the form of a mighty cloud, almost darkening the sun." He told his sister that living in a tent on the sand dunes of North Carolina in those conditions was by far the worst experience of his life. He said the mosquitos "chewed us clear through our underwear and socks. Lumps began swelling up all over my body like hen's eggs . . . misery, misery." They had mettle, however. They persisted.

They had grit and it was fueled by that key ingredient—fear. They used those feeling of fear and anxiety as fuel and turned what could have been threats to their success into challenges to be met head on.

3.

Langley was mentally done. He'd had many failures by 1902, he had taken much grief, and he couldn't stand the prospect of more bombardment on his reputation. His ego had driven him to the point where he was afraid to ask for help and afraid to admit to mistakes. He was above doing the hard work and clearly ashamed of the lack of accomplishment. He had always been a success. It was time he stopped the madness that was driving him crazy. He declared that he was not going to pursue manned flight; the repeated skewering in the press and his fear of failure were literally killing him. The public ridicule was something he was not equipped to handle; it only increased his fight-or-flight response. He had another hidden fear that was equally binding—but he never discovered it.

Despite his desire to abandon flying, his ship had already sailed. The US government had invested heavily in him and his partner, Charles Manly. Langley was sixty-nine years old and had been working on the idea of manned flight for seventeen years. He had an unmanned design that flew for almost a mile. In autumn 1903 his backers forced him to give it one last shot. His battalion of experts and engineers set up their latest craft atop a houseboat on the Potomac River, just south of Washington, DC. It was the same design as the glider that had flown for over a minute; this time Langley added a seat for a pilot. They strapped Manly into the modified machine along with a new, more powerful, fifty-two-horsepower engine and prepared to launch. It would be the first manned flight.

All eyes were on Langley, including those of the Wright brothers, who were getting constant updates on Langley's progress. They had turned down offers for additional funding, believing the influence of outside investors was not worth ceding their control. While Langley was scared he wouldn't have enough money, the brothers focused on controlling what they could control and not letting fear of other events distract them. When asked why not take the money so no one could build a plane faster, Wilbur replied, "Fear that others will produce a machine capable of practical service in less than several years does not worry us."[4] They were happy to learn from experience and had kept enduring through failure after failure. They had built wing structures based on what they learned from the best minds in aeronautics; their plan was to adopt the late Lilienthal's design, which they tested in their modified wind tunnel. This was the shape universally regarded as "the best design for manned flight." It worked on the model; however, in real life it was useless. After several weeks of trying to make the Lilienthal design fly the men scrapped that shape and acted with confidence and belief that at this point they knew more than their celebrated heroes of flight. They were no longer afraid of failure, or afraid of doing what no one else would do. They had the courage to trust their own designs. They had learned how to channel scary moments and butterflies into the energy to act. The neuroscience behind what the Wright brothers learned is in the pages of this book, but the dream they had—the impossible, audacious goal—was their mission and in their hearts. That's what drove them day in and day out.

While, according to the papers, Langley prepared to amaze the world, the Wright brothers finally got to test their new wing design on a manned glider. On a calm day in Kitty Hawk the men carried the craft to the top of a tall powdery dune; it was golden and smooth with the wind blowing straight off the ocean. They were sweating from carrying the machine. Wilbur hopped aboard for what became a near-fatal failed attempt, as the glider nosed down like a lawn dart diving into the sand. That didn't stop them, however. They figured the flyer needed a weight rebalance and they adjusted, then adjusted again. Finally, after a radical adjustment Wilbur took off again. The machine climbed higher and higher until the plane's nose pointed nearly straight up and the wings began to stall and stop producing lift. This was the exact same deadly chain of events that had killed Otto Lilienthal and it nearly killed Wilbur, not just once but again and again. Still they pressed on, with Orville yelling every time the plane started to nose up too high and Wilbur diving it forward. It wasn't long before they found a winning combination. They just needed more data and testing on their steering system before it was really ready to be powered with an engine. They agreed with outsiders who speculated that it would be a nearly impossible task for them to do on their own among the desolate dunes of Kitty Hawk. However, they were fueled by the fear of failure, the fear of not giving their best, the fear of not changing the world. They had a belief that they had to keep trying. As Orville would say about their courage, "there was some spirit that carried us through."[5]

That motivation wasn't the key to their success, but it was a big part of it. The principal ingredient the Wright brothers possessed and Langley lacked was evidenced in a note Wilbur sent back to Octave Chanute regarding a chance to publicly present their work. Chanute had asked if Wilbur would give a speech to the Western Society of Engineers in Chicago, explaining what they were working on. It was his first invitation to speak publicly about their "insane and absurd" activities. Wilbur was asked by the elder statesman for his input on the structure of the meeting. In a rare bit of authentic insight into his personality, he responded to Chanute that he had no input because "I will already be as badly scared for a man to be."[6] However, that terror didn't stop him from delivering a speech that would go down in history. The Wright brothers never stopped feeling scared—but they learned what to do with their fear. They used fear as fuel.

Back on the Potomac, Langley and Manly fired up the engine and launched "Aerodrome A" off the houseboat. It was a frigid October morning in 1903. After mere seconds the machine sank like "a handful of mortar,"[7] according to one of the journalists aboard the houseboat. Manly, nearly drowning after his cork floatation vest was caught in wires below the icy surface, eventually swam to the boat and assured everyone that they knew how to fix the problem and would make one more attempt on December 8. They had more engineers, more experience, and vastly more resources than the Wright brothers. However, Langley refused to change his design from the once-successful unmanned craft even though they added a pilot to the mix. Langley was deeply afraid of change; sadly, he never realized this disastrous hidden fear. He (and the press) thought he was ordained to succeed. He was not. The flight on December 8 ended the same way, with Manly swimming for his life through the frigid waters of the Potomac River. Langley had a stroke and died just a couple of years later, a broken man whose fear of failure allowed the press and the public to mock and ridicule him into the grave, and whose hidden fear of change put him in a fixed mindset that ultimately kept him from being a world-changing success. In the latter part of his life, his decisions were driven by fear; his reputation became so important to him that he harbored a fear of losing it, which changed his mindset from looking for opportunities to running from fear.

Just one week after the last Langley flight on the Potomac, on December 17, 1903, the Wright brothers magnificently launched a man into the wild blue yonder not once, but four times in a row. Fear was fueling those flights. After Wilbur made the first flight, the brothers promised to take turns at the controls. Wilbur's first twelve-second flight nearly crash-landed, slamming him to the ground at twenty miles per hour, but he yelled at Orville and the team to quickly get the plane ready to relaunch "while I'm sharp." Hands shaking, mouth dry, and pupils dilated; Wilbur learned that he had a higher level of sensory perception and was much better handling the plane when fear had prepared his body for superhuman performance—although when asked later whether he was scared, he replied, "Scared? There was no time to be scared."[8] The truth is that his amygdala was on full alert; however, he learned how to control that change and transform that feeling of fear to excitement.

The Wright brothers had that singular ingredient of courageousness that allowed them to be curious and fearless in the face of monumental odds. They succeeded not just because they were courageous (as you can see by Wilbur's great speech even after his admission that he was terrified of public speaking and his willingness to get back on the plane crash after crash) but because they used fear as fuel to create superhuman performance where all the money and talent in Washington couldn't. In fact, the *Aeronautical Journal* summed up the Wright brothers' winning formula best: "Never in the History of the World had men studied the problem with such scientific skill nor with such undaunted courage." Courage is the ability to recognize fear and compartmentalize it where you can either be unhampered by it, or better yet, where you are able to use it for the ultimate fuel. Courage, in fact, requires fear.

If you look throughout history from the Wright brothers, to Christopher Columbus to Nelson Mandela to Tom Brady, you will find greatness fueled by fear. There is a science and process to using fear. Until recently, finding that formula has been through trial and error, or fortunate upbringing, or a perfect storm of circumstances that drove greatness. We have only had the technology to discover neural insights (the inner working of the brain) in the past few years. Fear is the most powerful force that affects our lives and our society. Usually it is a negative force, as Gandhi famously said: "The enemy is fear. We think it is hate, but it is fear." Learning to use fear and not be rendered weak and cowardly by the people who try to use fear against us is one outcome of adopting the fear as fuel methodology.

I chose the Wright brothers as an example of using fear as fuel because for most of my life I, too, was a victim of my fears; you see, I was deathly afraid of flying. I missed out on countless opportunities, harbored a deep shame and guilt, and mentally tortured myself every time I was near an airplane. We all have traumas that determine our future, that write to our mind's hard drive and control subconscious decisions. That original fear is your Fear Frontier, which you'll read about as one of our most powerful driving forces. Then in my thirty-sixth year I had a life-changing experience that brought me face-to-face with my original Fear Frontier, as you'll read about. That moment changed my entire life forever. After choosing courage over fear and deciding on strength over weakness I would overcome the terror of flying. Paradoxically, I found a great joy that had been locked away from me for the first thirty-plus years of my life. In addition to becoming a commercially rated pilot, competing in aerobatics and flying thousands of hours, learning to use my fear allowed me to live the life of my dreams and go beyond success to significance. I found the quality of my decisions determined the quality of my life, and the more courage and confidence I had making those choices the more positive and amazing the outcomes could be. If I can do it, anyone can.

In *Fear Is Fuel* my goal is to give you the science and the tools to transform your life the same way Wilbur and Orville Wright changed the world. You can be a bike mechanic working in Dayton, an administrative assistant just starting at Google, or a high school teacher from Fort Worth—it doesn't matter. You already have all you need to change the world if you find more fear and learn how to use it to fuel the life of your dreams. If you scare yourself every day.

To effectively use fear as fuel you'll need to search inside yourself for some important clues, then adopt an effective framework based on the latest neuroscience. I've tried to make the explorations and courage-creating exercises as simple as possible. Feel free to skip around the chapters in any order—there are some exercises that might resonate with you now and others that you may want to save for later, after you gain a better understanding of the workings of the brain. I've written the chapters so they stand alone, so if something catches your eye go ahead and start there. My sincere hope is that this book challenges you to think differently, that it helps to change your life, and that once it does you take that knowledge and become a vehicle for positive change in the world.

Patrick J. Sweeney II
January 2019
Chamonix, France

Eight Tips to Get the Most Out of This Book

There is one over-arching quality that you need to cultivate to get the most out of this book. The fact that you bought this book shows that you already have a certain amount of this virtue. What is this mysterious trait? Curiosity.

How can you develop more curiosity to really benefit from the science and research in this book? Ask yourself why at least three or four times for every question you face. This simple act of wonder and not assuming that you know why, but rather asking yourself, "How do I know why?" will be the biggest step in filling your internal database, your subconscious hard drive, with information that will make you courageous and help you make radically better decisions in your life. The more you can wonder, the better your results will be toward living an amazing life.

Have a real desire to become courageous—to learn to use fear and not be manipulated by it—then ask yourself as you read each chapter, what can I take away from this chapter, what can I try right now that will build my courage? Committing to action—to becoming courageous—will by definition change your mindset from cowardly and fear driven to courageous and confident, learning to use fear as fuel.

Try to understand the various frameworks explaining how the mind works. There is a lot of science in this book, but I've tried to make it as simple to understand as possible. The reason it's important to understand things like free energy and valence is so you can see how the brain can change, and know that anyone has the power to change his or her brain. Accepting this possibility is critical to making progress toward living the most happy, fulfilled, and successful life possible. If you get at least a basic idea for some of the theories, you'll understand that change is possible for just about anyone, and that will actually make it easier for you to re-wire your own mind.

Take notes! If there is something that you find interesting, make a note or highlights so you'll have a summary to go back and read (see next point).

Review your notes every quarter—check back in and go through the book every three months until you reach your goal of a coura-geous life and have learned how to use fear as fuel.

Figure out your Top Three takeaways from the book and write them down on Post-It® notes. Stick them on your bathroom mirror, computer screen, and refrigerator, places you'll see them every day. It's an easy and free way to take more control over your life.

Give the book to someone and make that person your account-ability partner; make a commitment to share your ideas and details of your journey once a month over coffee or a glass of wine. Just knowing that you are accountable to someone else will really help you focus on making lasting change.

Take care of your body. There is extensive research proving the direct connection between diet, exercise, and mental health. Eating a diet low in carbohydrates and sugar, exercising regularly, and stress-ing the body with not just workouts, but things like cold showers or days of fasting will all help build a more courageous mind and keep the architecture of your brain stronger and working better.

I

FEAR

How about a dose of reality? The first part of this book introduces you to fear, because fear is what our most primitive brain wants us to believe is reality. We *should* be afraid of what people in our tribe think of us, because we might get rejected and not find a mate. We *should* be afraid of going away from our cave because we might get attacked and die; we *should* be afraid of standing up on the highest peak because we might fall off. Never mind that the view is spectacular and the journey is life changing; our fear-based mind does not care about happiness, fulfillment, love, or joy; it only cares about passing our genes along to the next generation. When people are locked into a life filled with fear and anxiety, constantly being victims of other people, being victims of *shoulds* and not creating courageous opportunities for happiness and true success, it's because they are prisoners to the survival part of the brain. Fear is holding them back. To change that reality, you first need to learn the root of all fears, how fear governs our lives, and most importantly how and when fear tries to take over so you can stop it in its tracks.

You'll learn a basic vocabulary to apply throughout the book: what fear is, why it's individualized, what causes it, and the new science behind exactly how our minds work. My promise for this section is that if you find more fear and learn how it shows up in your life through your mind and body, you will have tremendous opportunities to improve your life, your organization, and the world. This is the start of your user's manual for a courageous life.

1

○—

Fear Fluency

Nothing in life is to be feared, it is only to be understood. Now is the time to understand more, so that we may fear less.

—Marie Curie

1.

You can tame fear or fear can tame you. It is a fundamental choice. Fear can cause any one of many different emotions from uncertainty all the way to terror, but fear itself is the combination of inputs from our body's physical reaction to an event. Fear tries to tame us by taking over our central nervous system. You can learn to keep that from happening. Fear is not an emotion; it's the combination of reactions to sensory responses. Before you can tame fear you need to learn the language of fear; like any other language as we start to pick up expressions and phrases we begin to understand more and more.

At 4:30 every morning for the past eight weeks a group of sailors, who look like they have lost a year-long battle with a tsunami, gather relentlessly to fight their fears. A penetratingly cold wind whips spray off the Pacific Ocean into their faces. Looking out from puffy, red-rimmed eyes, the men still manage to sprint into formation on a slab of black asphalt that could have been a parking lot or basketball court in any other life. Eerily, silhouettes of about one hundred pairs of feet are orderly stenciled in white paint a perfect arm-span apart in all directions. Less than half of the painted feet now have real boots, filled by men, standing upon them. The other half have ghosts and terrible memories clouding them. Empty pairs echo of failure and fear. The men don't look at the empty places, however. Chappie fights back images of his spot being empty tomorrow; he's forcing his mind to focus on getting through this moment. Clearly, this place has a special purpose. Each remaining sailor puts his left foot and right foot on a painted set of prints. Several weeks into the world's toughest physical training, some of the men actually have to consciously focus on right and left to make their feet comply. This is the Grinder. It is the infamous location of Navy SEAL physical training or PT. It's also where the bell lives.

When most people get cold, they'll sprout goose bumps, then start to shiver. Think of the last time you got cold enough to shiver or make your teeth chatter. You probably had the luxury of being able to put on a jacket or crank up the heated seat while the defroster blasted out increasingly warmer air. If there was any uncertainty about how or when you'd warm up, you might have felt the twinge of uncertainty or anxiety. You probably had one big advantage over these sailors who were chosen for Basic Underwater Demolition SEAL (BUD/S) training or SEAL training. Your advantage was the fact that you knew you could do something soon to make the cold stop. There was an end in sight for you, so there really wasn't much to be afraid of.

There's only one thing the men on the Grinder can do to escape the bone-numbing cold or to ensure that they live through terrifying underwater fights blindfolded, getting stripped of their air source, or shot at as they climb a thirty-foot wall drenched to the bone, forearms pumped with lactic acid pooling in their muscles like a blazing river of pain under their skin. But most of these men would rather die than use the sure way out. They will be wet, cold, and sleep deprived for five more days now that it is the start of Hell Week. Terror of all sorts has been their constant companion and isn't going away anytime soon. Interestingly, they would find different ways to describe the fear or anxiety or terror to themselves and others. For the frigid cold and relentless challenges that have penetrated their organs there is only one known end in sight. That's the bell. If one of them staggers over to the "drop area" as it's called, and pulls the rope on the bell, he rings out to the world that he is a quitter; he is not physically tough enough to become the most feared and fearless of the world's warriors. The pressure is even more intense because the Grinder, and the bell, sits in the center of a series of buildings, like a quad, that houses active duty, combat proven decorated SEALs. These experienced frogmen can look out, can stare out, can cast judgment out, on all the sailors outside suffering on the Grinder who think they might be good enough to wear the coveted trident patch of a Navy SEAL.

What started out on day one for Chappie and the other hundred or so candidates eight weeks ago with sets of push-ups and pull-ups in front of a screaming instructor has steadily escalated. Challenges have increased every day for the past eight weeks, gradually building up to a pinnacle of suffering and agony called Hell Week. It's no coincidence that each day has been designed to progressively build their ability to deal with fear and stress. Sailors learn how to override their primal survival mechanisms (like wanting to get out of the cold, fight back at someone screaming in their face, or run when they are being shot at) and still be able to function using a high level of intelligence, sound decision making, and maximal speed.

Chappie is Doug Chapman (not his real name) one of those men in BUD/S class 228 in the winter of 2000. The US Navy has created the greatest courage factory ever devised; the members are fluent in Fear. Over the course of six months mere mortals are converted to real-life superheroes. SEALs are the most elite of an elite fighting force. Now Chappie was about to start the worst experience of his life—Hell Week—the torturous test of courage and will that will teach him an entire new lexicon when describing emotions. Hell Week goes well beyond the physical challenges you may see or even participate in at civilian events like the Spartan Race, the Tough Mudder, or *American Ninja Warrior*. Those adult recesses are child's play compared to not sleeping for days, having live ammunition fired overhead, and knowing that trainees die every couple of years because they are pushed beyond the limit. BUD/S is the ultimate training for pushing out your Fear Frontier, which is an original trauma that is planted in each of us when we're just a child, usually before the age of ten or twelve years old. How you process your experience with that trauma at the time ultimately determines your courage later in life.

Chapman learned many of the same techniques you'll learn in this book. Some he learned at BUD/S, others helped get him there. One of the most important techniques he had learned long ago, on his high school swim team, was self-talk. It's a technique the instructors at BUD/S highly recommend and teach daily. They have been using many of the same techniques for more than fifty years, but neuroscientists are just now dissecting why and how many of them work. We have the technology to understand how everyday mortals can learn to use neuroscience-based techniques to transform themselves.

USING FEAR AS FUEL METHOD #1

Tackle one fear at a time. Learn to face the fear, get used to your bodily changes, and expose yourself more and more to that specific fear.

Most frogmen think their training has enabled them to erase fearful thoughts or experiences to become brave, but neurologically speaking they are wrong. You can never fully erase a memory. For the SEAL who might have fallen out of a tree as a child and became scared of heights, or was trapped underwater after the canoe capsized and became afraid of water, he can never erase the memory of that traumatic event. We can only change neural associations of an emotion with specific events.

When we are traumatized, we form two memories at the same time: the event specifics and the emotions we felt. Neuroscientists from Harvard University have shown that you can never erase what's called a semantic memory (the events and facts). What you can do instead is write stronger emotional memory in the area of your brain responsible for what is called the executive function. We can consciously recall specific moments along with an original memory that was written with the help of two parts of the brain called the amygdala and hippocampus. SEALs write positive memories specific to the things they experience; they create specific bravery. For example, if one of them almost died in a river as a kid, when he gets out of the pool the first day he might think "that wasn't that tough, I'm a bad ass." And that's the first step to a new emotional association with water.

When I interviewed Dr. Mo Milad at Harvard's neuroscience lab,[1] he explained that rather than erasing old fearful memories, when we create courage and face our fears we actually write new, more powerful memories, with more positive outcomes in an area called

WHAT'S IN A MEMORY?

The past has a powerful impact on our future. There is no one true reality, just our own individual reality made up of your collection of memories. Your reality is made up of all the things ever entered into your brain's hard drive. Those memories make up all your Prior Beliefs, and that is what creates your particular orientation to things happening around you.

Three of us may walk to the edge of a cliff and have a very different perception of the reality and a dramatically different view of the future because of our memory database.

I'm a rock climber, so I'll put the cliff in the context of my recollection of solving tough climbing problems, or choosing an aesthetically pleasing route. You might be a horticulturist and wonder what kind of alpine flora is sprouting up through the cracks. The third person might think, "What the fuck am I doing on the edge of this cliff? I'm going to die!"

Reality is based on past experiences, real or imagined, and current perceptions. So if you want to change reality you have to change your memories. It helps to keep in mind that you can only change your reality and memory, too. You can't control what other people think or feel. There are varying strengths of past events based on the power of the electrical charge between synapses as well. Electrical charges and wireless brain waves change strength with the emotional intensity of a memory. The fascinating aspect of this neuroscience is that we can create memories and populate our hard drive just by imagining them, and the subconscious will see those as if they really happened. That changes your reality. Imagined events are usually weaker signals than emotionally charged experiences that create lots of free energy and activate the amygdala; however, a high volume of small visualizations can help rewrite powerful emotions. If you think we can pick and choose our reality—you're right!

the prefrontal cortex (PFC). That's what Chapman was doing every day by finding more fear: he was writing new memories that would allow him to make high-quality choices in the face of fear, rather than just focusing on survival. You can think of this courage-creating process in the same way as Leonardo da Vinci would continue to paint on top of a canvas that didn't turn out as he had planned. Our memories can be painted the same way—stronger, more visible memories layered on top of old ones you want to cover up. Facing fears one at a time takes a long time, but if your goal is a completely courageous life and making the best long-term choices in all aspects, it will take a very long time to get there.

Chapman, a thirty-seven-year-old Kansas native, recalls what went through his head when he started getting scared or dejected during SEAL training a decade ago: "On the O-Course [obstacle course] I think it was the first time in my life I was thinking about just getting through something, instead of winning. Yeah, I was afraid at first, trying to climb a thirty-foot-high rope tower when my forearms were burning already from pulling myself up ropes and walls the first couple of minutes. But I made it. When I did I told myself 'I just got over that wall. I did it. Now I'm mentally and physically stronger.' I built up another chunk of confidence, and I did something even though I was scared. The truth about BUD/S is no one congratulates you for doing your best or beating your record. You had to tell yourself that you did it. You have to be your own cheerleader. Yeah, it gets tougher each day, but so do you."

You get bolder by writing new emotional memories over the old scary ones. Bravery increases when an original future-envisioned outcome (falling or dying or breaking a leg) gets overwritten by the memory of successfully getting through something that was difficult or that you expected to fail at again. Succeeding. Changing your expectation. Drawing on your past successes in the face of danger or failure and focusing on those. Doing more than you thought you could. You feel physical changes and most of the time we think of those changes as feeling "scared." It's important to realize that what you feel isn't your fault, and it's not good or bad; it's just your body's chemistry changing. That's why we need to get you fluent in fear so you can learn courage and change your life for good.

The physical exertion is only a small part of what makes BUD/S so difficult. The real challenge is the mental fortitude to face everything and accept responsibility for getting through these physical challenges. Only about 30 percent of the men who start Hell Week make it through to the end. The navy is mining men from within their ranks who already are courageous and strong; then they teach them how to channel their fear, use it as fuel, and build up a level of courage that makes them unstoppable. SEALs end up getting so good at tapping into these superhuman powers that they learn to use their mind and their fear to do what soldiers for centuries have required heavy drug doses to pull off.

The good news for you is that researchers are just now proving that anyone has the ability to make their body produce even more powerful performance-enhancing drugs than any synthetic drug with just the mind. By using your fear as fuel, you can produce a change that is even stronger and more effective than the Germans' crystal meth.

Marcus Letrell is another celebrated Navy SEAL who inspired the movie *Lone Survivor* by battling almost two hundred Taliban soldiers with his three teammates (all of whom died in the ambush). When we met in Washington, DC, at the Walter Reed Medical Center he told me that surviving BUD/S comes down to believing in yourself: "If you ring that bell you've just given up on everything you believe in and yourself. My attitude was you'll have to kill me or kick me out, or else I'm going stay in BUD/S." He made the choice to face everything and deal with it as courageously as he could.

The US Navy created Navy SEAL training in the 1960s. Since then they have had decades to figure out the formula for ultimate courage, and judging by those who have become war heroes, saviors of nations, and great leaders it appears that the navy found the ultimate strategy for taming fear and using it as fuel. Or have they?

2.

The white light of fear can blind us to making good choices in our life. White light is made up of many frequencies, just as fear can be made up of different ingredients. The fact that you can tame one aspect of your fears and yet not necessarily be completely courageous is a paradox that takes some explanation. The reason this paradox exists is just coming to light through the latest psychological and neuroscientific research presented here. If you go back to your high school physics class you might remember that white light is actually made up of different wavelengths of color; similarly, fear is made up of three different components, like slices of a rainbow. You need to understand these primary colors to really light up your life (sorry, couldn't pass that one up). Where else to find out what's at the end of the rainbow than Ireland? It wasn't a leprechaun and pot of gold

I was after, but rather answers to some of the most perplexing questions about courage and fear.

After traveling the globe from neuroscience oracle to oracle it was clear that to live a passionate and balanced life of courage there are three types of fears that we can tap into or hide from. While it might be easy to think of fear as having three legs like a stool, that analogy lacks the interconnectedness that Dr. Shane O'Mara was getting at. Fears are even more entwined than the legs of a stool; that's why I use the image of a Terror Triangle, as shown in figure 1.1.

If you are not conscious of all three and haven't created an awareness of different kinds of fear, you don't have all the tools you need to live completely courageously.

There is more to fear than meets the eye. Taming fear is not as simple as mentally willing your arteries into crystal rivers before torpedoing out of a C-130 transport at 30,000 feet over enemy territory or kicking down a door to darkness where your body could be permanently separated from its soul by an unknown terrorist.

Terror Triangle

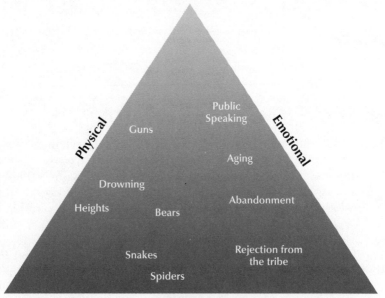

Figure 1.1.   The Terror Triangle: The Three Types of Fear

It's not as simple as overcoming physical terrors. You might be surprised to learn that there are many lessons SEALs can take away from someone as fragile as a Buddhist monk sworn not to harm even a worm, or even J. K. Rowling, the writer who created the wildly successful Harry Potter franchise.

Inside the fortress-like walls of Trinity College in Dublin, Ireland there are literally answers to millions of questions. The Long Room, made famous by its only cinematic appearance in *Star Wars*, has thousands of books from hundreds of years ago. The biotech and engineering buildings bustle with cutting-edge research. However, I was looking for something not yet published or peer reviewed. I wanted to figure out those spectrums of color that make up the bright light of fear, and why they intertwine to make courage or fear part of our life. Dr. Shane O'Mara was the man to start me along a journey to finding the answer. I first met Shane at the Science Gallery at Trinity. Shane has the classic Irish features that make him look like a middle-aged Dennis Quaid. Tall and confident in his walk, and firm and direct with his handshake, Shane received notoriety for his research proving that torture is no more effective than coercion for interrogating prisoners. We met for coffee just next door to the Department of Neuroscience and Psychology building at the ever-energetic Science Gallery on Trinity's main campus. There's always an exhibition that combines science, art, and performance, making the gallery a unique spot; add in the first-floor café buzzing like a beehive in spring and you've got a very lively place to meet.

I was thinking of the courageous Indiana Jones and his comical fear of snakes when I asked Shane a set of questions.

Why are some people able to conquer some fears and not others?
Can we split fears up into two, three, or even ten separate categories?
Do the sources of different fears overlap?
What creates courage?

Shane cautioned me that fears can't be put into simple distinct buckets because the ways the brain interprets many fears are related, like different lights having differing amounts of one color. One of the things O'Mara's lab has shown is that we have two very quick-acting systems in our brain that make instant "snap" decisions. One system that recognizes familiarity of a task or person (he's shown that when seeing a person you use your subconscious to instantly assess how friendly he or she is) and the other system how difficult something is (with people it's how competent they might be at a given task). These snap decisions draw on your history and different neurological pathways. They also are filtered by your experiences, the way a blue filter on a camera lens will block out the colors of the sky. As I was wrestling with a theory of types of fears that are inputs to our emotions O'Mara told me that, based on his most recent work on mice, you need to know where you're going to know where you are.

In Dublin, it seemed like Guinness might be a better inspiration than the espresso we were enjoying, but Shane and I kept talking and it planted the seed for my Terror Triangle. I had to mull over his advice before I'd come to the epiphany that led to figure 1.1. I had distilled the inputs of fear into three spectrums, but it was clear that depending on the fear it could have more of one component and less of another—but seldom was a fear made up of just one of the factors. If you can classify your fears, you can understand where in your reality they are coming from as well.

Fast-forward six months to a small hipster café in Brooklyn. On a near perfect, Indian summer day in mid-September, I had ridden a city bike along the East River and up over the Brooklyn Bridge, dodging roller-bladers, runners, and crazy homeless people singing show tunes like Ethel Merman. I was off to see "The Man" when it came to fear. I had an idea for classifying fears I wanted to run by Dr. Joe LeDoux from New York University. LeDoux is considered the fear Yoda; he's written the leading books on fear and anxiety including his 2002 classic *Anxious*. I had come up with the Terror Triangle concept and I wanted his approval and input.

As we sipped cappuccinos, Joe explained that the combination of our physical reactions, personal interpretations, and past memories makes up our feelings of fear and interpretations of courage. Each one of our neurons can be thought of as having a bell curve of action. Everyone will be at different points of the bell curve on millions of different neurons. Some will have the smallest fraction of action (way on the left side of the bell curve) and others a huge amount (way out on the right). LeDoux believes a person's personality is the sum and multiplication of all those individual bell curves. You can think of this idea like looking at a huge flat screen television that has eighty billion pixels (the number of neurons in our brain) and each pixel has an infinite gray scale from the whitest white to the darkest black. The beautiful black-and-white images that can be created are going to be different to represent each one of us because each neuron has slightly different activation, so no two people (even twins) are going to experience and interpret fear the same way. The amazing thing is that we can change the picture on the screen, and literally change the energy that goes to different neurons in our brain. That is part of the idea called neuroplasticity, the fact that your brain can change at any age.

Two important takeaways from LeDoux's theories are that we should never beat ourselves up for how those neurons are distributed; it's not our fault; it's only our physical makeup. And second, we can change those bell curves and the power to each neuron at any age, so feeling scared or weak can change if we want it to. As I'd find out later, there is even a special pathway to courage, which a four-foot-long snake and an fMRI machine proved to the world, as you'll see later in the book.

The Terror Triangle Gives You Wings

The Terror Triangle also can be used to understand your daily levels of energy. Because fears are specific to physical, emotional, or instinctual inputs, battling those fears saps your energy. You can think of starting each day with three full tanks of energy on each side of the triangle; what you do during the day will raise or lower your energy levels. Leveraging the triangle is easy if you think of every decision point and choice you make during the day as being more toward one side of the triangle. For instance, not answering a call from your spouse is a choice on the emotional side of the triangle, skipping a trip to the gym is on the physical side of the triangle, and deciding to take the train instead of flying is some combination of an emotional and instinctual choice. Being able to classify the type of fear will help you keep your decisions balanced and based on opportunity rather than fear.

Know that for physical choices if you treat your body well by eating healthy, exercising, and turning your moments of anxiety into fuel, then your physical energy increases. That's why simply making the choice to walk around your building for a meeting rather than sit in a conference room will increase your energy for the rest of the day, or taking the stairs at your hotel will help your long-term health as well as immediate sense of well-being. Likewise, practice gratitude and loving happiness with your partner, family, and co-workers and you will witness your emotional energy blossoming. However, the converse is true. If you haven't found your hidden fears yet and aren't working on turning them to fuel, you are going to be subconsciously fighting them all day and by mid-afternoon you'll be exhausted. Just being afraid to suggest to your boss that you walk around the building for a meeting because you don't want him to think you're out of line or rocking the boat will suck the energy out of your tanks.

The Fear Frontier

If you want to speak fluently in fear, you need to be able to talk about what is happening in your life at any moment in a way that both you and others can comprehend. Imagine yourself at 10,000 feet above Orange, Massachusetts, bouncing along in a noisy Twin Otter high-wing plane, feeling the effects of summer turbulence. A stranger you met an hour ago with long hair, a bushy beard, and the eyes of a madman is now strapped to your ass, shuffling you toward the open door of the plane for your first parachute jump. Both of you will feel the by-products of fear—changes in your mind and body. If you ask most instructors, even after thousands of jumps, they will almost all tell you that they always feel some level of fear and it helps them focus. Many are actually addicted to that chemical change in their body; they love the fear and use it as fuel. If I ask you, the person jumping with him, likewise you'll say that you feel fear. However, it is likely much different from the instructor, even though you both say it is "fear."

That's why we need to understand our level of fear and what part of our brain is in charge at any given point. Fear is only an input—we have three sources of fear; physical, mental, and emotional. They live in the small Terror Triangle on the far right of figure 1.2 and feed our fear responses. The triangle's three inputs can provide an infinite variation of scary events that can range emotionally from Chill on the left side to Terror all the way on the right. The height of the individual peaks of emotion is the level of change in our body's physiology because of the fear input.

What you might notice is the two humps behind the individual states of fear. The one on the left represents when we are emotion-

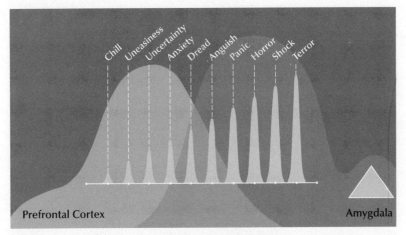

Chill · Uneasiness · Uncertainty · Anxiety · Dread · Anguish · Panic · Horror · Shock · Terror

Prefrontal Cortex · Amygdala

Figure 1.2. The Fear Frontier and Fear-Based Emotions

ally in control because the newest, and smartest, part of our brain, the PFC, is in charge and allowing us to observe, orient ourselves to the situation, and act optimally. Somewhere between Dread and Anguish is where most people are taken over by our survival brain, run by two small glands at the base of your brain called the amygdala. The amygdala is famous for handling the fight, flight, or freeze response and you'll hear plenty about it soon. Just know that you never want it to be in charge. Where the graph of the PFC crosses over the amygdala between Dread and Anguish is your Fear Frontier; it's where you stop thinking in an effective, calculated, and rational way and start reacting with a survival response.

The goal of *Fear Is Fuel* is to change the graph to look like figure 1.3.

In keeping with LeDoux's idea, if you can get to the courageous end of the bell curve for all three components of fear, you'll push out your Fear Frontier and live a courageous life. It's not enough to tame one fear factor on the triangle, as you are about to see.

Your Fear Frontier and Terror Triangle are related and drive subconscious behavior most people are unaware of. Because of the way you built your mind's hard drive of memories and emotions, you have hidden fears as well. Your hidden fears are the toughest ones to tame and uncover. Once you identify them, however, you can eventually learn to use them as fuel. Uncovering hidden fears and learning to use them as fuel is what pushing out your Fear Frontier is all about. The Fear Frontier doesn't exist in one physical

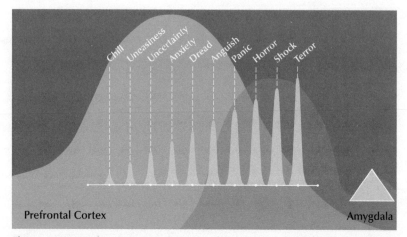

Chill Uneasiness Uncertainty Anxiety Dread Anguish Panic Horror Shock Terror

Prefrontal Cortex   Amygdala

Figure 1.3. Moving Out Your Fear Frontier to Still Act Rationally when in a Higher State of Emotion

place in the brain; rather it's the myriad connections of millions of different neurons in various parts of the brain all working together in an incredibly sophisticated behavior and perception network of both wired and wireless communication.

Consider the implication of knowing that there are three kinds of fear as you sit in front of our former Navy SEAL who now has to refer to himself as *retired* Chief Petty Officer Doug Chapman. He and I sit at a shaded picnic table in La Jolla, California, the ocean breeze swishing palm leaves overhead. Uncomfortably, I shift my eyes toward the ground after a tear rolls down his tanned and chiseled cheek. His throat labors convulsively; he manages just a whisper explaining that his marriage is crumbling and the job leading a hot new start-up has him hanging by his fingernails to a business development role after his investors replaced him as CEO. In short, despite having a world of physical courage, his life was not following the script that he set for himself. Despite being fearless in the face of battle, the warrior who was slumped in front of me in La Jolla had not been able to translate his physical bravery to courage in career and relationships. The root of his problem goes back to his Fear Frontier.

You can't help but rethink fear when you are in front of a real-life Captain America and you witness him crying because he's finally coming to grips with the subconscious, hidden fears he was afraid to explore at any other time in his life. When he was in the Teams the thing that mattered most was physical courage. Chapman, like all SEALs, was world-class at focusing on a task even when his life was in grave danger. He knew his job and was brilliant at it; with physical fears he pushed his Frontier of acting optimally all the way out to Terror. He now realizes that outside of navy life he needed more than physical courage to be his best and live that dream life. Chappie was scared in a way he had never been before. Without the Teams he didn't have a tribe; he felt like his identity was at stake. He was in search of a silver bullet. Like many people he had not yet realized that he harbored hidden emotional fears of abandonment, fear of failure, an identity crisis, and fear of commitment that were ripping him apart from the inside.

The realization that a Navy SEAL would have been terrified of failure (or scared of anything for that matter) came as a surprise to me. Like many people, I used to have a completely erroneous view of fear. I thought the feelings and anxieties I felt were only happening to me, and that I was just a sissy and needed to toughen up. I didn't discover the truth until I finally faced the ultimate fear. Sitting with Chappie made me realize I was never alone—that inner fears could be as bad or worse than fear of outer threats.

On that sunny seventy-degree day in La Jolla, I wondered why Chappie hadn't been able to live a life of courage in his marriage and business and reach his true potential. He had successfully made it through the courage factory that the US Navy calls BUD/S—he had proven that he was literally one of the most courageous men in the world in combat. His tours of duty in Iraq earned him a whole chest full of fruit salad (lots of very colorful ribbons that signify many medals won) on his dress uniform.

BUD/S is designed for training just one of the three components of courage—he was without a doubt top of the world in one aspect: physical courage. Warriors don't have a need in combat for the two other forces of fear. The reason he was scared outside of a military or combat situation was that his training was as specific as it was effective.

To find a Hollywood happy ending in real life, however, Chappie needed to recognize the other two sides of the Terror Triangle—emotional and instinctual fears. Then he had to find his Fear Frontier. Once he saw the difference among the three fears, it would be up to him to identify their role in his happiness and success, and train those areas in the same way he faced physical fears. He had learned how to do it with physical fear, so I was sure he could apply the same process to the other two categories of fear.

The first way of using fear as fuel—to face one fear at a time—works well for that specific fear, and it can carry over to similar fears; however, it doesn't help you cultivate a total mindset of courage and curiosity that transcends other fears. The other drawback of this one-at-a-time approach to conquering fears is that you never create the subconscious neural networks for courage. You miss the understanding of how to use fear in any situation for better decision making and optimal outcomes. To create that mindset of courage you have to rely on neuroscience.

USING FEAR AS FUEL METHOD #2

Recognize physiological changes in your body created by an amygdala hijacking and focus on turning feelings of fear to sources of fuel using the BASE framework.

As I listened to Chappie's story, suddenly my mind switched channels to images of a colorful functional magnetic resonance imaging (fMRI) brain scan I had recently seen at a seminar in Zurich, Switzerland, hosted by a French-born Buddhist monk named Matthieu Ricard. Ricard lectures around the world on happiness. His adult life began as the caricature of a meek intellectual—a molecular biologist by training who converted to Buddhism in his thirties. Today he travels the world telling his story. He uses his science background to combine some of the most cutting-edge technology like fMRI brain scans with techniques in meditation and mindfulness to help make the world a better place. The scans he shared in that Zurich lecture showed different parts of the brain that were activated for different types of fears and happiness.

Ricard is known as the "happiest man in the world" according to *Time* magazine, and his technicolor brain scans were proof that he had tamed fear in physical, emotional, and instinctual realms. If this unassuming intellectual could conquer fear in all three territories why hadn't a decorated Navy SEAL been able to do the same thing?

What is the secret to getting courageous in all aspects of life? Ricard's philosophy is that we have to be able to, on demand, develop a state of mind that deals with the ups and downs of life's challenges. We need to build our own inner resources.

Just a dozen years ago if a Buddhist monk, or even a psychologist, prescribed actions or treatments you would have had to take it on faith that it worked. Until somewhat recently, psychological treatments were often viewed with skepticism, because it was difficult to replicate or measure results with scientific rigor. We are just now at a point where neuroscience can show what is going in the brain and psychological approaches like cognitive behavioral therapy (CBT) or ACT can address those issues. Most importantly, we know why and how to use fear as fuel instead of running away from it as people have for so long. Much of our understanding and measurement has to do with the root of all fears you'll read about later.

There is a progression you'll learn in this book that follows a formula you can use to change your own life and the lives of your team, organization, or family members, too. We're starting with the bottom box and building your fear fluency now. See figure 1.4.

The primary reason most of us cannot live a complete life of courage is the same issue our Navy SEAL was facing: we have never been shown how to discover our Fear Frontier and push it further out the performance spectrum on all three sides of the triangle. We've never been told we need more fear in our life, and that the

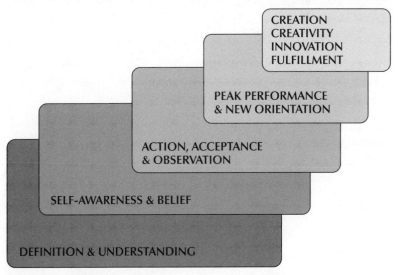

Figure 1.4. Building Fear Fluency

fear is our ultimate source of fuel. It's not just the source of fuel; those three components are our source of energy as well.

3.

In the United States, more than one in five people are clinically diagnosed with a mental illness, including depression or anxiety. The US Psychological Association lists over five hundred defined phobias. You might have one, or many, of these. I can't imagine how many I had.

We have learned that 33.7 percent of the population will be affected by a mental illness in their lifetime.[2] That harrowing statistic is getting worse in our current political climate and parenting environment. After analyzing thousands of surveys from my fear seminars and speeches I was shocked to discover that more than 80 percent of people believe that they have some sort of fear holding them back from being the most successful and happy version of themselves. Most of the respondents were what most people would consider successful presidents and CEOs of large companies! In all the people I've helped discover their Fear Frontier, nearly every one of them had hidden fears they didn't know existed until we helped make them aware of those fears, and then labeled those fears and eventually pushed out their frontiers, and how they reacted to other fears.

I will not only lay out a blueprint to forge your own temple of courage but also build a shield against manipulation by fear, bullying by dogma, and interference in your life by others. When you push out your Fear Frontier you will live a life that is created by you instead of a life that happens to you. That means creativity, innovation, and fulfillment will become your constant companions.

Fear Is Fuel came about to expose fear and the people who manipulate it as the ultimate frauds they really are. In order to become courageous you first must destroy everything you think, know, or believe about fear. What led me to write this book is what happened to me after I came head-to-head with my greatest fear, and what I discovered on the other side of that Fear Frontier.

At six years old I planted the seed for my Fear Frontier: an original traumatic moment that kept recurring in my brain with severe negative emotions attached to that episode. When my mind recalled those events and emotions my survival instinct took over and I wanted to fight, flee, or freeze. When we hit our Fear Frontier we don't act optimally or even rationally. We let fear be in charge.

Chappie confided in me that his parents had driven him home from a swim meet one night to find their front door swinging open in the autumn breeze. The house had been broken into and all their valuables stolen. He was ten years old and his feeling of safety at home was shattered. He felt violated and at the same time vulnerable. Those same feelings that channeled him to become a warrior, fighting for others also made it difficult to trust others and be truly vulnerable. As we talked about his past, he could start to see what was familiar about those feelings he had as a child, and the problems he had with his current wife. The Terror Triangle helped explain what was happening in his life and helped him make choices that would ultimately lead to happiness and success.

There are only two ways to make decisions: out of fear or out of opportunity. When you make a decision out of fear, it almost always leads to regret. When you make a choice based on opportunity, it will always lead to learning something and getting closer to your goal. When your amygdala—that small gland at the base of your brain—hijacks your body, it wants to make every decision based on simply surviving. The amygdala always wants to fight, flee, or freeze. It will do whatever it thinks gives you the better chance of living to send your gene pool on to the next generation. Fear only helps you to survive; opportunity makes you thrive.

After thirty years I figured out how to embrace fear and use it to fuel greatness. Neuroscience has recently proven that there are many parts of the brain associated with creating and recalling memories. We use the amygdala, the hippocampus, and if emotions run high, a region called parahippocampal cortex. Scientists used to think that just the amygdala harbored memories, but they were wrong. It's a very complex network of interconnected neurons throughout the brain. There are many regions working at the same time so we can simultaneously write new memories and recall critical life-saving information we may have learned in the past.

Understanding this complex memory creation and emotional association will be the key to shortcutting a path to courage and fearlessness by using the fear response to power your life.

For me, and many others who never had the advantage of modern neuroscience, we had to learn to use fear as fuel by pushing up against the fear with a near-death experience. Ironically, that was the best thing that could have happened to me, but it doesn't have to happen to you.

4.

I was stretched out on the lime green shag carpet in the living room, imagining that my GI Joe figurine (he wasn't a doll because only girls played with dolls) was in the Vietnam jungle on a secret mission. My brother was next to me, occasionally sabotaging my mission. I imagined his voice was the Viet Cong psychological operative blaring brainwashing messages over a static-ridden PA speaker in Hanoi. I was working Joe's kung-fu grip, mounting him on the six-wheel bright yellow all terrain vehicle when my mom and dad broke up the jungle warfare operation by lumbering into the room like giants. Dad plopped down on the couch with a grunt after Mom turned on the "boob tube" as they called it. It was summer of 1976 and Boston's favorite newscaster, Chet Curtis, was the man everyone turned to for the latest news in Beantown. My parents were no exception. Just as Chet started in on a story about notorious gangster Whitey Bulger, he raised his right hand up to his ear as if he had to focus on hearing the message from his director again because the first time didn't make any sense. Suddenly he blurted out urgently, "This just in, an apparent plane crash at Logan Airport, we're going live to Rusty Allen for the details."

The image cut to a middle-aged anchorman whose dark hair contrasted against his chalky skin, the words coming out of his mouth were a ghastly combination of a desperate cry and an angry yell. He was trying to converse professionally into his microphone on the tarmac of Boston's Logan Airport. "More than one hundred people are believed dead as the pilots were unable to execute the instrument landing in foggy conditions just an hour ago. The devastation is horrific!"

The pilots flew a Delta DC-9 too low on an instrument approach and slammed into the sea wall, cartwheeling the plane down the runway smashing it and its contents to pieces. There were body parts, luggage, and flaming wreckage strewn up and down the tarmac.

My jaw slacked open and I froze, letting Joe slide from my fingers and land on the soft shag carpet as I watched this scene unfold in monochromatic reality on our RCA black-and-white TV. I didn't know it at the time, but the neurons in my mind were firing and wiring.

Immediately two memories were etched in my mind's very sophisticated hard drive: a semantic memory of the facts of what just happened and an emotional memory of what I felt because of those events. My stomach knotted. I was scared. Because there was high emotion creating the memory, my amygdala was activated, which made the memory even more unforgettable—the sensation fired more synapses in my brain because of the power of the event. I engaged all the potential high energy on the far end of the bell curve that Joe LeDoux describes, so it was written deeply in my memory. My heart pounded. Emotionally, I empathized with the passengers, I imagined what it would feel like if I was on the plane, or if my parents were on the plane. I created my first primary Fear Frontier—a terrifying association of an event with an emotion that would become the foundation for most of my fears for the next thirty years.

Trauma is usually associated with a single event, or the same repeated event that is similarly traumatic. Your own original anchor events, if unchecked and unresolved, will plant a seed of fearfulness within you that will have repercussions throughout your life. If succumbing to fear continues, if you never learn to use it, then you have an orientation and view of reality that will feed a lie of anxiety and dread. You will be stuck in a loop that keeps courage out of reach.

Everyone's personalities are shaped by childhood traumas. You eventually find defense mechanisms that become ingrained. Figuring out your Fear Frontier is the first step to identifying fear and then using the right defenses to get better at everything.

If you were that six-year-old kid, and you'd never even seen a plane in real life, you'd still have a blank slate. Just a couple of weeks after the crash my family was ready to fly from Boston to Atlanta, Georgia, to visit our Uncle Teddy and Aunt Ginny. They had a litter of puppies and one of them was reserved for us—our first dog (appropriately named Rhett Butler by my Dixie-loving aunt). Our hand-me-down luggage was packed up for an exciting week-long trip south of the Mason-Dixon line, the first family trip we'd ever taken in my six short years on earth.

The family hauled bags from the parking garage into the airport. Picture a Delta logo on the tail of a DC-9 through the hazy smoke of the terminal. That was my amygdala's trigger. It was a sensory input (information that was collected through vision and the visual cortex) that sparked the amygdala, hippocampus, and prefrontal cortex into simultaneous action—they would all fire the same neurons again and again when I thought of flying or Delta. My subconscious brain thought I was about to die. It was time to survive, or so it thought.

When my amygdala sensed this threat, my palms got sweaty, my mouth got dry, my heart raced, and I held my breath. Those were my signals for survival; fear would change my body the same way each time my subconscious detected a threat. There was a chance according to whatever data my senses had collected, that a threat existed that might make me extinct. Either my inherited memory or my learned memory recalled a threat and activated my threat response system—through the amygdala in that instant. Immediately my two memories from the crash were retrieved from my brain's hard drive and brought into real time. A fierce flight reaction was taking over my six-year-old body—I had to get out of that airport. I kicked and screamed and cried, trying to pull away from my parents. I nearly drew blood from my mother's soft skin. People in the airport stopped to stare and see who was apparently torturing a tomcat. My mom and dad tried to comfort me. I got louder and redder in the face, tears cascading down my scarlet cheeks. In an attempt to get away I ripped at mom's arm like a cat trying to scramble up a tree. I threw such an apoplectic fit that we finally got kicked out of the airport. We did the only thing we could do—we drove the seventeen hours from Boston to Atlanta. Yup, that's right, we drove. Our week-long vacation suddenly turned into three days in the car and a few days of fun. Even worse is the fact that I still hear about it at family gatherings today, more than forty years later.

When I saw the Delta logo on the tail of the plane, I recalled the traumatic event of a few weeks earlier, and as my mind relived those facts, it also felt the emotions I associated with the event. In 2016 neuroscientists at Harvard University led by Dr. Scott Orr discovered that within ten minutes of a trigger event your associated emotions will be activated.[3] That's when I could have rewritten the emotional memories or made them extinct (if either my parents or I knew how). I'd never be able to get rid of that semantic memory; the facts of what happened will stay with me forever. However, I could have changed the emotional association. In this case I didn't.

In fact, I made that emotional memory stronger because those feelings were reinforced by my fight for survival and meeting resistance from everyone (my parents and the poor lady working the gate for Delta), so as emotions got hotter my electrical impulses got stronger across the neurons and the memory became more deeply ingrained. I wired those neurons together.

The crash and our subsequent trip to the airport anchored a Fear Frontier in me that would be the foundation for a lifetime of anxiety and fear. Anytime I felt my heart racing, or my palms got sweaty, or I stopped breathing, I had to run. I slept with the light on in high school. When I heard thunder on the playground I'd run for the house to hide safely away from "deadly" lightning. There was a neighborhood bully named Hubba whose favorite pastime was putting a giant rubber thumb on his hand and watching me whirl into hysterics as he chased after me. I was fearful of life, and it amplified my feelings of worthlessness and insignificance.

As the son of a first-generation Irish immigrant living in the blue-collar Boston suburbs, the expectations for me were pretty low. No one in my family went to college. When we were young my dad worked from 8:00 in the morning to 5:00 at night selling shoes; he'd stop at home for a quick bite and a nap and then deliver liquor from 8:00 p.m. to 11:00, cutting out in time to get to Boston's first data center, where he learned to tap letters on a keyboard from midnight to 7:00, entering data on keypunch cards. We lived with my grandparents in a duplex, and three nights out of most weeks we'd have Bisquick pancakes for dinner because it was all we could afford. Being a coward and being poor provided one great benefit: it gave me ambition.

However ambitious I might have been to get out of our blue-collar Bisquick world, the seeds of cowardice were growing throughout my body like thistle, making any kind of accomplishment twice as hard as it could have been, blocking out the path to courage.

"Coach, I think I ate something bad for lunch, can I go sit in the locker room for a bit?" I lied to my baseball coach after I heard distant thunder. He probably saw the terror or shame in my eyes and realized I was unconsciously holding my breath; he would reply, "No problem; why don't you hit the showers and call it a day." Of course that fear-based decision led to regret. I never became the baseball player I wanted to be, since it's tough to get better by skipping practice.

When I was scared I tried to lie about it, but lying led to destructive feelings of guilt. Guilt, shame, and fear were my constant states of being. Because I wouldn't get near an airplane I missed out on spring breaks, I turned down exchange programs, I never got to Disney World as a child—all because I was petrified of something statistically safer than sitting in a car. It turns out it was the fear that almost killed me, not the flying. It took thirty years to find out if I could ever get over my fear of flying, and when I figured it out it unlocked a world I could have never possibly imagined. The same could be true for you, but you only find out on the other side of fear.

2

∽

Forget What You Think

Fear is the main source of superstition, and one of the main sources of cruelty. To conquer fear is the beginning of wisdom.

—Bertrand Russell

1.

The University of Southern California (USC) campus in 1987 was a muted brick patchwork of rosy lines separating tumbleweed-colored squares reminiscent of ancient Spanish missions. The idyllic setting was shattered by a 6'3"-tall freshman lumbering across the courtyard dressed as a janitor, as out of place as a bikini in church. The adventurous teen was about to play a prank on one of his best friends. His plan was to barge into an American Literature lecture where his friend was fastidiously taking notes and claim he was sent to clean up some student's vomit. As he burst through the door and launched into character the students and professor stared slack-jawed for a solid thirty seconds before they finally erupted in riotous laughter. The prankster was a Sports Information major who got a great thrill out of playing the janitor and catching the class and its esteemed professor completely off guard. He ducked back out the door before anyone had a chance to stop him. It turns out the last laugh might just be on him.

As luck would have it the professor caught sight of him the next day in the school café. Before the prankster could bolt to safety the Lit teacher did the opposite of what our unwitting comedian expected. Rather than the dressing down the freshman braced for, the professor got such a laugh out of the janitor character that he invited the young man to come back anytime he wanted to (in character of course). This amazing life story, however, was just getting started.

About six months later the make-believe janitor's friends invited him to a show at the world's most famous improv-comedy club called the Groundling, on Melrose Avenue in Los Angeles. The student was pulled up on stage during an audience participation skit, and sadly, the result seemed to be a disaster.

To be truly happy and successful you've got to recognize your fears and use them to power greatness; if you miss the opportunity to do so you'll be imprisoned in a cocoon your entire life and never embrace all that life has to offer, and all that you are meant to bring to the world. Celebrated figures throughout history have experienced breakthrough moments of courage by facing their fears. These epiphanies come in many different forms; yours can too. The good news is that if you miss the opportunity to use your fear, there will surely be another one. Oftentimes the event seems terrifying until it's over and you look back on it. There is no courage without fear. If you don't feel fear and you take action, there is no courage in that deed; it's just action. If you feel fear and act thoughtfully in the face of it, you are living a life of courage. Once you recognize and use fear, the life-changing results are always the same, even if the path to getting there is different. When you funnel your fear you'll not only change your life, but you'll change the world by bringing your true gift to the rest of us. Until you find the courage to be the authentic you, you will not be able to find your true self; you'll be too afraid of what others think, or what bad things can happen, or how things might change if you actually become you. You are not alone; millions of people have yet to discover their authentic, honest, courageous selves.

I work with a lot of executives and CEOs, many of them worth tens of millions of dollars, many who have asked me to help find their true and authentic self. Not knowing your true self is a prime symptom of unprocessed, hidden fears. Hidden fears smother our intuition and gut instincts. If you don't know what it feels like to sense a full-body yes, or a full-body no, to be in touch with your physical sensations of truth, you aren't really living. Hidden fears hide the real you, just as our janitor discovered (thankfully for all of us who love the Christmas classic *Elf*).

That USC student who got pulled up on stage was so petrified that he couldn't deliver his one line; in fact he couldn't utter a word. He experienced one of the three survival responses brought on by fear, the one indicative of the highest level of fear, the most primal—he froze. Like a white-tailed deer spotlighted by a bank of halogens. However scared he was, being up on stage and making a fool of himself was not nearly as bad as he had secretly feared it would be. He had a fear of public speaking that had been holding him back and he was forced to face it. He had experienced the worst possible failure—he blew his "one chance at fame." In that moment he realized the truth: his fear was not nearly as bad as he imagined, and it changed his life.

Freezing on stage was a traumatic moment that opened a whole new world to him. The student confessed that "even in that moment of abject fear and failure" he found it utterly thrilling to be onstage.[1] That was when he realized that his true calling was to be a comedian. He found the hidden fear he hadn't even realized he had—the fear of failure and rejection on stage—and he realized the fear was nothing but a farce, a movie he played in his mind. He faced his fears head-on and came out laughing; he learned to get excited by them. For the next three years he took classes to learn the skills and art of comedy and stagecraft. He tamed the fear of failure and rejection by facing it head-on and using a similar framework to *Fear Is Fuel*.

Despite moving back home for two years after graduation, taking classes, and making little money, Will Ferrell was having the time of his life. Facing his fear and realizing that he could tame fear, and even turn it into fuel, was what helped create one of the great comedic actors of our generation. Even as an established star Ferrell still has fought stage fright,[2] but judging by his results, now he uses the energy that once rendered him speechless as excitement to perform. He also disproved the common fallacy that says you only have one shot at your chance of a lifetime.

Athletes, actors, and explorers aren't the only ones who learn how to use fear as fuel. The greatest leaders in history have figured out how to tame fear and go beyond making us laugh; they have used its power to change the world once they learned how simple it is to actually strive to do the deeds.

RECOGNIZING FEAR AS FUEL

The largest collegiate rowing regatta in the United States is the National Championship Dad Vail rowing regatta held every year since 1934 in Philadelphia. After a year competing for the University of New Hampshire, the pinnacle of our season was racing against almost sixty other universities. There were ten heats of six boats in our category. The first heat we took five mighty, boat-rattling strokes off the starting line. Then my up and back motion ground to a stop as my sliding seat derailed and jumped off the track that guides it back and forth (our coach later said I rowed like a puppy trying to screw a golf ball, but I still contend it was the fifteen-year-old boat). We came to a splashing halt, the thick wooden handle of the oar driving into my stomach. I scurried to put the seat back on. With it back in place, we raced in a terrified frenzy from last place through the five other boats to win the heat. Unbelievably, the same thing repeated itself in both the quarter- and semi-final—with us fumbling to a stop then coming back and eventually winning each race. When the finals rolled around I was so petrified the seat would jump off that we raced off the starting line like it was a 100-yard sprint instead of the 2,000-meter Olympic distance. Fear fueled us as we pulled ahead of the competitors by more than four lengths. We disregarded the mental governor that usually drives pacing in athletic events and went full out from the start. We won with as much relief as elation. In retrospect it was the first time I realized that fear could actually be a fuel and "pacing" is often fear-based. It confirmed what Sir Edmund Hillary said: that fear can help you extend what you believed your capacity was.

By all accounts the freshman member of the New York State Assembly had it made. He was just elected to his first office, his family was loaded, and he was a pretty good-looking kid with an attractive young wife. A real Hollywood couple. The problem was he was sick much of his upbringing, he lived in the shadow of his successful father, and he realized, after the boss of the New York Senate ordered him how and when to vote, that he was not his own man. He was afraid to stand up for himself, and he was afraid he'd never live up to his father. He harbored a hidden fear that seemed impossible in its irony—he was afraid of success. He never had a frightful moment like Ferrell on stage, or me in the hospital (the near-death experience you'll hear about soon), but he lived through so many moments in his life where someone chipped away at his psyche that he felt that the statue left over was as weak and fragile as an Irish crystal decanter balancing on a wobbly shelf. He knew if he didn't make a change he'd never be happy and fulfilled. He longed to be an epitome of courage and heroism, but he just couldn't take action. The catalyst of the change came when his mother and wife died on the same day.[3]

After experiencing the greatest loss imaginable in one day, he faced his Fear Frontier with no attachments and a realization that a fear of loss had been keeping him from the life of his dreams and reaching his true potential. He left almost immediately from New York to the Badlands of North Dakota with the goal of setting up a ranch. He brought two of his hunting buddies from Maine to help him build a house and herd cattle. His revelation around loss and impermanence helped him learn how to live in the present, enjoying every moment of life, doing his best to live a life of courage and integrity.

The boy who was in the shadow of so many in New York set up two ranches with thousands of acres before he came back East a man of confidence and courage. When he retuned from the West, Teddy Roosevelt was a changed man—confident, courageous, and with a wide sweeping vision of success not just for himself but for his country. His rise from scared and sickly New York State Assemblyman to New York governor, leader of the Rough Riders, adventurer, and ultimately the US president who did more for outdoors and parks in our country than any other president was another example of how taming fear can lead to a life of success we can't even imagine until we cross that frontier. In my favorite quote of all time, Roosevelt shares his belief that it is not the critic who counts, rather the man who gets in the arena and experiences both victory and defeat. Roosevelt advises that once you suspend judgment about winning or losing or pointing out where others failed, you can live an entirely different life. He shared his ideals in a 1910 speech he delivered at Paris's Sorbonne University that has inspired millions. It's commonly quoted as the Man in the Arena:

> It is not the critic who counts; not the man who points out how the strong man stumbles, or where the doer of deeds could have done them better. The credit belongs to the man who is actually in the arena, whose face is marred by dust and sweat and blood; who strives valiantly; who errs, who comes short again and again, because there is no effort without error and shortcoming; but who does actually strive to do the deeds; who knows great enthusiasms, the great devotions; who

spends himself in a worthy cause; who at the best knows in the end the triumph of high achievement, and who at the worst, if he fails, at least fails while daring greatly, so that his place shall never be with those cold and timid souls who neither know victory nor defeat.[4]

3.

What about me?

Will Ferrell was a big, funny, gregarious kid. He was born to be a co-median. Teddy Roosevelt had rich parents; he was already way ahead of the game and had tons of advantages.

What about me?

I'm an administrative assistant and work for a temp service, sure I went to a great university. Really, I'm just a glorified secretary. I studied really hard and went to law school but dropped out after a se-mester. My parents are so successful, yet I'm a complete let down. I'm afraid I'll just end up getting my "Mrs. Degree" and live a life making peanut butter sandwiches and picking up kids from soccer.

If that sounds like a familiar dialogue it is a classic fear-based mindset of a victim. The victim mindset is one that believes life happens to you, not by you. *Fear Is Fuel* is built on the premise that there are two ways to make decisions in life; one is based on fear and the other is based on opportunity. People who make decisions based on fear often do so because they have an overpowering vic-tim mindset. It is often the default mindset that comes naturally to so many of us, because of all the data that was put into our mental hard drives growing up.

Our minds process decision-making information with a filter built for survival in a prehistoric world. Fear-based decisions help our genes make it to another generation, but hold us back from hap-piness, fulfillment, and success. We didn't choose our parents, we didn't choose the language we learned growing up, or the town we were born in, or the color of our skin; we didn't choose any of the things that create our orientation to the world. However, as adults when our prefrontal cortex is fully developed, we can either rein-force our childhood survival data and those fight, flight, or freeze connections in our brain or we can rewrite and improve the process-ing power in our mind's hard drive. It is the process of rewriting the data and actually erasing primal shortcuts that helps us remove upper limits on our happiness and success. Getting out of the same thought patterns allows us to use what were once fears we ran away from as new and powerful sources of fuel. The great news is that you, and anyone, can learn to do it. And if you stick with this book you'll have a guaranteed path to courage—even if you consider yourself a glorified secretary.

There was a girl from Texas who had the same challenges that you might be facing. She was stuck early in her life and fell into the trap of being a victim; she let her decisions be dominated by fear and intimidation. As a young, shy girl growing up in Abilene, she was often scared. Thanks to affluent and driven parents who gave her a great education, she was admitted to Stanford University where she worked hard and did well, but it was intimidating. She kept her head down, didn't rock the boat, studied, and got good grades. After college she was afraid of losing her parents' approval; primal fears of abandonment or disapproval seemed to be the motivator of her major life decisions. She relied on the database built up as a child Her dad was a judge and that influenced her path toward becoming a lawyer. Her Stanford diploma got her into UCLA law school as her father wanted, but the journey only lasted one semester before she was so miserable that she quit.

She became a receptionist at a real estate office. She broke down after spending her life doing what her parents expected her to do; she was unknowingly living in fear of rejection from the tribe and it finally took its toll. Eventually she found herself a secretary at a temp company called Kelly Services in 1976. In 1977 she got married. Peanut butter sandwiches and soccer mom shuttling were not far off.

If you look back on how her database was developing as she matured, one of her biggest Fear Frontier traumas manifested itself when she was a young adult. She lived in awe of her father, who was a prominent attorney, judge, and law professor. Like many children, she was afraid she would never be able to fill his shoes, so when she failed out of UCLA law school after just one semester she was devastated. She became another person who thought her "one shot" was blown. When I first met her in Miami, she confessed that her dad nearly crushed her dreams for good when he told her, "I'm not sure you'll ever amount to anything."[5]

I listened to that story in the Green Room of the Fontainebleau Hotel in Miami. I was the opening speaker for a Young President's Organization conference and Carly Fiorina was up after me. It was

2016 and she was one of the most successful businesswomen of all time. In fact, she was running for president of the United States.

After failing out of law school and getting married, Carly uncovered her hidden fears when she and her husband moved to Italy. She credits teaching English to Italian businessmen for helping her learn to take risks and yearn for challenges and assignments that were tough. After the time in Italy she faced her fears of rejection or abandonment and asked herself, "What happens if I end up being all alone? What is the worst case?" She was scared but she decided to act, not react. She had the choice to make a fear-based decision or one based on opportunity.

Carly decided on a future filled with opportunity. She really wanted a career in business, despite the business world being considered a "man's world" by many women at the time (in the early 1980s). Carly went back to earn an MBA from the University of Maryland and then went to work for Lucent Technologies selling phone systems to the government.

Imagine a shy, pretty, Texas girl walking into a room full of Department of Defense, former military tough guys. Many of this old guard were used to back-slapping, strip club boondoggles funded by unethical salesmen trying to get the big contract. How would she ever win in that terrifying boy's club?

Carly decided she would use fear as fuel and turn those situations to her advantage. One of her classic stories was a sales meeting with the old boys' network; she decided to face everything head-on and accept responsibility for the outcome. Carly stuffed socks into her pants and went into the meeting bragging boisterously that her equipment was the same as all the other sales guys. That's a move that took more courage than she would have ever thought possible, and it was also one that caught the old boys totally off guard and had them rolling on the floor in laughter.[6]

It wasn't long before her career skyrocketed once she figured out how to use fear as fuel. Carly became adept at facing challenges head-on with calculated risks that, according to the *New York Times*, fueled her

> focus and ferocious effort, a dizzying climb up the corporate ladder, culminating in more than five years as the chief executive officer of Hewlett-Packard, by far the most prominent American company that

a woman had—or, to this day, has—ever run. Fiorina, in a phrase, made history.[7]

Secretary to the most famous female CEO of all time.

Gangly prankster to one of the most successful comedic actors of our generation.

Sickly, spoiled rich kid to someone who changed the course of the free world.

All three of those transformations, in one way or another, were fueled by fear to people just like you. They were no different. We all have fear, anxiety, insecurity; that is hard-wired into our survival mechanisms. You are the only one who can make the choice to use it to your advantage in today's world or let those fears keep you afraid and living in a cocoon. There's nothing stopping you from adopting the same mindset Carly, Will, or Teddy did.

4.

Your Framework for Courageous Life

To learn to use fear as fuel in the fastest and most effective manner possible, you need to follow a framework based on neuroscience that also uses the best ideas from past successes. This is the second method of learning how to use fear as fuel; the neuroscience approach. Keep in mind that the first method of using fear as fuel is attacking one fear at a time (that's often a major component of exposure therapy and a component of cognitive behavioral therapy, which teaches patients how to identify and dispute unrealistic or unhelpful thoughts and fears, and then develop problem-solving skills); the third and last method is dancing with the angel of death.

There are four steps based on my research interviewing dozens of neuroscientists and psychologists and working with hundreds of CEOs, professional athletes, and special forces operators. It's like getting your body in shape; it's not easy but the following steps can be adopted by anyone and understood by anyone, so it's simple. The amazing thing about the neuroscience method is the speed. I had the CEO of one of the world's largest motion picture studios, whom I mentored, tell me it was like putting five years of mindfulness training on fast-forward and getting the same results in a few months by learning the ability to control your own mind and subconscious decision making.

You can climb these rungs to courage no matter where you are from, how much money you have, how much education you've received. The only thing that matters is your willingness to try the *Fear Is Fuel* framework and know that if you keep up with it, your life will change. First, you have to decide if life is going to happen to you and you'll make decisions out of fear, or if you are going to face everything, accept responsibility, and create a life you author, making your decisions based on opportunity.

The framework follows these simple steps:

1. **Feel Your Fear**—Figuring out how your body manifests fear physically will let you know when your amygdala and limbic brain are active and when your subconscious is trying to take survival action. I detail the principle called Free Energy in chapter 4, which becomes the fuel for your amygdala powering regret. The amygdala and limbic system activation creates physical changes I call your fear tells. Those physical sensations can let you know you are primed for peak performance and about to react. They also warn you that you will have to take control quickly to clear your working memory and resolve the uncertainty so your amygdala doesn't make you fight or flee. Learning how and discerning when this happens helps you understand when you have to take action.

2. **Find the Fear to Fuel It**—The second step is purposely putting yourself in "fearful" situations to exercise your survival system, make it stronger, and then learn how to clear your mind so you create an environment that becomes the precursor to happiness and greatness. You have to get used to the feeling of fear to turn that same feeling into excitement, motivation, fulfillment, and fuel. You have to be able to shut off the amygdala when it tries to take action. This takes practice.

3. **Build Blocks of Courage**—Optimize your mind and body to effectively deal with scary situations. We will use the BASE method to rewrite the internal hard drive that now makes 75 percent of your decisions subconsciously. This includes a technique I call VETing, learning from every situation to rebuild your mental hard drive, believing you created everything that

happens to you, and optimizing your body, diet, and environment for courage. It's setting the playing field for a champion.

4. **Use Fear for Peak Performance**—Turn survival-driven fearful situations into opportunities to in some way or another use fear to unlock superhuman performance. Eventually you will let go of future-based decisions and will be living in the present all the time in a state of peak performance, fulfillment, and happiness.

To get to the state of peak performance, fulfillment, and happiness, you've got to destroy everything you think you know about fear. The biggest lie we're told is to avoid fear. *Fear Is Fuel* is anchored on my philosophy that you need more fear and more positive stress in your life. Our bodies and minds have been built over thousands of years with very sophisticated systems that must be fired up and run around the track regularly to stay high performing. One thing you'll learn is that it's not enough to use just one system either—you've got to exercise the entire machine, and since the world today is so much different from the world eons ago when our brains were designed, you've got to train your brain for what is important in today's world.

3

~

Fear Tells You About You

We suffer more often in imagination than in reality.

—Seneca

1.

Phil Hellmuth looked down the smooth green felt of the poker table. In the middle, a mountain of chips were just pushed to the center. "All in," said the diminutive character sitting to Hellmuth's left. For a moment Hellmuth observed, then oriented himself, trying to see if his foe was using an intimidation tactic, bluffing with this half-million-dollar bet, or if he really had Hellmuth's two pair beat.

Hellmuth would go on to win the World Series of Poker fourteen times, amassing a fortune of over twenty million dollars. Playing cards. He believes that the secret to winning at poker is 30 percent reading the cards and 70 percent reading the opponents. Every player has a series of tells, their unconscious reactions to both good and bad situations. A great poker player can read those tells like a Hemingway short story.

Slowly Hellmuth counted out a half million dollars of his own chips, preparing to call the bet. With a mind as fast as Big Blue, his statistical knowledge told him that with the cards showing on the table and what was in his hand, he had greater than an 87 percent chance of winning. Knowing the cards were only 30 percent of the equation, he didn't slide the chips into the center of the table just yet. He wanted everyone to think he was about to.

Like an assassin having second thoughts before choking the life out of a sleeping victim, his hands stalled before they laced around each side of the stacks, ready to push forward and call the bet. His hands put enough pressure on the chips to advance them ever so slightly. As he initiated the push he looked up and stared at his opponents eyes; he focused on the pupils. In that split second, Hellmuth noticed his opponent's pupils get bigger; he saw black flooding inside the icy blue iris and realized that the other player was watching something he liked.[1]

Hellmuth's advantage was perceiving his opponent's positive response to counting out chips to call. When someone's pupils get bigger and you see more black, that generally means there is something good happening; when the pupils get smaller something bad has just happened. Hellmuth folded. The third player didn't fold. He went all-in as well and lost $500,000 to the full house that their opponent was so happy to have in his hand. Knowing that tell, the change in his opponent's pupils, saved Hellmuth half a million dollars and powered him on his way to slaying all the players in the tournament. Knowing your fear tells will save you a lifetime of mediocrity and senseless suffering.

Poker players spend a lot of time looking for the reaction of their opponents. Some unconscious reactions can never be controlled— that's why you see so many players (including Hellmuth) wearing dark glasses during games. They can't regulate the reaction of their pupils.[2] It's not just pupils; there are all sorts of different tells. One player toys with their chips, one starts talking more, another bites their lip or doesn't move. Those are all actions that poker players call tells. You are going to use knowledge of tells, your own tells this time, and the same basic principle to build your courage.

To live an absolutely extraordinary life you need to know when fear, and more specifically the amygdala and limbic system, is trying to take over, make the choices, and take action based on survival. The amygdala should be just an early warning system; however, it was designed to be a rapid reaction force for humans living in a much more dangerous world. You are going to figure out your unconscious physiological response to fear so you'll know when your amygdala has been activated and wants to take over. That two-million-year-old-piece of software sitting at the base of our brain wants

THE INFLUENCE OF HIDDEN FEARS

We have no choice as to what we were taught growing up. We spoke the language our parents did; we lived in whatever home was provided for us. The choices others made for us shaped who we are, including our parents' definition of success or happiness, and what they found fearful or threatening. Early fears may have been so traumatic that we block out the conscious memory, but subconsciously those high-charged events live on. Maybe you were left alone as a child and strange people came to your door. You've had a hidden fear of being alone, and maybe have jumped from relationship to relationship and avoid being alone. That's a traumatic influence hidden from you yet driving your actions.

Fears are concealed deep in our subconscious because your fear network picks up things you never consciously see. Humans knowingly focus on one or two things at a time, collecting about 10 percent of what we absorb consciously, but our amygdala picks up raw data from the bigger scene that we seldom see, 90 percent of the information. Our subconscious fuels our perception of different events and creates our orientation and Prior Beliefs of the world. If your parents had a car repossessed or they couldn't afford new shoes for the school year, you may think getting a steady job, making $100,000 a year at a stable company is the best choice you can make—no matter how miserable you might be. Your hidden fear of not providing for your family locks happiness away from you because you fear you won't have all that you need. You're wrong. We don't have to let our hidden fears hold us back; we just need to rewrite them: shine some light on them and they'll scatter like cockroaches.

to run the show when it senses a threat, even if the threat has a one in one hundred million chance of harming you; it doesn't care. Once that lizard brain and primal survival network have sprung into action, then you can make a choice, but most people never see it that way, because they don't recognize their tells. You have the ability to use fear, and the physiological change in your body, as fuel. Or you can let it cripple you. Creating the subtle awareness to notice slight changes in your physiology takes those who practice meditation years to master. Scaring yourself every day will shortcut that process by months and possibly years. Don't get me wrong; there are many times in your life when the fear response can be helpful;

a burning building should cause you to flee, a gun pointed in your face should cause you to freeze. I'm not suggesting that the survival instinct is always bad; I'm saying it's always bad if you can't decide consciously whether to heed the message, and get in control enough to make the best possible choice.

Sensing something the amygdala thinks is dangerous, scary, or threatening triggers a reaction in your body for survival. Depending on how urgent a threat is, the physical reaction is turned up higher and higher. If you step in front of a bus, the reaction is powerful enough to get you to jump out of the way and that's good. When the amygdala is activated gradually by an email, a call, or a conversation and crosses the line to take over action, that's when we go from rational decision making to fear-based actions. That point is our Fear Frontier and often people don't know that threshold has been crossed. Unconsciously we operate at less than full brain power when the amygdala is reacting. Most people don't understand that the neurological process of survival, the fear response, occupies precious processing energy in their brains. You are going to learn to turn that survival effort and energy into radically better decision-making capability.

The first step toward the life of your dreams is hacking your mind to make the best decisions you possibly can at that moment of amygdala activation. It's not easy. Knowing when your amygdala is taking control and how to override it quickly, to use the higher brain function, is the cornerstone of optimal decision making. That's the basis for using fear as fuel.

I speak to more than 40,000 people every year, helping them learn to create the life, career, and company of their dreams. I always ambush a handful of unsuspecting victims to come up on stage and sing with me. Spoiler alert: we never actually end up singing, but public speaking and singing are among the most common fears. Even picking people from the audience gets an amygdala response without doing anything remotely dangerous or threatening. I scare people in real time. Like being dealt a pair of aces at the start of a poker game; getting scared has the same effect of unconsciously causing your physiology to change. You have your own distinctive physical tells when you get scared. You need to learn what they are and recognize them when they begin to manifest. Letting your fear reactions take charge only ensures that you survive. Reaction is the opposite of a well-thought-out decision to thrive.

Imagine, half-awake one morning, you open your front door and jump back uncontrollably when you see something long and skinny coiled in the grass. Had you stopped to take a snapshot of what you were feeling in that instant, you might notice that your shoulders are tensed up, pulling toward your ears, or your legs are shaking, your mouth is suddenly dry, and your palms are sweaty. Another person might feel nauseous or clamp his jaw tight. Those changes in your body are examples of your fear tells. You might also notice when you get an email from your boss's boss or a call from your biggest client that your shoulders tense up and you feel a tremble in the leg—maybe not as much as when you thought the garden hose was a snake, but it's the same reaction. Your tells belong to you. You need to learn them and know when to jump back from a possible snake or take a moment to treat that upset client with caring and curiosity.

Find Your Tells

Time for the first critical exploration in the *Fear Is Fuel* program; you need to find your tells. You probably know an easy way to scare yourself; most of us have a replicable fear—a fear of heights, spiders, public speaking, enclosed spaces, dogs, and so on. Sometimes just watching a scary movie can elicit your survival reaction (which should tell you how useless that response can be in today's world). To use fear as fuel you need to know when the amygdala activates and tries to hijack your behavior. You also need to know how to find your way to an area called the subgenual anterior cingulate cortex (sgACC) to create courage; you'll learn all about that in chapter 8. Understanding which network in your brain is currently driving the ship is why you have to find your tells; if it's your survival network and not your success network you've got to switch captains in a hurry, before you slam into that *Titanic*-sinking iceberg.

The best way to recognize which system is in charge is to plan a frightening activity right now. Schedule it on your calendar as your first step to using fear as fuel. Walk out on the edge of a fire escape, stand up and make a toast in a crowded restaurant, ask that woman in marketing out for a date. Do anything that is out of your comfort zone and do it from the perspective of an experiment. You want to watch what happens. Sometimes you need help to recognize the changes.

Ideally you should bring a partner with you for two reasons—one, to record your reactions and make sure you are scaring yourself and two, to make sure you don't completely lose it. Set up a time to frighten yourself—even if it's going to the local climbing gym, or giving a presentation at work, you need an event where you'll actually get a genuine amygdala activation and engage that lizard brain and the eons-old decision-making logic that lives there. It's better if you know when the event is and have time to worry about it, because you can start to feel your body changing in anticipation of the event. You might even notice something happening now in your body as you think about the possibility of doing something that scares you. That's great, and so exciting! These are the changes we need to recognize.

Anticipation magnifies fear, because fear is all about what might happen; fear is hardly ever about what is really happening right now. Asking your husband to hide in the closet some random morning and pounce out might scare you, but it won't give you as much information about your tells as if you were waiting backstage for twenty minutes before you give a TEDx talk. Once you have scared yourself, take a careful survey of your body and notice as many changes as you can. Ask your partner to watch your reactions as well to see things you might not notice.

Write them down in a journal or a notebook or on your computer. Some examples of common fear tells include:

- Butterflies in the stomach
- Sweaty palms
- Tight jaw
- Tense shoulders
- Trembling hands
- Shaky legs
- Hot flashes
- Tight back muscles
- Racing heart
- Chills
- Choking
- Goosebumps
- Shortness of breath
- Dizziness
- Dry mouth
- Need to urinate
- Feeling faint
- Ringing in your ears
- Diarrhea
- Higher-pitched voice
- Confusion or disorientation
- Shallow breathing
- Inability to remember things

It's crucial that you become aware of your body's reaction to that fear cocktail created by the amygdala. When your senses send information to your amygdala, that data is processed very differently depending on how much connection you've developed between the prefrontal cortex (PFC) and amygdala. The PFC can be thought of as the adult supervision, the center for happiness and fulfillment, the high-level brain. It's also the newest part of our brain and as I said, it doesn't fully develop until our mid-twenties.

The amygdala handles lower-level, primal, lizard brain survival and procreation; it has one letter in its alphabet soup of life and that's an F. Everything it cares about starts with that letter—fight, flight, freeze, food, and fuck. The amygdala is at the center of our emotional survival network. If you went to a party school, like my alma mater the University of New Hampshire, you no doubt came across that drunk fraternity brother or sorority sister who had absolutely no adult supervision, saying what they want, yelling at everyone, peeing in the most convenient spot and usually ending up in a shrub for the night. The reality of Frank the Tank or the Sixteen Candles girl that you might remember was not just behavior driven by alcohol; it was driven by their stage of neural development. Most kids in college are between seventeen and twenty-one years old and the PFC has not yet fully developed, so there is a wide degree of variance in teenagers' behavior.

The good news is that a self-discovery journey finding your fear tells will help you grow as well. As you get more and more comfortable with fear you will *react* less and less and *act* more and more.

One of the critical aims of a life-changing fear expedition is that compulsion, or anything unplanned, is eliminated from your life during stressful situations. Your goal should be to limit most knee-jerk reactions. You should plan how to act and find the best strategy for your desired outcome. That requires thinking beyond the now. It requires being in control.

If you react while your amygdala is in charge you are only going to respond with a freeze, fight, or flight response. You will make a single point-in-time choice—in other words you only answer one question: "What can I do right now to stop this threat?" You won't think about the consequences two or three levels later after making that first choice. If you recognize your body's tells and you can control your thoughts, your body and your actions might feel the same but your decisions will be much richer. This is the beginning of controlling your inner self and owning your mind and soul—catching yourself saying, "I'm scared, but I'm going to look at the situation from an observer's point of view." It's a great sign that you are starting to take accountability for the world you create.

As you get in touch with your fear tells, it won't be long before you can separate the body, mind, and soul and truly be in control. Your body collects the data from different senses and provides that information to your mind, which interprets the input and will infer likely outcomes of action. The mind can interpret the data in many different ways but the soul provides the plan for how your mind will focus and how you will see the world based on your goals and desires.

MOTIVATION FOR THE LAST ONE PERCENT

Insecurity and fear drove my second-place finish in the 1996 Olympic trials. My motivation was to prove myself and stand out as someone who was a valuable member of his tribe. Everything was about me; making myself confident, getting myself recognition, salving my fears. It wasn't until later in life, when I found true confidence and courage, that I became motivated by causes greater than myself; that's when my results skyrocketed.

Had I had a different mindset in 1996, I might have had an Olympic medal. I realized this when I met Alex Gregory. Alex was a talented rower for Great Britain as a youth and made his first National Team in 2004. He finished eleventh in the quad in the Junior World Championship. Not bad, but certainty not great. Instead of improving, he stayed at the same level for years. He loved the identity and life of an athlete, but it was bleeding his parents and supporters dry, financially, while he traveled the world seeing the sights. It took him five years to finally break down and realize that he was only rowing for himself; his family and friends had given everything for him, only to watch him live a vagabond life.

He told me when we met in London in 2016 that a moment of clarity had changed his life. He realized his motivation was about himself and not doing something for those who helped him. He chose to do something to inspire people. Winning was the best thanks he could share with those who cared about him. It became about others, not about him. When our motivation goes beyond ourselves, we can accomplish anything. Alex went on to shatter his past performance levels and win two Olympic gold medals.

2.

Do you have any hidden fears? That's a trick question of course—if they are hidden you'll have to say no. Before my own courage transformation, I had many hidden fears but no way of knowing it at the time. Unless you've spent time in self-reflection and analysis, you likely have very little idea what your hidden fears are. It took me more than thirty years to unpack the baggage that was holding back my authentic self. When I did finally figure out my fears, my entire life changed; yours can too.

People create different defense mechanisms for fears. Sometimes running away from your fears is a literal action. When I turned twelve years old my family started moving around every year or two; my dad's job took us from opportunity to opportunity. I was terrified each time we moved to a new town. So I ran. I was literally running away from my fears.

At fourteen I ran the Chicago Marathon, 26.2 miles, and finished. It was enough motivation to focus my fears or numb them out, so I ran another one the following year at fifteen, the Maine Coast Marathon (because we had moved to New Hampshire). I was slow, but just finishing earned me respect, especially from adults who knew how tough a marathon really was. Eventually in high school I won the New Hampshire State Championship for cross-country skiing and went to college to ski on a Division I ski team. I used to go to sleep every night praying for an Olympic medal in skiing—but it wasn't meant to be. My second year of college X-C Skiing evolved and with a change in technique I was no longer competitive. The athletic director suggested, if I wanted to find a new sport, that I try rowing. I was afraid of losing my identity as an athlete, so I jumped at the chance. It was a life-changing move, with a lesson that didn't sink in until much later for me, but it is one I've never forgotten. When something disastrous happens in the present, as scary as it may be at the time, the resulting change often works out to be a much bigger benefit in the long run.

Division I cross-country skiers are notoriously fit. Fitness, not technique, helped me set a new UNH record on the rowing machine (Concept II Ergometer). Being part of a team, and outside on the water, made me happy as well. I loved our early practices, frigid adventures with icicles hanging off the riggers and our coach buzz-ing his Boston Whaler launch up and down the river like a maniac lost in a maze, just to break up the ice. We won a Division II national championship in the four-man boat and I was hooked.

After I graduated from UNH I got a job working for a group of entrepreneurs. However, my thoughts were never far from rowing; not surprisingly, it showed in my work. Before long it was clear that I was distracted but I was not sure why; I thought making money would make me significant; my parents had told me that if you get a good job and steady paycheck you've made it. It was evident that my boss was getting ready to fire me, so I decided to save face and quit. It was a coward's move, but the outcome allowed me to accept a tryout, and eventually join, the US team training center for row-ing in Boston called BRC (Boston Rowing Center). At the time my belief in the reality set by my family and our Irish-Catholic upbring-ing had me torn—I was the first to graduate from college, I had a great job and a steady girlfriend; what was I doing throwing all that away? Was I mad? Yet with rowing, I thought I had found my path to significance. I really enjoyed pushing my body and trying to get better. I felt that I was in a state of flow every time I got into the boat. It was the only place where I found that feeling.

Hidden fears conceal themselves by creating a fight response, making us want to be "right" rather than curious, or often those fears hide themselves in a set of rules we feel compelled to follow. Archaic rules are truly meant to be broken, but oftentimes breaking the rules is a really scary thing even if it makes the most sense. If there is a rule you adhere to, or believe, have you asked yourself why? *Fear Is Fuel* is all about curiosity and having the courage to ask why. If you ask why, that creates a deep motivation that can power your whole life.

Because of hidden fears and not knowing my tells, I missed the opportunity to impact others and possibly even get an Olympic medal (see sidebar on last one percent). I spent six years training full time for the Olympics in rowing. The ups and downs of politics and my own fears eventually led me to row the single scull with my own agenda, rather than the team boats that were so much fun. I did well; rowing changed my life and probably saved it as you'll see.

Even with a second-place finish in the 1996 Olympic trials and experience in World Cup races across the world, I feared that no one was going to hire a dumb jock, so I went to a top five business school for my MBA. I focused on my studies six days a week and did really well at the University of Virginia. With my newly minted MBA I got an opportunity in the technology heyday of 1998 to help these new "dot-com" companies build data centers. I was helping to pioneer a new area for Trammell Crow, the largest US real estate company, and it was where I conjured up the idea for my own company, ServerVault. Because I lacked awareness of my hidden fears and how to know when my amygdala activated, the fear of failure and fear of rejection drove me to make bad decisions. Like my Olympic finish falling short, my first company could have been a billion-dollar unicorn, but it wasn't.

ServerVault was one of the first managed hosting companies (the precursor to the internet cloud today). It was a success but with poor investment leadership. I took the fastest venture deal offered to me. I feared that if I didn't lock the deal down, the investors might change their minds. I was too scared to be patient. I learned a ton about entrepreneurship and investment from ServerVault. However, I was often a reactionary leader with investors and customers because I was constantly afraid. I never found my true self, and that fear cost me with investors. I should have been having a blast and living in the present enjoying the moment, but I was always worried about tomorrow and things I couldn't control.

The hidden fears I didn't recognize soon became self-fulfilling and the investors acted more and more aggressively, as the dot-com bubble deflated. They also didn't have experience with downturns and cycles. In retrospect, I had to find courage before I could see how I was letting myself be manipulated at every turn by those I thought had power over me. I was living in fear every day, but didn't know it. I dealt with the stress by drinking. Six or seven beers each night during the week, more on weekends. Rather than discovering my fear tells, I numbed them.

Eventually, with the help of our very talented CFO, Jim Zinn, we sold ServerVault. After that up-and-down experience, my entrepreneurial arsenal of knowledge was well-stocked by many of the failures, mistakes in judgment, and experiences I'd been through. For my next act I was determined to put those lessons to work. I went to summer school at the Massachusetts Institute of Technology (MIT) to find the latest technology. This period of my life was driven by one goal: "forty by forty"—to make myself a net worth of forty million dollars by the time I was forty years old. Wealth equaled self-esteem. I'd find significance in money. I was sure courage lived in a big bank account. I kept numbing out my hidden fears and ignoring those fear tells, and it was starting to have a disastrous effect on my health.

At MIT, radio-frequency identification (RFID) was the hot technology. I learned as much as I could about RFID and met as many experts as possible. This was the opportunity I had searched for; I'd dominate this new industry. I founded ODIN Technologies in 2003. We became the leaders in RFID software and services, and I even wrote the book *RFID for Dummies*, clearly not for an intelligent reader like yourself!

I was still the same faint-hearted kid who wouldn't get on the plane in Boston, except I had gotten really good at convincing myself (and others) that I wasn't a wimp. With five or six beers in me I could stumble onto a plane if I had to—however, if there was a train or highway that was feasible I'd jump on those options, claiming (to save face) it made more sense than wasting time in an airport. Fear was still eating away at me. I'd find out soon that it was consuming more than I could have ever imagined. I still had no idea that my fear tells were always present. My tight chest, constant shallow breathing, tension in my neck, grinding my teeth at night, all tells that were painted over with pints of Guinness. I'd lull my fear tells to sleep every evening starting at about 6:00 p.m. It didn't take long to almost kill me. It's the type of thing that could happen to you.

ODIN started out with three employees, which became six, then twelve and soon it doubled again with no end in sight. We were true to our core ideology to "hire only the best." Because of that mission we developed an amazing team. I was afraid I might be judged as not hard working so I had to be first in and last to leave. "Face time" was as important to me as contribution. Hard work measured in time was part of my parents' reality, and it was a rule written into my brain's subconscious hard drive that I never questioned. By now I had a $120,000 Hummer H1 and other expensive toys that were just objects to hide behind.

If what I was doing sounds familiar, you are likely harboring hidden fears reining in your happiness and success. My routine was well crafted to ignore fear tells and keep me running from all the things that haunted me, all those hidden fears. On a typical morning I'd wake up early feeling guilty about drinking, so my first stop at 5:30 or 6:00 a.m. was Gold's Gym in Ashburn, Virginia, to sweat out the Guinness. It was the only time of the day when I occasionally felt a state of flow. It was also a moment when I should have realized I was acting in the mindset of my genius, but I never recognized it as an opportunity because my amygdala was constantly activated making knee-jerk survival decisions. I always felt that I had to fight to gain any ground.

After the workout I'd walk across the parking lot to ODIN's offices for early team meetings stuffed into the conference room. I would scarf down some donuts or bagels between meetings where I would make high-pressure decisions about hiring, firing, and expanding. I continually created some crisis hurtling down at me like Wile E. Coyote running from a giant rolling boulder. I'd grab a Snickers bar and wash it down with a couple of Diet Cokes to keep the engine roaring. I never knew if I was making the right decision, and my only guiding light was my forty by forty objective. It was all about making me rich, with maybe a sliver of helping other people grow and doing some community good, but I never had the courage to even discover what I was passionate about. Every day I'd try to figure out what other people wanted me to do.

Fear has a terrible way of clouding decisions and authenticity. The trouble is, unless you become aware, you'll never notice that you're acting in fear because it comes naturally to us. Each choice I made was single level—a one-time reaction, not a thoughtful multibranch action. Five nights out of seven I was out at some networking reception, venture capital dinner, or charity event. Seven or eight cocktails would keep me in good humor until about 1:00 in the morning. Then I'd usually force a bleary-eyed drive home. The last thing in my head before it collapsed on the pillow was a feeling of guilt, followed by a silent commitment to get up early and "sweat it out." An hour or two later my wife would elbow me sharply to get my teeth-grinding to stop. At 4:30 or 5:00 a.m. the alarm would buzz and I'd numbly start the cycle all over again.

This was 2005 and the economy began to bubble back to life. My friends would drag me on their private jets for trips all over the world partying with the rich and famous, living what seemed like a charmed life. But it wasn't. I couldn't get on a Gulfstream without four or five Bombay Sapphire and tonics. I couldn't be at an event just to enjoy the moment; it was always about what was coming next. I seldom made a decision based on opportunity and do not remember once going to bed with the conviction of knowing I was true to myself. Then one morning the material armor and outward shield shattered. This is what might happen to you if you're not careful.

I dragged myself into the gym as usual, seeing the same crowd.

"What's up, Danny?"

"What's up Sweendawg?"

"Lats and legs this morning, baby. You?"

"Clangin' and bangin' some massive shoulders like grapefruits!"

After the obligatory fist bump, I dropped down in front of the lat pull-down machine for my first set. I pegged in two hundred pounds and grabbed a wide grip. Immediately, I felt a sharp pain shoot down my left forearm. It was so painful that I skipped upper body and worked my legs. Must be a pulled muscle. Maybe a stretched tendon. I could always come back tomorrow for lats and arms. Tomorrow came and the pain got worse. It was the kind of pain that makes you think you should go to the doctor, but you're afraid to. Afraid of what he might tell you because you were too scared to deal with the truth. I didn't have the courage to face bad news.

By the time day three rolled around I could barely move my arm. It was scarlet, angry, and looked like an overstuffed Christmas stocking. Did someone put an iron on the cotton setting and duct tape it to my arm? The pain finally overcame the fear and I was soon in Dr. Wyman's office. His initial thought was that it looked like a staph infection. Time for some blood tests and a course of antibiotics.

"The nurse will call you back with the results of the blood test this afternoon," he assured me.

The nurse never called me. The doctor did.

That moment changed my life. My doctor told me there was something seriously wrong and he didn't know what, so he wanted to get me checked in to Johns Hopkins ASAP. It was the top hospital in the world. They could fix it if anyone could. I soon became the battleground for a fight between a rare form of leukemia, the knowledge and skill of the world's best doctors, and God's will. I was bathed under the sterile blue lights of the oncology center, standing in front of the mirror wrapped by a white cotton gown flecked with miserable little blue flakes. Looking at myself in the mirror I realized this outfit was no different from the gown ninety-year-old stroke victims wasted away in. It wasn't the armor of a thirty-something millionaire. I looked in the mirror and studied my skin as it reflected a cadaverous pallor, accentuated by the red rings around my eyes.

I was beyond terrified. Plus I had no way to dull the fear. Hopkins didn't provide a fridge stocked with Guinness.

Your body responds to threats with the three Fs. I had passed the first two fight or flight phases of defense and started moving into the final, most primal, freeze stage—the point at which your body believes there is nothing left you could possibly do other than pretend you are dead and hope the threat leaves you alone. Playing possum. I fostered a victim mindset my whole life, so naturally I felt that this was completely out of my control. For more than thirty years I had wired my neurons to eschew accountability—so they defaulted on the efficient, most worn pathway in my mind. The sole exception was in athletics; I knew if I worked hard in rowing I'd get results. The path between working hard (fighting) and results seemed well wired for athletics. Still, the most efficient neurological network was the route that said I was a victim; someone else was doing all this to me. Lucky for me, I started wiring a new pathway before it was too late, but it wasn't before I thought I had died. On the second day at Hopkins Dr. McDevitt came in and asked my pregnant wife and me if my "affairs were in order." I knew that was doctor speak for being totally screwed.

We had a one-year-old daughter, Shannon, and my wife was six months pregnant. I was facing my ultimate fear—death. A funny thing hit me at that point though, for the first time in my life I started worrying less about my fears, and more about my daughter, then about my wife, and finally about our unborn son.

Two days later I was in the operating room. A rare leukemia created rogue T-cells that attacked my healthy white blood cells and demolished my immune system. An operating room, with its highly resistant bacteria lurking around, is the last place you want someone with no immune system, but I had no choice. They operated and took out the staph infection and soon I was recovering alone in a dark hospital room with the ethereal glow of various machines casting a spooky green hue on everything. I got up to go to the bathroom and that's when it happened.

Everything went dark and I started to see in tunnel vision like the end of a tough race. I was losing my footing like trying to stand up on the Teacup ride at a carnival. Then I saw a staticky bright light like the TV scene from *Poltergeist*. I thought, "This is it. I'm dying." I never heard the little old lady saying "Stay away from the light,

Carol Anne." But it still seemed like I was in that movie, and I didn't want to go.

A cold rationality engulfed me and a strange thing happened—I started to see past the veil of my fears. This was the dance with the angel of death at its crescendo. I was seeing the reality of life in a whole new way. I had an epiphany about my fear. I realized that it was the same movie playing over and over in my mind. It was always a horror movie; it was always a fight. It was always about me. It was different with the Olympics; I had learned how to use the fear as fuel on the race course thanks to my coach and the psychologists at the Olympic Training Center. I had used fear as fuel in athletics, so why had I confined it to the race course?

The angel of death is really the one controlling life. Everything we have, everything we are, everything we love can be taken away in the blink of an eye. One heartbeat away. Sitting in the hospital bed with more tubes and wires hooked into me than the Space Shuttle I decided that the only real truth in life is death. We have rules and constraints entered into our subconscious database and we blindly believe they are all true. They're not. This I saw clearly. Curiosity is the secret to living a happy, successful life. Being right, doing what's expected, believing rules are unbending, and running scared are ingredients for a miserable life.

For the first time in my life I realized that the movie in my mind could be a love story, an adventure film, and, hell yeah, even a comedy. I was the producer. A pretty miserable character of a father came to light when I pictured my one-year-old daughter eventually recalling a memory of her late father as the guy too afraid to get on a plane and take her to Disney World. Time to take on my flying demon. "Fuck all this fear," I thought. A few new flicks were about to be released and featured on the movie theater of my mind. I envisioned the first blockbuster was my family riding the highest roller coaster at Disney and I was laughing. Life suddenly wasn't about amassing a fortune. Living wasn't postponing what I wanted to do to an eventual retirement or thinking a big house or club membership would make my wife happy. It was about now. Happiness was about being grateful for every day. I realized that my mind had many uncovered layers—gratitude, authenticity, curiosity, and courage. I wish I had known those existed thirty years earlier. Helping others peel back to those layers is the reason I'm writing this book.

Ultimately my fears, and that constant fear cocktail of cortisol, adrenaline, and oxidative stress that I numbed with alcohol caused me to be susceptible to leukemia, and contributed to the demise of my immune system. It was why I felt terrible all the time. Analyzing the situation from the perspective of a producer of my life I believe the choices I made put me in the hospital. Fear was eating away at my immune system with a constant low-grade stress. Alcohol, diet, stress, and sleep habits were fueling the fall. If I made myself sick, why couldn't I make myself better?

I learned techniques at the Olympic Training Center to eliminate fear on the racecourse, to literally change my perception of reality. My mind could shift what was happening to my body. That was a skill for racing I became very good at. Could I heal myself in the same way? I had some amazing doctors, and without giving away the end of the book—I died.

USING FEAR AS FUEL METHOD #3

Dance with the angel of death. Live the knowledge that your origin is your destination; this world is temporary. Live in the present, grateful for everything you have with the realization that it could all be taken away in the blink of an eye.

No, of course I didn't die! You're reading my story. I made it out of Hopkins. I thank God, my coach, the docs at Hopkins—because for the first time in thirty-five years I was about to learn what it was like to really live.

My time at Hopkins became a race against the clock. I put the Olympic visualization techniques to work. I could literally close my eyes and watch warrior cells start to spill out of my sternum, coursing through my body searching out rogue white blood cells tainted with leukemia. I'd watch a ray of energy shoot out like a laser gun demolishing each rogue cell into oblivion. It was 24-7 working, praying, and visualizing to treat my body the way I should have in the past: with respect and love.

My body was recovering slowly, but my mind changed overnight. A friend of mine from business school was my chief operating officer at ODIN at the time. When he saw me getting sick and after I had been admitted at Hopkins he sent an email to my wife and said "good luck to Paddy, but I've got to think of myself and I'm quitting." I would have been so pissed off and furious and feeling like a victim in the past ("How could he do that to me, now?") but after the sickness I had none of those reactions. I thought for the first time; I wonder what doors that will open for us? Amazingly I wasn't upset or stressed at all. In the end, his fear-based decision caused him to miss a seven-figure payday when I sold ODIN.

Among the many lessons I learned as I lay in that sterile hospital bed was that I was much more motivated by taking care of my kids and making sure they were raised strongly and confidently than I was in making forty million dollars by the time I was forty. It dawned on me that it was the opposite of my rowing motivation, and ultimately gave me some insight as to why I didn't end up with an Olympic gold medal. Ego-driven motivations for self-respect and self-esteem will never lead to greatness. Fear and ego can lead to riches and fame, but then there is never enough if it's always about the future and never about the present. Unless you know your fear tells you might end up like me and just keep trying to numb them out and cover them up.

Authenticity and confidence are the foundations of greatness, not the other way around. Constantly looking for outside validation to gain respect or confidence only amplifies feelings of inadequacy. But love—of spouse, of children, of family, of friends—that can inspire people to charge into a burning building. Think about it—what would you do for someone you love?

My wife and I walked out of Hopkins, an IV bag tucked under my arm and a calm in my heart that I had never felt before. The grey, chilly mist of November dulled the dilapidated neighborhoods around Hopkins, but I was grateful to be taking it all in. Then I saw it. A red leaf floating in a cesspool-brown puddle. The edges were tinted yellow and deep rust veins etched through it. As clichéd as it sounds, it was one of the most beautiful things I'd ever seen. I stopped to notice it and took a deep breath. Three weeks earlier I would have been annoyed that it was raining and I was in Baltimore. I would have stomped right by without even seeing it, worried about what was next.

Every moment of every day took on a new meaning of gratitude and beauty. I wanted to keep my promise to myself and my family of overcoming my fear of flying, so after reading more than a hundred accident reports on the FAA website, I finally got the courage to take my first flying lesson at Leesburg Executive Airport. I could feel my fear tells just thinking about flying, and because I wasn't drinking I started dealing with them first by just breathing as I had learned at the USOC Training Center. Just reading about accidents had my heart racing. I breathed deeply and kept reading. I wasn't going to stop.

I resolved that even if I were crying and screaming I'd get my private pilot's license. The angel of death showed me the ultimate fear, and what I felt now wasn't close to that night at Hopkins.

The first two lessons were impossibly anxiety ridden. Every bump, noise, and change made me jump as if I were in a dark room and a gun was fired right next to my ear. I was sweaty and shaking, and my mouth felt packed with cotton. Sandy dryness choked off my words when I tried to speak. My fear tells were crystal clear; I recognized the ferocious bats charging against my stomach walls and pushing up my throat. Walking out of the private plane terminal felt like stepping into a super-high-definition movie; everything was sharper, my hearing and eyesight seemed to pick up every detail, colors were more saturated, noises had more depth. I remembered every detail as if it had happened dozens of times. I didn't know it at the time but the powerful fear cocktail that my body produced because of the activated amygdala was being used by my prefrontal cortex to consciously recognize more details. My survival response was being tempered by my courageous decision to keep going even though I was scared. I was finding a new superpower and rewiring my brain; I was using fear as fuel and felt like I had the power of a superhero.

By the third flying lesson I started to learn more and more about the physics and the plane design. I was making choices based on a new reality—one of statistics, data, and physics rather than a single news report that had planted a seed of terror in me thirty years before. My instructor was a patient and talented Dutchman named Ray DeHaan (aka the Professor). Ray radiated confidence. His passionate attitude conveyed the excitement of launching into the wild blue yonder. Like Navy SEALs I was getting more and more exposure to my Fear Frontier but rather than let the amygdala react I was consciously taking control. It took a few weeks, but eventually I fell in love with flight. I had turned fear into fuel, faced everything, and accepted the responsibility for the outcomes. It was liberating beyond description.

Eventually when my mental hard drive recalled the idea of airplanes and flying, I no longer conjured up emotions of terror and loss. Now, I felt pride and respect and even sex appeal. The movie I was playing in my head was me in an olive drab jumpsuit with "Maverick" on the chest, a classic pair of Aviators blocking the sun as I high-fived Goose. This was a lifelong love affair in the making.

After twenty-two hours of flying with Ray, I soloed and earned my private pilot's license. I felt my fear tells but didn't need to numb them out. Never in a thousand years would I have believed I would be flying a plane by myself, especially with a goofy twelve-year-old kid's wide-eyed grin on my face. During my first solo cross-country I stared at the void next to me where the Professor had sat for several months, then I looked down six thousand feet below to the Shenandoah Mountains. I felt such an overwhelming sense of pride and accomplishment it was intoxicating, like a dream. Not with Olympic training, not with selling businesses for millions, not winning jujitsu fights against tougher guys, did I ever feel this exhilaration. Nothing compared to taking on my original Fear Frontier and obliterating it. I had found the self-confidence, courage, and self-esteem I was missing for so long. My daughter Shannon and I were definitely going to Disney, and anywhere else in the world we wanted to see. My life had changed completely.

It only took about six months for this newfound love of flying, and the complete rewriting of my emotions associated with air travel, to cast an incredible halo effect on the rest of my life. Confidence begets confidence, as I soon found out. I was feeling my fear tells still, but I was no longer afraid of them. I stopped running and numbing. You can find the same courage and confidence, but you've got to take that first step.

With a newborn son at home and my daughter turning two years old, my routine changed as well. I started the day with my wife and a cup of coffee, hoping the kids would stay quiet long enough for us to enjoy each other's company. I was so appreciative of fresh air and the outdoors that we began holding team meetings at ODIN by walking around the building out in the sunshine. My talented CFO, Jim, came from ServerVault to ODIN to help with my next entrepreneurial adventure. I started to appreciate his sage advice more and more. I realized that so much of what was written on my subconscious database was because of my parents' fears and an immigrant family's value of what is "right" and what is safe. Or simply what had always been. Thousands of years ago tribes created rules that helped them survive, but many of those rules hurt our chances of happiness and success today.

Fear was still present when a client would call or an employee would quit, or an investment would fail, but now helping others and enjoying the present was building my courage, and it felt great. I discovered the real me. I found my genius. I recognized my fear tells but they never scared me; in fact, I'd often feel something scary, breathe to get present, and then laugh about it.

Flying is one of my great joys in life; it's an incredible source of fulfillment, challenge, and freedom. I don't believe in regrets but I do believe in learning lessons and sharing knowledge. I would love to have discovered flying earlier, but if I had, maybe I wouldn't be inspired to help millions of people uncover their hidden joys and passions. I couldn't believe that fear kept flying locked away from me for thirty years.

What great unknown joy has fear locked away from you? What happiness are you trading for a misconceived idea of safety or rules?

Going from petrified flyer to aerobatic competitor is one example of a dramatic change in lifestyle that not only led to an immediate change in happiness, but also catapulted my professional success and fulfillment with significantly less effort. Imagine every day of your life being a day of wonder, and everything you love and are passionate about manifests itself each day. What if everything you touched turned to gold? How would that make you feel? Never mind working for the weekends and praying for vacations or wishing to win the lottery. Find your fears and make every day the day of your dreams; you deserve it.

As soon as I became a private pilot I wanted to do more in flying. I went on to get my instrument rating, then my commercial license. I got certified for flying float planes on the water and now compete in aerobatic competitions. Can you believe that the kid who wouldn't get near an airliner now purposely puts himself in a tiny plane, alone, upside down, spinning at breakneck speed toward the ground pulling five Gs? That scenario would have been the ultimate nightmare for me before my illness.

FEAR OF FLYING HACK

After most of my speaking engagements, someone inevitably comes up to me and admits that they are afraid of flying, or their partner is afraid of flying, and they are missing out on seeing the world.

I tell them they can fix it with a little knowledge and the BASE method, and I always scribble a quick hack on a napkin that works wonders. I write this:

- First 3—30 percent
- Last 5—50 percent
- 22,000 years

What it means is that the first three minutes of any commercial flight, and the last five minutes, combine for almost all of the fatalities. The rest are mostly ground-based collisions happening during taxi, the rare in-flight icing scenario, or the incredibly rare mid-air collision, according to the FAA database. The simple idea is setting your watch for three minutes; feel free to be scared all you want the first couple of minutes (or until you get to 10,000 feet); then enjoy the flight, turbulence and all. Do the same thing at the end. Accept that turbulence may feel uncomfortable but it won't cause a crash, and expect it to get bumpy at some point so you're ready for the ups and downs. The 22,000 might be the best one—if you flew every day on a commercial flight, you would have to do so for 22,000 years to get in a fatal crash based on safety statistics from the past sixty years. This limited bit of knowledge, if you believe in it, should help limit the free energy and uncertainty that causes fear during the flight.

If you are a scared flyer, even if you never take the controls yourself, just the ability to get on a plane anytime, anywhere, and feel confident traveling to a new and exotic place can build a courageous mindset that is life-changing. As you'll read later, experiencing other cultures and geographies will also build your subconscious database to make you happier, more creative, and better able to deal with new and challenging situations.

Getting comfortable with fear means that there's nothing stopping you from trekking in Nepal, skiing in the Alps, starting a business in Hong Kong, rock climbing in Italy, speaking at a conference in Las Vegas, scuba diving in Oman, mountain biking in South Africa, or pub-crawling in Ireland. If you or someone you know is being cannibalized by guilt and shame by not getting on a plane, share my story with that person. I hope knowing of my transformation, and how amazing life is on the other side of your Fear Frontier, is enough to change anyone's world. In fact my editor, Suzanne, hadn't flown in eight years out of fear, and had not taken her children on big trips. After reading this chapter she booked two flights and chose courage! You can too, and open a whole new world of excitement for you and the ones you love.

I am writing this book, lecturing, and hosting shows on fear so that other people can get the tremendous life-changing benefits of courage without having to creep to the edge of their grave and then fight their way back out after a tango with the angel of death. The tools in *Fear Is Fuel* won't eliminate the ups and downs of life, any more than training in a sport every day guarantees you get better each day. When training both your body and your mind there are ups and downs, but the progression is always up—it's just not straight up. Learning your fear tells is the first way to start making your progression to a better life.

Despite what I thought about being the only person feeling scared, worried, and constantly running away from my fear with booze, I found that I was not alone as I researched this book. In fact, I was shocked to learn about many iconic figures of courage who started their lives the same wimpy way I did. I found confidence and courage because I realized that my daughter Shannon needed a daddy who wasn't afraid to get on a plane and take her to Disney World, or show her the world. Who could you be if you started that company, or made that phone call, or followed that intuition? Who would you be if you had the courage to be the person everyone who counts on you needs you to be?

4

◦‿

The Root of All Fears

What you are afraid to do is a clear indication of the next thing you need to do.

—Ralph Waldo Emerson

The forty-something Silicon Valley billionaire crossed his legs. Immediately, one of his $2,000 Louis Vuitton sneakers, supported by the bottom leg, began pistoning up and down. Clearly this man was unaccustomed to waiting for people, but he seemed resigned enough to sit in a hundred-year-old old classroom with a handful of other "students." In 2019, the people surrounding the neurological equivalent of Socrates are not interested in the questions of life; rather they are interested in the questions of artificial life: robotics, artificial intelligence, imaging, machine learning, and a framework for the brain. The entrepreneur from Silicon Valley is creating a new version of Alexa or Siri that predicts human needs. He is one example of a weekly migration from all over the world to University College London. They come for the Monday lunchtime "Ask Karl" sessions that are open to a select few. Karl is in such demand that he almost never meets with people one on one; rather he has his assistant, Maddy, nudge suitors into these weekly sessions.

Interestingly enough, the quest for the holy grail of artificial intelligence (AI) might actually be what solves one of the most vexing questions Socrates and philosophers throughout history have pondered. What is the root of all fear?

Answering that question and creating a framework to talk objectively about things like fear and courage, even anger and depression, things that are nearly impossible to objectively measure today, would help millions of people escape the bounds of fear, anxiety, and helplessness. If you can understand the inputs that change the outcome of any equation, you can change that outcome. When it comes to mathematical equations, there are few men who can compare to Karl.

A worldwide race toward finding the optimal design and architecture for AI has meant that the money follows the brains. The biggest brain of all belongs to the aforementioned neuroscientist in London, Karl Friston. He is the inventor of several software systems and imaging technologies responsible for breakthroughs in the study of the human brain. There's a measurement called the h-index that academicians covet the way athletes focus on heart rate. It's a score used to measure the impact of a researcher's publications. Friston has been estimated as the most frequently cited neuroscientist in the world and his h-index is twice that of Albert Einstein. To say someone is a shoo-in for a Nobel Prize is ludicrous, but I, and most neuroscientists I know, would bet money on Karl.

At the Wellcome Trust Centre for Neuroimaging at University College in the heart of London, Friston "pays the bills" by developing mathematical techniques and systems to characterize how the brain is wired and responds in various situations. His passion, however, is something he developed ten years ago called the Free Energy Principle (FEP). The FEP is a theory that is so complex Einstein would guffaw at attempts to explain it (maybe that's why he's not cited as often as Karl). I'll give it a shot because, after all, I once wrote a Dummies book, so I do simple.

The amount of information in this book is nearly overwhelming. I've organized and explained the neuroscience as well as I can after interviewing almost three dozen scientists and psychologists (many who spend their day talking only to mice). I've read hundreds of peer-reviewed technical studies. I've gathered personal stories from more than five hundred CEOs and presidents to fill this book with as much wisdom as possible. This next revelation might, however, be the biggest idea in the book. Here is a mic-drop moment from my research:

Free Energy is the root of all fears.

If you consider different kinds of fears, some are passive (things that happen to us like getting old, dying, etc.) some are active fears we create (asking someone out, starting a company, talking in front of an audience); there are also internal, instinctual, survival-driven fears (rejection from the tribe, abandonment, failure). However, if you step back and look at them, every fear we have is rooted in a fear of the unknown or a state of uncertainty we may not be able to handle. Free Energy is the space between what your mind can imagine and what is happening. Free Energy is the unknown.

Why is Free Energy so important for your fear journey? To become truly courageous you have to either eliminate or get comfortable with the unknown. We can contend with whatever happens and live our most amazing lives by using our fear as fuel and reminding ourselves that we can handle anything that comes our way. If you can imagine dealing with the worst, you can handle it, as you'll find out in the next chapter. If you can understand where fear originates you can create expectations and actions that get you comfortable with the uncertainty, the unknown, the root of all fear.

The first place to start understanding Free Energy creation is the database of our mind. We all have prior beliefs that are based on our lifetime of memories. In your brain, you don't have a model for the world; you have a model for *your world*—one that exists only in your brain. As you both experience and imagine new things, you build an updated subconscious database in your mind enabling you to soon see things in a different light (of experience).

Experience and imagination change your roster of possible outcomes. The more memories you have to reference, the more you can create different hypotheses (or guesses) about the future. Expanding your beliefs changes how you make decisions for the better, as you'll see.

Even visualization can change your way of thinking. Most people go through the routine of their day without considering all the potential disasters that could happen, or even without being open to the occurrence of a spectacular windfall. It's true, if you imagine yourself getting T-boned by an eighteen-wheeler running a red light and you see paramedics cutting your lifeless body from a crumpled car, it's not going to be the nicest experience. But imagining that scenario can give you a kind of power. You'll feel fear in your mind, and you'll order your life knowing that death by an eighteen-wheeler is a possibility if you are out driving today. Your subconscious brain will actually assign a likelihood of that happening; it will predict that occurrence and assign a score to that expectation. Your subconscious database feeds the survival system that only cares about mitigating risk. If the image is vivid enough in your mind, it might keep you from texting and driving or it might give you the courage to call in sick and work on that book you always wanted to write. And if you visualize the crash, or any other fear, and engage it with all your senses, it will definitely make you more familiar with the feeling of fear. The same would be true for something positive. If you have the chance to give a presentation and you imagine yourself getting a standing ovation, and killing it, that adds to your database of beliefs as well. You'll prepare for an expectation and future that has you doing great, getting promoted, and being proud. The good feeling in your mind and body wants to manifest itself in your reality. Preparing for a vast array of outcomes is one reason leading companies have *pre*-mortem meetings with their project teams. The companies do not want to be caught off-guard if a project goes south and they aren't prepared, so they get together and brainstorm all the possible bad outcomes (you'll learn more about this technique in chapter 9). Visualizing and imagining things creates a memory; however, actually experiencing something firsthand makes the memory much stronger.

Our subconscious is powered by that very sophisticated database, made up of a lifetime of memories, both real and imagined. That virtual database holds every memory we've taken in and every emotion associated with those memories. We also have memories we've only imagined that get stored as well—the more senses we use in our imagination, the stronger those imagined memories can be. The more powerful an emotion associated with a memory, the easier it is to recall that memory. That database is our Belief, and for the mathematical equation you'll see in a minute it will be called Prior Beliefs (PB). Some memories are buried beyond the recall of our conscious mind, but all the data we have stored can influence our actions at some level. Most of our hard drive data is not our doing; we don't choose the inputs during our first ten to twelve formative years. Our languages, geography, and family structure all were chosen for us, and we are only aware of a small conscious part of what we remember. Crazy as it sounds, 90 percent of what we sense and experience is observed by the subconscious brain in order to help us survive and pass our genes on to the next generation. That leaves only 10 percent that we consciously notice. The conscious mind is the equivalent of a trickling stream of data while the subconscious is as powerful an information flow as Niagara Falls. The subconscious constantly catalogs threats (or what those around us teach us are threats) and opportunities beginning as early as in the womb.

The first entry into our database comes at birth from our DNA. The next layer comes from family and caregivers who decide what language we will speak, how many people we share our cave with, what education we get, and most importantly the limits, taboos, and rules we need to follow. A hundred thousand years ago these actions helped us to adapt and survive. Today we may be told we can't handle having kids, or we are not smart enough to become a pilot, or someone is better and more deserving so we shouldn't apply for that grant, or $100,000 a year salary is incredible and you should be happy with that, or birth control is wrong if is based on technology. These are the stories, and often rules, that entered our database because a parent or teacher or priest or friend or some other important figure in our life propelled an idea toward us when we were young and absorbing everything without question. A lot of times people push ideas because rules have always been there, even if they make no sense in today's world. We can and must take control over our lives as adults to change and repopulate our database. There is no limit to your capacity to achieve once you realize that you control your outlook on the world.

MEASURING FREE ENERGY AS THE ROOT OF ALL FEAR

Your world is created by what populates your subconscious database; those Prior Beliefs (PB). Everything you've ever seen, sensed, or done in your life becomes the most powerful inputs. To give you an idea of how inputs could be hypothetically weighed, look at the inputs to your database this way:

Experiences—A memory added by experience has a strength of 10 on a 1–10 scale because you see it, smell it, feel it, taste it—it's real and you associate emotion with it.

Genetics—The next component that makes up your PB is DNA and epigenetics (things passed down directly from your parents). This is the basis of Instinctual Fears in the Terror Triangle. These memories would be a five on the relative memory strength scale.

Imagination—Last, you have your imagination; daydreaming, dreaming, visualizing, and meditating. Those are all another source

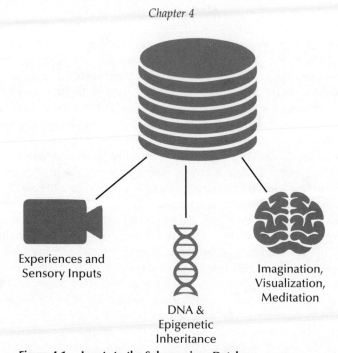

Experiences and
Sensory Inputs

DNA &
Epigenetic
Inheritance

Imagination,
Visualization,
Meditation

Figure 4.1.   Inputs to the Subconscious Database

for creating memories, but less powerful than an actual live experience. They would have a strength of one or two.

See figure 4.1.

When an event takes place during your day and you need to act, you will come up with a bunch of guesses about what you should do to get a desired (or expected) outcome. If you enter a dark room, your hypothesis is that if you went over and turned the switch on, the outcome would be unsurprising as the lights popped on. You are predicting with a high degree of certainty (or precision) a cause and effect. The prediction of what to do was your hypothesis (H). The more hypotheses you have the more outcomes you can imagine and the lower the chance of generating Free Energy. I'm going to repeat that because it is on the critical path toward courage: *the more possible outcomes you can imagine or experience, the less Free Energy your mind will produce because you reduce the uncertainty.*

After you come up with your H you will act. This leads to either one of your expected outcomes (EO) like the lights coming back on, or you get electrocuted with a bone-jarring shock, which was highly unexpected. The shock surprises you and that creates a Free Energy gap between the reality you expect and what is actually happening. Imagine you're in a crowded subway and the moment that you put your hand into your pocket and your wallet is "just not there": that's another kind of unexpected shock.

Your Personal Reality (PR) is made up of all the hypotheses that you could think of that would happen in that situation. When you get pushed outside your PR, Free Energy is created. Your goal as a balanced, closed system is to get back to your reality, get back into balance. We can distill our emotional experience down to an equation to help us realize what changes will impact our experience of fears.

To put it in a very simple mathematical formula:

Your Prior Beliefs (PB) multiplied by the number of Hypotheses (H) you can come up with leads to all the possible Expected Outcomes (EO):

$$PB \times H = EO$$

Our brain subconsciously assigns odds to each possible outcome. Our brain doesn't need these odds to add up to 100 percent. We can imagine that hitting the light switch has a 50 percent chance of turning the lights on, and that screaming for your Dad has an 80 percent chance of getting help and there is a 30 percent chance of running into a piece of furniture. Expected Outcomes are assigned a level of confidence, or a weight (W_{EO}). If you add up the weight of each expected outcome, that gives you a measure of your Personal Reality (PR).

$$\sum(W_{EO}) = PR$$

Don't worry, we're at the cool part now. I told you I'd keep it simple.

The potential Free Energy (FEp) is equal to Expected Outcome minus Personal Reality.

$$FEp = EO - PR$$

Ta-da! That is the root of all fears. Now let's look at why you should care and how we can put it to work changing your world.

LEFT IN THE DARK WITH FREE ENERGY

Imagine you are six years old and having dinner with your family. You are sitting at the dinner table, clandestinely feeding your brussels sprouts to the dog; maybe some music is playing in the background and the lights are shining brightly in the kitchen and dining room. Everything is normal. Then all of a sudden you hear the THUNK of power going out through the entire house. The room is flooded ink black with the absence of light, the music stops, and everyone is shocked into silence.

A typical American six-year-old has not put a sudden power outage into his experience of life yet. Because his internal database is still small, he does not hold the Prior Belief that reality can be normal sitting at a table with your family eating dinner and then the world goes black. This is a classic Free Energy moment—his idea of reality, his Prior Beliefs, has no scenario where dinner takes place in darkness. He did not sit down at the table with one of his hypotheses being "we might eat in the dark." That Free Energy moment will fuel his amygdala to flee this threat of darkness and get back to a normal state. Let's say the Free Energy production on scale of 1–10 is a 9 for six-year-old you. You're freaking out.

Now consider a second scenario. Your mom knew there was construction down the street and they would have to shut off the neighborhood power at some point. She sits you down and says; "Honey the nice workers down the road might have to take our electricity away for a little while tonight, but they promised it will only be for a few minutes." Your mom put information into your database that, while not as powerful as living through the actual event, still created a new memory and added to your Prior Beliefs. You can imagine a new perspective on the world with that information, and a certain amount of precision and probability are automatically assigned to your hypothesis. Now, relive the scene and see how the equation would change: the house goes dark, you're still a bit freaked out, but you sort of knew it was coming. Your Free Energy is now a **6 or 7** on the same scale.

Last, think about what happens when the power goes out. Mom grabs a flashlight, Dad lights some candles and tells you not to worry; it's like going camping and it will be fun, he promises. You absorb everything and live safely through the experience. A new experience in real life increases the size of your database; your PB database grows. A week later when the lights go out again, you recall all your Prior Beliefs, remembering the fun night of flashlight shadow animals on the wall and roasting marshmallows over a candlestick and your Free Energy scale this time is a **2**. In short, certain states of living become excitingly familiar.

In Free Energy the database in our mind is called Prior Beliefs, PB, or Priors. Let's refer to it as **PB** for Prior Beliefs. Imagine that all the information in the universe would fill up the database to a score of 1,000. That's a God-like knowledge of everything, impossible for man or machine to achieve. Compare that to a baby being born with some instinctual knowledge. She comes out with a PB Score of 5. You are likely somewhere in between 5 and 1,000 if you are reading this book. The three inputs you saw earlier create your PB—all the experiences that entered your world both consciously and subconsciously through all your senses; your genetic makeup, your parents' fears, and new additions to that genetic makeup; and then things that you can imagine, visualize, daydream about. With that scale to give you a perspective to look at the world, let's compare Free Energy using the formula.

If you go back to your lights-out dinner as a kid and compare you and your mom it might look something like table 4.1.

You can see from that simple equation that the six-year-old you had five times more fear potential in that lights-out situation than your mother, and of course way more than God (and Alex Honnold) because they are both fearless!

Table 4.1. Prior Beliefs

	Six-Year-Old You	Your Mom	God, Zeus, Vishnu
Prior Belief (PB)	50	100	1000
Hypothesis (H)	7	10	Infinite
Expected Outcomes (EO) = PB x H	350	1,000	Infinite
Total Weight of Expected Outcomes $\Sigma(W_{EO})$	200	350	googleplex
Potential Free Energy $FE_p = EO/PR$	1.75	.35	0

The whole point of this exercise is for you to realize that you, and only you, can control the inputs that create free energy. I'm not even trying to come close to the work of Karl Friston or any of his colleagues, who will chuckle at the simplicity of my formula. My goal is to suggest a framework of applying the levers of free energy to your life. Yes, it's simple and subjective, but it can be extremely powerful if you want to get out of simply surviving and learn to thrive. Looking at the example above you can see what factors are important to reducing Free Energy, like having a big database of experiences, and many hypotheses that stem from that knowledge.

Fear is the gap between what you expect and the element of surprise, which determines the amount of free energy. To help you get your arms around the concept, you can think of free energy as fuel for our amygdala and the limbic system, the region of our brain that handles our survival and fear responses. See figure 4.2.

The amygdala and our survival network's job is to keep us alive so we can pass our genes on to the next generation. Because of the massive subconscious database in our mind, we have certain beliefs or ideas about what things keep us safe and what actions might put us in danger, no matter how remote the likelihood of harm actually

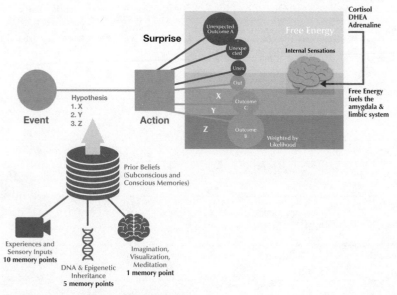

Figure 4.2.   Free Energy Production

is. When we expect a certain outcome (that's our hypothesis) and something unexpected happens, that creates surprise. Depending on how big the surprise is determines how much free energy is created and how powerful the sensations we feel in our body. For many people just the idea of an uncertain outcome is enough to keep them from wanting to try new, different actions. When we don't try new and unusual (novel) paths our internal database (PB) doesn't grow. Fear creates an adaptive risk-averse approach to life, and we don't try new things. We stop growing. If you have a negative bias toward new experiences, you will not try them and never have a chance to change that belief from negative to positive. Chronic anxiety is a byproduct of sticking with the same Prior Beliefs, being locked into one hypothesis and never trying to prove it wrong. If you don't think a different approach will work, the negativity bias kicks in, so you won't turn a new hypothesis into an action because you are already convinced that the outcome will be negative. You never have the opportunity to gather evidence that proves otherwise. It's like a hamster stuck running on the Habitrail wheel who believes the tunnel next to him doesn't lead anywhere so he keeps running on the wheel and never discovers that the tunnel leads to a big pile of food. This hypothesis lock is exactly what happened for thirty years with me and flying. When I finally broke out, I discovered how wrong that one hypothesis was, and fell in love with flying planes and traveling.

I said at the outset that the Free Energy Principle is a very complex theory and Friston uses intricate terms to describe the principle in detail. His language means many people who are not scientists find the descriptions intimidating, but he does this very purposefully. Friston can make deep connections between just being/surviving or existing in a particular form, and the experiences and belief that you have about the way you engage with your world. Friston believes that there is a benefit to connecting the dots between the math of what is going on inside you and the psychological descriptions most people put on your behaviors. It's like describing a financial transaction; there are terms that make things very specific, and anyone who knows finance can understand what high interest rate means or a low interest rate, or the term of a loan, or the principal vs. the interest—all things that affect what it looks like to finance a house, for example. Friston believes that if we create this very specific framework, we can attack some of the biggest problems with mental illness.

The road from medical student to professor at University College London first wound Friston through a mental institution where he interned and began forming many of his landmark ideas. During his training he met once a week with a group of psychopaths and schizophrenics at an institution. One of his patients was a normal-looking, somewhat frumpy middle-aged woman who could pass for your weird British friend Nigel's Auntie Em. However, her model of the world and her actual observations were so dramatically different that it was clear she did not have the same connections or capacity to rationalize the difference. She had lost the ability to correct her errors and come back to a balanced state. Her biology was flawed. Her brain ignored many of the seemingly clear observations coming in from her senses. When there is a dramatic difference between what your senses are telling you and what your expectations are of reality, that's when the wheels come off.

For Auntie Em, her continued effort at reconciliation drove her psychotic behavior. In the incident that got her incarcerated, she had received extensive sensory data input (what her eyes were seeing, her ears were hearing, and her hands were touching) that a particular woman standing in front of her had brown hair and blue eyes and was pleading with her to stop; but that didn't align with Auntie Em's expectation of reality. Consequently, her mind was not willing to change its course and accept what her eyes and ears were telling her. She ignored the sensory input that would normally help us correct our prediction errors. She was set on a belief of a personal reality and ignored the sensory data because of a fault in how she dealt with conflicting information. She lost it. The reality gap caused her to decapitate her next-door neighbor with a butcher knife because she believed she was a giant crow intent on pecking out her eyes with a foot-long beak.

Auntie Em's beliefs didn't align with what her senses were telling her, and she couldn't close the gap, so she sided with her beliefs. Unless you have a biological issue, you have the ability to close the gap.

The foundation of *Fear Is Fuel* is that we need to scare ourselves every day. To be more like the heroes you'll read about, from Orville and Wilbur to Cato, you should seek out more fear, and face that fear, by both experience and by imagining all possible scenarios, good and bad. The techniques you'll learn from the courage exercises will help you gain more confidence that the absolute worst seldom happens, and in doing so you continue to limit the amount of free energy you produce. By aligning our sensory data with our big picture of what could happen, great or horrible, we create an accurate view of almost any reality, a view where we minimize prediction error.

The reason it is important to have an understanding of free energy is that if we learn how to measure fear, or at least understand what components go into feeling fear, then we can see how changes in our life will affect our perception. Think of me for a moment like your guidance counselor in high school—the guy who really pushed you to take a statistics class—not because I think you want to be a statistician, but because knowing things like the odds of something happening, if one thing causes another thing, or if it is instead correlated, all are concepts that will help you think better.

The point is, you don't need to know statistical formulas in depth to benefit from the concepts. The same is true for my concept of the Free Energy Principle as the root of all fear.

There are two ways to create free energy in your body and engage the limbic survival system (that's where the amygdala and all its cohorts live); one is what we all face every day that starts with your experiences in the world, from the bottom up. That's the example of the lights going out at dinner. You had an expectation of reality and that prediction was flawed so from the bottom up you had prediction error that caused free energy. The way to limit that error is to be able to predict more possible outcomes, create more hypotheses, learn new possibilities.

The FEP tries to explain why we limit our life or our "states of being" into a relatively small and familiar attractive set. What happens from the bottom up is that we create expected outcomes of the world and when we are wrong about what we think, that results in a prediction error. The way that most people behave is to avoid what we consider highly improbable states—like jumping off a cliff, having low blood pressure, being unloved, or being homeless. Our neurological network puts a high degree of precision on our predictions. We believe our own story. When we have a big gap in prediction error, we experience uncertainty, which creates free energy. These are states that based on our understanding of the world we would be surprised to find ourselves in. If you can measure that surprise mathematically, then you can describe a guide for behavior that helps avoid or at least minimize surprise. Free Energy is the measurement of that surprise—the sensory cues taking place. The

THE FREE ENERGY OF BRUTUS

Brutus looks like a lion. He's our 125-pound Leonburger. He's as sweet a dog as you'll ever meet, with soft brown eyes and a completely chilled-out disposition. Like you, he is a closed system that resists breaking down and doesn't experience entropy, or a desire to come apart at the cellular level. He goes to sleep and wakes up (twenty or so times a day) basically the same, as you do.

The Free Energy Principle states that your Personal Beliefs all were created in the past and your Expected Outcomes happen in the future. Those are two of the biggest influences controlling free energy. In other words, the greatest source of our fears is in the past and the future. Limiting free energy and fear is best done by staying in the present like our big, furry pooch. Brutus gets scared and produces free energy when the smoke alarm goes off because I'm cooking and it surprises him. As soon as the noise stops, he forgets about it, and lets the past go. He doesn't worry about previous events, and he's not fixated on future possibilities. He's entirely in the present and because of that dogs produce much less free energy than most humans. Letting go of what's already happened and being present in the moment is a great way to reduce free energy and get your tail wagging again.

average surprise, or the surprise you expect following an action, is mathematical uncertainty or entropy. If you believe that then the motivation of all our behavior is to avoid uncertainty, avoid the unknown, avoid fear, then you can move to increase or learn other expected outcomes.

The way Free Energy is created is what Paul Badcock,[1] a professor at the University of Melbourne in Australia, calls bottom-up or top-down. If the first way we experienced free energy was bottom-up, we found out after we got more information about a situation, an error in what we believed, and the surprise was in the error. Top-down is signals you send to the rest of your brain that make predictions about the future. The situation might be just the way you think it is, but free energy arises because the outcome is not represented the way you believe it would be. Think of things that have not happened yet. The future can create excessive free energy for people who make predictions about things they cannot control, or worry about the what-ifs (the foundation for many anxiety issues).

Each one of us is our own creator of free energy and we are fueling our own fears. This is how anxiety and anger issues often arise. One example of self-creation of free energy is my wife spending a lot of energy worrying about our absent-minded twelve-year-old son walking to school. He has to cross a busy road on the way. My wife can envision all the negative or surprise outcomes that could happen, which causes her to worry. She knows what the event is (our son crossing the street) and she can weigh all the possible actions that lead to various outcomes and form various hypotheses (H), yet she can't take any actions to get her expectations back to a state of normality. Because she is worrying about something she can't control, she can never impact or even know the event outcomes because she's not there. She produces free energy so she can't reduce her fear. The only outcome is by definition going to be a surprise. This creates an unhealthy amygdala activation with associated stress hormones such as cortisol impacting her body. The only way she can eliminate the top-down Free Energy state is to not worry about what she cannot control. If you cannot control an outcome, you must focus only on controlling your reaction to that outcome. See figure 4.3 for what top-down free energy production might look like.

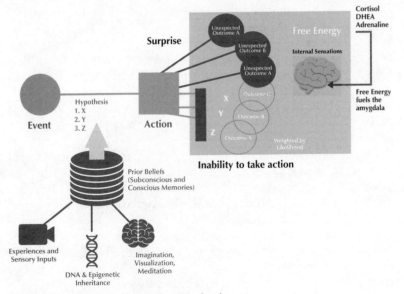

Figure 4.3. Top-Down Free Energy Production

The good news is that there are many methods to resolve that self-creation of free energy. One reason that cognitive behavioral therapy (CBT) and schema therapy work so well with patients who have trauma or anxiety is that they modify Prior Beliefs very effectively. Those therapies build up the subconscious database by challenging existing beliefs and giving patients techniques to increase both PB and H—the two biggest influences on the production of free energy in our simple equation. Understanding why CBT works so well when someone with severe fear or anxiety issues enters therapy with a psychologist exemplifies why we can reduce our fear of fear, create courage, and change our lives to be happy and successful. Just the process of trying to reduce free energy can provide a neurological reward and change the chemical functioning of your brain.

The Free Energy Principle states that whenever we make a choice our motivation is to gather evidence to minimize surprise. One way to do that is to seek out new and different experiences. This is called novelty seeking, finding new experiences to prove or disprove hypotheses (neuroscientists would call this epistemic value). Back to our hamster on the wheel, novelty would be getting off the wheel to explore the tunnel. If you choose to search out novelty, it can be very fulfilling and enlightening emotionally. You may even find it addictive, as the hamster would with a big pile of food at the end of the tunnel each time he scurries through it. Extreme athletes or "adventurous people" who travel, try new sports, or perform in front of audiences are a perfect example of novelty seekers. They still feel their same fear tells, but because they have built up a database with new experiences and created different hypotheses, they are in a state of arousal that can be seen as self-fulfilling excitement. Instead of locking out other hypotheses, they seek new ones. Ultimately that's where you should be.

Like other major changes in *Fear Is Fuel*, choosing to seek novel experiences that expand your PB is simple but not easy. It comes down to making the choice to try something different and then having the confidence to know you are in enough control of your world to have enlightened feelings from novelty seeking. When you make a commitment and experience fulfillment from doing something new and uncomfortable, it is an amazing part of life that opens up an entire vault of happiness, excitement, and exploration. Part of the truest adventure is exploring within yourself, and novelty seeking helps us better understand ourselves and nurture our curiosity.

The exciting aspect of novelty seeking is that you can always find new things to try. Trying new things can be as mundane as changing your greeting to coworkers in the morning or as wild as hiking the Great Wall of China.

Rock climbing was one of my first and favorite areas to seek novelty. At first it was just the climbing but each year I find ways to challenge earlier hypotheses and expand my orientation to the world. I climb a lot and generally have feelings of excitement, extreme focus, and timelessness; because rock climbing requires so much focus, and the stakes seem very high I can get in the zone quickly. I experience a wonderful state of flow. But it's not always roses and unicorns. The exception usually comes at the beginning of the season when I practice falling. When you lead climb, you pull a safety rope, tied to your waist harness, along with you. Your partner holds the rope taut from the ground below you. As you climb higher you clip the rope into a series of anchors that would stop a fall, assuming your partner holds the rope; it's called belaying. As you climb, if the anchor is in front of your face, the rope has a little bit of slack down to your harness; it goes from your waist up to about your face, back down through the anchor, and all the way down to the ground. If you fall in this instance you fall a few inches, just enough for the taut rope to pull tight and stop you. As you climb above each anchor, every inch of rope above that anchor equals two inches you have to fall to go past the anchor in order for it to catch you. To learn how to fall safely, and to get used to the idea of a big fall, I practice falling in a controlled environment indoors. I'll climb up a wall until the anchor is below my feet by a foot or two, meaning I'll fall the length of my body, plus the amount I am above the anchor, plus some stretch in the rope—maybe ten to fifteen feet of free fall before my partner catches me. The first fall or two of the season, my partner says I sound like the Hogwarts Express steaming into the station, because my four-by-four breathing is so loud (see chapter 7). It's scary and I've got a happy-hour sized fear cocktail coursing through my veins. But I do it, and it gets easier and easier with each fall. I seek out that novelty to disprove the theory that falling will kill or hurt me. I add a new hypothesis to help deal with the internal feeling, the bodily sensations, my fear tells, and frame them in an entirely new light. The more you disprove that uncertainty, the more attractive disproving that becomes. In fact, your mind produces adrenaline and dopamine, which gives you that great athlete's high and sense of

FINDING FEAR MAKES YOU FIT

Extreme sports are good for both the body and the mind. Sure, learning to rock climb, skydive, white water kayak, paraglide, ski, mountain bike all can keep you physically fit, but did you know those activities will change the neurological structure of your mind and increase cognitive capacity? A 2013 study in the *Journal of Health Psychology* found that high levels of fear are experienced by most practitioners of extreme sports. Adrenaline junkies who play those sports integrated intense fear into their worldview, or Prior Beliefs, creating a healthier and more encompassing reality. They are not afraid of fear, a common limitation for many people. Most of the subjects in the study experienced fear as "a potentially meaningful and constructive event in their lives." Many of the CEOs, athletes, and special forces veterans I interviewed for this book or coached in their businesses talk about fear as a normal part of life, not to be avoided but accepted, and as you know by now, to be used as fuel. It also helps propagate new neural connections as you get older, keeping you mentally fit as well.

flow. Novelty seeking is a great way to learn new things, eliminate free energy, and cultivate courage.

Learning rate can be one of the best determinants of how a person reacts to unexpected uncertainty. In a 2013 study, researchers found that the faster people can learn and increase the size of their Prior Beliefs the less free energy they are likely to produce.[2] Everything we think or believe is an inference to explain our sensations, our fear tells, and to minimize the surprise or uncertainty on feeling those sensations. If you can learn to interpret your fear tells as excitement you will not be surprised and therefore will produce less free energy. This process is called interoception, how our brain basically creates a hallucination of the world. This hallucination is made up of all the sensory inputs and then internally we piece all that data together and create a story around those inputs. That story is what we believe to be the world. Special cells in our brain take our inferences or conclusions about things and pass them through various parts of our brain to be analyzed. The cells responsible for this are called pyramidal cells. The deep pyramidal cells send your predictions or expected outcomes down deeper into the brain toward the amygdala, and the errors that your brain thinks are in your conclusion (prediction errors) will be updated and accounted for to reduce surprise—by being returned to the source of predictions to update our beliefs.

These pyramidal cells update our internal view of the world and that's how we learn. The faster we learn and update our orientation to the world, the more success we'll have in our life and career. The way to learn quickly and increase the size of your subconscious database is curiosity. Considering, imagining, or better yet, experiencing different states of being changes your world literally by changing your mind.

Curiosity takes effort. The brain doesn't like to use a lot of energy being curious. It would rather use shortcuts to reduce energy expenditure (you'll learn more about in chapter 10) called valence. Valence is the efficient tried and true method. If you don't use the shortcuts and are curious about what to do in response to something, it takes much more energy. You will need to infer and select the best way forward. FEP would say the goal of those plans is to minimize your uncertainty and update your PB.

Some of the techniques you'll learn later in the book will give you tools to not only update your existing PB, as you would in normal existence, but also to dramatically change what you think the possibilities are. In chapters 9, 10, and 11 you'll learn tools based on free energy to shatter your old beliefs and limits. When I explained some of these tactics to Friston he agreed that "You're absolutely right—creating new hypotheses expands the repertoire or model of things that could happen—by internally simulating them. Your hypothesis space is then more fit for purpose, in the sense that it affords a greater opportunity to resolve uncertainty."[3] That's the way a very smart man says the ideas you'll read about can help you create courage! Friston calls it revising your policy space to become courageous. If you made it through this chapter and picked up at least the concept of the root of all fears, congratulations—you've changed your perception of reality! That wasn't so hard, was it? You are one step closer to using fear as fuel, learning to make the production of free energy your friend, and empowering yourself along your courage journey.

5

❦

The Faces of Fear

To conquer fear you must become fear.

—*Batman*

1.

Abright yellow orb dances in the middle of the pink and purple horizon. A blurry reflection is mirrored just below the horizon off the shimmery Gulf of Mexico like a child's finger painting. "Another epic Pensacola sunset," thought Nick Bradshaw (not his real name) as he guided his $70 million F/A-18 Hornet back to the Naval Air Station just like hundreds of other evenings. He was calm, happy, and grateful for the scene painted in front of him. Then disaster hit and his whole life changed.

Bradshaw was a US Naval Academy graduate who rose through the ranks of pilots to become one of the elite. He reached the pinnacle of naval aviation by not only flying F/A-18s but for the past two years he had been an instructor, the best of the best. His short blond hair, chiseled jaw, and permanently affixed Ray-Ban Aviators gave him the central-casting look of a *Top Gun* character.

The sunset flight that evening was a routine sortie over the Gulf of Mexico, on the way home cruising along the east coast of the Florida Panhandle and up over Panama City. When Bradshaw was pointed due west toward Naval Air Station Pensacola, the intensity of the setting sun radiating on the horizon and the sparkling explosions of light off the waves below him created a neurological trigger in his brain that detonated a migraine headache accompanied by a temporary loss of vision. Bradshaw held the plane level and crushed his eyes shut, deep creases forming at their edges, his brow furrowed tightly as if the harder he squeezed the quicker he could force the blur to the edges and clear his vision. He shook his head like a Rottweiler trying to dislodge an earwig. Still, blurry spots and an opaque void persisted in the center of his vision. Bradshaw radioed the tower and reported unusual readings from his radar system. He asked for permission to head back out to sea for a few minutes to diagnose the problem. He was able to turn the F/A-18 due south and keep it level at 15,000 feet. His weapons system officer (WSO), working in the aft seat, had been asking what the hell was going on; Bradshaw brushed him off, saying it was nothing, a problem with his helmet. But the question came again with clear annoyance and worry in the voice this time.

After about fifteen or twenty minutes, Bradshaw's eyesight returned to normal and he brought the fighter home to base. The discussion between his WSO and Bradshaw was short and to the point. There are two lives in the plane together. If something was threatening either, they owed it to each other to say something. If Bradshaw's WSO went to their commanding officer, it would be disaster for both of them. No pilots would want to fly with a WSO they couldn't trust. Conversely, Bradshaw keeping a potentially disastrous medical secret to himself could result in disciplinary action and even a dishonorable discharge.

Bradshaw did the only thing he could do in the situation; he went to the flight surgeon (who normally gave annual physicals or prescribed the occasional antibiotic) and came clean. Bradshaw told the truth about what happened. After a battery of tests it was clear that Bradshaw had developed a specific type of neurological disorder called ocular migraines, where hyperactivity within the brain triggered by exposure to bright light flashes causes blindness. His flying days were over. Bradshaw felt nauseous; sitting in the sterile white office. He'd never been so scared in his life.

Bradshaw had no idea how to deal with the emotional fear that was strangling his world. The dark side of his personality and his hidden fears erupted front and center. He couldn't see any value being just plain old Nick Bradshaw. He was only significant if he was "Nick Bradshaw, F/A-18 instructor pilot." As a boy Bradshaw was valued when he brought home a trophy; he knew he would get overlooked unless he got straight A's in school or won the big game. So he developed a defense mechanism that was to win and become the best at his chosen field. Flying gave him that winning identity as an adult. This same man who had an uncanny ability to compartmentalize physical fear in the heat of battle, focus on his tasks, and put fear back on the shelf to execute some of the most physically and mentally demanding tasks imaginable had hit his Fear Frontier. This time it was emotional. Bradshaw had no idea how to deal with it. Tragically, just one thing came to mind.

As a child we all develop our own specific "Face of Fear." Despite our own personalities being uniquely individualized to us, there are similarities. Every Face of Fear has a healthy, happy, successful side and every Face of Fear has a dark side. Our individual relationship with fear and how we respond to a traumatic situation determines whether we succumb to the dark side and our talents enable a narcissistic, self-serving life, or we use our skills to make the world a better place and do our best to end suffering. You need to recognize your dark side before it's too late.

The Face of Fear that Bradshaw developed to make him one of the best pilots in the world revealed its dark side. The dark side in each of our personalities most often comes to light because we are afraid to face some or multiple truths. People who are excessively narcissistic, who lack empathy, or who are habitual liars are almost always manifesting those behaviors because of some deep-seated fear. Until they face that fear, they will have to keep the cycle of lying, taking advantage of others, and never being good enough. Because he hadn't worked on facing the fears of his personality in the same way he worked on his flying skills, he was in enemy territory in his mind. Bradshaw had an emotional fear of rejection; that shaped his behavior and became self-fulfilling. As long as he was a flight instructor, he felt he'd never be rejected, but he had just lost that. He couldn't cope with his emotional fear and was crippled by the uncertainty of not being the best. The fear of facing his true self also paralyzed his creativity; he couldn't imagine himself doing something else. His job *was* his identity. He lived, slept, and breathed flying. The personality and defense mechanisms he created as a youth were challenged and because he was not emotionally prepared for a change in his identity he believed the moment turned him into a failure; he felt rejected. Having never faced any significant failures in his life, he did not have an internal script to follow to overcome the attack on his identity.

His coping mechanism was the same as many other pilots who are suddenly and surprisingly grounded, Bradshaw hit the Officers' Club. Hard. It wasn't long before he was mixing whiskey into his morning coffee. Not long before his wife took his child to stay with her mother. His drinking during the transition period to a desk job became so severe that a month after he was grounded military police found him passed out on a December night near an alligator-infested pond, covered in mud. That led to a Navy-sponsored entrance to a rehabilitation center, where he tried to pick up the shattered pieces of a once high-flying career. He wasn't ready for the dark side of his personality and when it ambushed him, he was petrified of what it meant; he believed that without the trophy title of instructor pilot he had no value as a person. He couldn't handle the uncertainty of life without flying.

If you think about your friends or family, or even celebrities, you'll be able to think of someone with Bradshaw's personality type, and maybe even see the unhealthy, dark side that fed the fear that he was nothing without his wings, his identity. The root of that fear, of course, is Free Energy and the fact that he couldn't imagine a different reality, a reality without flying that was fun, fulfilling, and exciting. A mentally strong and healthy person with Bradshaw's personality doesn't get transfixed on one identity. That person will see value in and embrace all of his identities and be open to other beliefs—instructor pilot, husband, father, friend, son. Emotional fears cause people to fixate on the one aspect of their identity they know and trust; that's why so many succumb to constant fear and anxiety when that identity is crushed.

Nick Bradshaw could not deal with the threat to his sole identity; he couldn't embrace a new and exciting chapter in his life. Fear over-came him. Compulsive drinking numbed that fear. This chapter will help you to face the fear that can accompany a challenge to who you think and feel you are.

2.

"Wow, Laurie, for a girl you really crushed it; you almost beat all the boys!"

The gangly twelve-year-old blonde stomped off the court away from the judge who was counting her shots, a coach from a local high school. She clenched her fists as a wave of crimson flushed up her neck and cheeks, contrasting against her porcelain Irish complexion. Despite winning the Elks Free Throw Championship Competition for girls by sinking twenty-two out of twenty-five free throws, her jaw was locked tightly and she was sucking air through flaring nostrils like a raging bull.

Her dad saw her and waited. The corners of his lips turned up ever so slightly. She wouldn't make eye contact with him, even as all the other parents gave her words of congratulations. Her dad asked: "Are you mad? Well you should be pissed. Where did you blow it?"

She didn't answer.

He waited.

She still didn't answer, even though her breathing increased and the whistling of air through her nose was audible.

"Laurie?"

"I rushed the last two shots after that one bounced around the rim. I should have sunk at least one."

"Listen to me. Listen. When you are under pressure you can't think about anything but your routine. Not the last shot, not the next shot, just your form. Every shot the same. You got it?"

"Yeah." Pause. "Dad?"

"What is it?"

"That Coach said I crushed it—for a girl."

Cal's eyes narrowed and his shaggy brows pushed together. He took a breath as he thought of the best way to respond.

Growing up the oldest of four daughters might be a tough responsibility for some kids, but being the oldest of an Olympic silver-medalist dad[1] and Olympic team-member mom can either be a huge advantage or a crippling catapult to anxiety. It all depends on how your life unfolded as a child and how you faced important traumatic moments. It's those defense mechanisms that lay the foundation for your personality.

"Listen, Laur, that coach doesn't know what the hell he is talking about, you are a basketball player—not a girl basketball player. You could have won the whole thing—I mean you *should* have won. Don't ever settle for less. We're just lucky your mother didn't hear him say that to you; she would've kicked his ass."

With that, Laurie's lips finally curled up in a smile.

Her dad continued, "If you're entering a race; you're entering to win. If you're playing in a game, you're playing to help your team

win. Think of yourself as an athlete and compete against other athletes. Now it's time to put the day behind you and figure out what
you can do during practice that will help you win the next one."

Laurie's reaction was to go back and focus on being a student of
the game, to be the best.

Her parents had taught her repeatedly to practice in a very
thoughtful way, use the same movements and routines each time
she did something. Make every shot in practice perfect and you will
get used to making perfect shots. She would become a leading scorer
on every basketball team she ever played on because she disciplined
herself to approach every shot the same way—she had a routine that
never varied whether she was alone shooting after practice or had
ten seconds left in a championship game.

Laurie liked the compliments from coaches and other parents, but
what she yearned for was to show her mom and dad that she could
be an even better version of them. Like Nick Bradshaw, her value
and happiness came from being the best at her sport. She would
train harder and work longer than anyone. Coaches and teachers
always commented on her ability to motivate herself and be productive. Not only was she blossoming into a top athlete in school;
she was at the head of her class as well. Her thirst for being the best
was well paired up with a deep-rooted self-motivation that, thanks
to the support of her parents, was not limited by perceived gender
differences. Along with her self-motivation she developed an ability
to put process or routine ahead of fear and anxiety. Whenever she
was nervous in big games, important tests, or school presentations
she learned the ability to focus on her routine—treat it like practice
and push any fears or anxiety into the background. She had created
her own Face of Fear—a personality and defense mechanism that
had a very powerful healthy side; it would take her places most
fourteen-year-old girls would never dream of, and in fact it would
take her somewhere that wasn't even allowed by law when she
hatched the idea. The interesting thing about any Face of Fear is that
if you don't work to develop the healthy side, fueled by courage and
a willingness to tackle fear head-on, you will more often default to
the destructive dark side. It takes effort to be courageous and it takes
courage to push back your dark side when things get tough. Your
dark side is going to default to your own survival, your own place
in the tribe, and more destructively, your decisions will be driven
by fear, not opportunity. We all have our own Face of Fear. If we can

create an understanding of our own personality it will help us stay on the light side and overcome moments of falling to the dark side. Avoiding the dark side not only helps us to make choices based on opportunity, but it allows us to see things in the present from a place of love, courage, and happiness.

3.

"Are all three of your children from the same wife?"

The slightly oily sheen and cinnamon color of Tashi Lama's (not his real name) face gave it a vibrant luster that stood out in contrast to his matte maroon and mustard robes. The Buddhist monk and I were having a challenging conversation about some of the concepts of Buddhism. Tashi fled his native Tibet in 1993 and landed in Breckenridge, Colorado. He was teaching Tibetan massage and also helping people understand their past lives. Based on concepts of birth time, date, and location Buddhists believe they can gain insight into their past lives and even what age they are likely to die. I wasn't buying it.

"If they have the same mother, the same father, then shouldn't all children be born with the same personality?" Tashi asked.

"They are as different as chalk and cheese, that's for sure. It was clear before they even spoke."

"It's because they carry the challenges, attachments, and sufferings from past lives forward to this one, and they must figure out how to eliminate that bad karma. Knowledge of past lives should bring humility, recognition of suffering, and wisdom—taking time to figure out and work on changing their weaknesses into strengths in this life," he explained.

You might not agree with the idea of reincarnation and the philosophy of attaining enlightenment by eliminating the karma from your past sins, but Tashi was certainly right about changing your weaknesses into strengths.

Buddhists believe your personality stems from your past lives, but they don't speculate as to how many types of personalities there are. There's no right answer, but people who study people believe that there are anywhere from five to sixteen different types of personalities. You could literally spend a lifetime studying personality types, but thankfully you don't have to—I've got a shortcut.

My interviews with psychologists, neuroscientists, and even philosophers have led me to the realization that most people can identify with nine different personality types; your specific personality is created by the defense mechanism you develop in response to your early traumatic experiences. How you respond to your first Fear Frontier is what really drives your personality.

You learned in chapter 2 that when we experience our first traumatic experience or experiences that a Fear Frontier is created by forming two memories on our brain's hard drive—a semantic memory and an emotional memory. The memory of the specifics and events can never be changed, but the emotional association with the event can be altered at any time during our life. However, when we experience our first trauma we develop a defense mechanism against future trauma. This process creates the foundation of your personality. The way your personality evolves determines your biggest fears as you get older and also your defense mechanisms for avoiding those fears. If you start to understand the relationship between your personality type and your anxieties, you can use the knowledge of your specific fears to understand why and when you might drift toward the dark side of your personality.

It's crucial to identify yourself with one or maybe two of the personality types so you can start to investigate more about how you defend against trauma and fear.

Your personality, barring a major shocking event like the death of a parent or sibling, is ingrained by the age of twelve. You can modify your personality at any age, because of neuroplasticity. As you grow older you can shift toward the fearful side of your personality where decisions are made based on fear and survival, or you can lean toward the courageous side of your personality where your decisions are made based on opportunity. Your success, happiness, and fulfillment at any time depends on your choices; you are the only one in control of how you react to your future. When you get to the point where you can see yourself behaving on both the good side and the bad side of your personality, you create the feeling of watching a movie of your life. There is a significant difference between watching a movie and acting in one. Watching the movie, being the observer, is what we should strive for. We want to be the director or producer. That's the first step to being able to assess any situation rationally.

My Dad's favorite movie is *The Godfather*; we must have endured it fifty times growing up. Michael Corleone battling the dark side of his personality is what creates the pain and torment of the movie. I always wished he'd realize he was going to the dark side, before it was too late. That's the benefit of watching it from the observer's perspective: the fog of emotion is lifted and you can see clearly. You don't have to be Michael Corleone, or in the Mob, to think about the fight you had with your parents, the time last week at work when you flew off the handle and called a coworker an asshole, the Sunday you sat watching a full season of *Breaking Bad* instead of working on your house. To help you learn to be the producer or director of your dream life, let's use Hollywood for a little help.

Because of dramatic extremes, movies are a great way to recognize healthy characters or tragic ones. You don't want to be like poor Darth Vader, who waited until minutes before dying to look into Luke's eyes and finally connect with true joy. That's why before you get ambushed by a tough event (like our pilot Nick Bradshaw did) I want you to cast a character type for your life. This will allow you to watch your own movie and mentally shape the actor.

A firstborn child with Olympic athlete parents, Laurie Coffey believed, and still believes, that the worst thing that could happen in life is to be insignificant because you failed to use your talents and opportunities to achieve greatness. However, she doesn't believe, like Bradshaw, that her identity is her talent. For Laurie, the healthy side of her "Face of Fear" was driving her to be highly self-motivated and determined to be productive. More than anything Laurie refused to let anyone put a limit on what she could achieve, and she had a strong enough confidence to believe she was valuable no matter what she chose to do in her life.

As a top scholar and champion athlete, Laurie could have gone to any Ivy League school, but she had other dreams. Each US Senator and Congressman can recommend five students to attend the US Naval Academy at any one time. That effectively means they can nominate one new incoming student each year. Laurie went on to get one of those coveted nominations. Her dream was to fly the Space Shuttle one day. She also thought it would be amazing to fly F/A-18s like Maverick from the movie *Top Gun*. The funny thing is, when Laurie hatched those dreams of fighter planes and Space Shuttles, women were not allowed to fly planes in combat. There were no female F/A-18 pilots. That never stopped her from believing in lofty dreams, mostly because she never delineated roles based on male or female. She thought it was ridiculous to define herself so narrowly. The navy lifted the ban on women fighter pilots in 1993. Laurie's personality was a true asset in the high-pressure, high-stakes environment of the Naval Academy, especially as a varsity athlete. Because of her sports career and her parents' experience, Laurie learned to face her fear head-on, recognize it, and tell herself not to attach undo importance to it. Neuroscience has shown that this idea of compartmentalizing fear is one of the optimal tactics of dealing with fear while at the same time using that fear cocktail your body creates under stress as a source of superpower. That's why you need to find more fear, to practice putting it on the back burner while you go on with your task at hand.

Laurie Coffey went on to graduate from the Naval Academy and become not just an F/A-18 pilot, but like Bradshaw an instructor teaching other pilots at Naval Air Station Pensacola, and a combat pilot flying dozens of sorties in support of Operation Iraqi Freedom. She learned to use her personality to the fullest to get what she wanted in life and become a member of a group of less than one-half of one percent of all naval aviator fighter pilots as a woman. But ask her and she'd never want to be put in that category; she'd just want you to know she was one of the best pilots in the world. Period.

Laurie's life took a different trajectory with a new baby girl, whose father wanted to return to his farming roots and put an end to their nomadic military life. It was clear that they had different goals and dreams; consequently, they broke up. After she had her daughter, Laurie reprioritized and adjusted to a new normal that wasn't what had been planned. She realized she wanted to be present with her young daughter, not always out on deployment or living on an aircraft carrier. Just before her daughter's third birthday Laurie altered course and sought a position teaching at the Naval Academy. She wasn't flying anymore, but no longer being an F/A-18 instructor didn't send her into an emotional tailspin. She was in touch enough with her personality to know that her genius lay in being great in all of her day-to-day actions; greatness wasn't wrapped up in her title, or career, or sport. She continued in the navy, taking on challenging assignments and opportunities to lead and serve, and retired this year after a twenty-year career; she finished up running logistics and operational planning for the European fleet at a dream location in Italy with her daughter.[2]

4.

Early traumas and our Fear Frontier shape our personalities. While getting yelled at by a coach or told you are "not as good as a boy" might not seem like a major trauma to adults, it's enough to activate the amygdala in a child and create a physiological response. Remember that children don't have a fully developed prefrontal cortex, and just about every experience is a new (and often scary) one. How we respond to those traumas becomes a defense mechanism that shapes our actions through our developing years and still shapes our actions as adults.

If we have the support to face anxiety head-on and can tame fear, we will seldom experience the dark side of those traumas. As you'll find out below when you read about the different personality types, Laurie Coffey would be a classic Jerry Maguire personality based on my Hollywood persona ranking. She was happy and successful because she had mastered the most valuable qualities of that personality.

If you take a look at the other side of a personality like Jerry Maguire or Lieutenant Pete "Maverick" Mitchell from *Top Gun* (not surprisingly both played by Tom Cruise), you may recognize some of the signs of a person who never came to grips with their fears. They might be amazing on the physical side of the Terror Triangle, but emotional and instinctual fears still derailed their success and haunted their daily lives. This changes radically when they come to grips with all aspects of their demons, which is of course the climax of the movie.

Understanding your personality will help you uncover your hidden fears and give you early warning of personality traits that might hold you back in your career and relationships. Specific personalities share common fears, because they share traumatic life-shaping events and defense mechanisms.

This is a Hollywood version of the personality type so you can figure out your persona and even do the same for your colleagues, family, and friends. People spend a lifetime studying different tests and philosophies—it is a very complex art—however, this is an intro into the science of personality evaluation and will serve to get you reflecting on how you have developed your current relationship with fear.

Who do you think you most resemble and what are those strengths and weaknesses? Why does your boss or spouse act a certain way when there is pressure or a deadline? Creating some insight into yours and others' Faces of Fear will help you think twice before you let the amygdala drive you into a reactive action. The act of trying to categorize personalities will help you better observe action in yourself and others as well.

5.

The following nine profiles emerged from a combination of psychological tools and behavioral science research. I've put them here for the same reason that we worked to discern your fear tells: so you can start to see certain behaviors happening consistently in you. Your goal is to identify behaviors that seem familiar and create a strategy for dealing with them.

Awareness and preparation are often enough to keep you from succumbing to the dark side and guide you down the path toward happiness, success, and courageous leadership no matter what challenges present themselves. After you read through the nine personalities you might identify with more than one; that's great—you'll have twice as many exercises to try! Once you get good at defining your own type, you can recognize traits in others and better understand why your spouse (who might be the Innovator persona) doesn't say he's unhappy until three weeks after something happens and he finally blows up, or why your boss comes up with the greatest ideas but then she fails to prepare all the way with them, just like Lucky Rogue, who has never read a manual once in his life!

Over the past fifteen years I've taken dozens of personality tests and surveys, mostly in an effort to figure out how to hire the right people for my technology companies. One weekend I binge-watched countless reruns of *Gilligan's Island* to see which of the Seven Deadly Sins the characters represent (while fueling the age-old beauty debate: Ginger or Mary Ann). I attended writers' workshops on character development based on personality type. I took acting classes and learned how to insult people's specific personalities like Shakespeare. I wanted to try to see what it was like to be all nine personalities. I even dressed up with eight other CEOs in our opposite persona and went out to dinner at a very public restaurant, completely acting the part of my opposite. The bottom line is that there are so many different types of tests and workshops that you could spend a lifetime self-evaluating and trying to figure out your exact combination of variations (and many people do). That's a ton of work, and you're already super-busy, so I'm giving you the Cliffs Notes version to get you started. Knowing yourself is the foundation of using fear as fuel. This is another step toward self-knowledge and discovery.[3] When I was grinding through my MBA, I took a semester-long career management class at the University of Virginia's Darden School. After all the tests and evaluations we went through, they recommended I become a park ranger; that one came as a surprise but was closer to my genius than I could have imagined.

Understanding yourself better and reflecting on the why, being curious, will help you take the position of an observer so you can assess every situation. Here are nine Faces of Fear to help you look at yourself from the outside. Which one are you?

Read the first part of each one of these personas out loud and see which one feels the most like you when you hear it.

1. Inspired Leader

You are a proud member of your tribe; you like being part of a team or organization. Most of the time you avoid confrontations or rocking the boat, but when you must, you can motivate and inspire your team. You're outgoing and engaging and will walk through walls to protect your values or ideals.

The reason you are so effective is that you bring up the fears all of them were thinking about and tell why you chose courage and opportunity and won't succumb to fear taking over. In turn, this gives you security and guidance, and most of the time the Inspired Leader type is serving the greater good rather than himself.

Greatest fear: The inspired leader needs a tribe, so the greatest fear is being rejected by the tribe.

Birth of your personality: Your Fear Frontier had something to do with an event when you were by yourself—being beaten up by a bully, maybe getting lost trying to find your way home, or even being punished for standing out and doing something different. Your defense mechanism became to rely on friends to help you deal with things and to keep friends around you; you learned to look like them, act like them, and not rock the boat—always be a team player. When your principles are challenged, you can be a powerful leader.

Compulsion: Going with the flow and being uncomfortable venturing out on your own.

Strategy & Exercise: **Your courage has to come from within; you are the most comfortable person with fear, so take on any challenge and show the world what courage looks like, even if you do it alone.** Do something that makes you feel insecure—hitchhike to dinner, wear a really wild outfit to work, like a beatnik or punk rock outfit, act out in a nonconformist way to prove to yourself that you don't need a tribe to fuel your courage and greatness.

2. The Lucky Rogue

You're strong and in control not just of your destiny, but of any situation. You're charismatic and can get people to push out of their comfort zone and try something new and challenging. You always want to be improving your skills; whether it's taking on a new language or sport, or learning how to program software, you want to master it. You don't mind a confrontation and sometimes get mad when people don't follow your lead.

Greatest fear: Fear of being controlled by others or being out of control; this can lead a lot of Lucky Rogue types to be claustrophobic or fearful of things like flying, where they are not the person in control.

Birth of your personality: As a child you may have been punished or hurt for showing emotion and feelings; you could have often had conflicts or arguments with your parents. Crying when something bad happened may have been met with disapproval or even punishment from an authority figure, so to defend against this you learned to repress your feelings and become fiercely independent.

Compulsion: Needing to be in control.

Strategy & Exercise: **Your strategy should be to create significance in the world while at the same time being sensitive to every individual. You can be the kind of leader that people would walk through fire**

to follow. Your desire to be independent and self-reliant, or even a hero to others, makes you quick to be the one to pick up the check or volunteer to do something tough. Take a week and accept all the gifts that come your way without hesitations. When someone offers to buy you a coffee or lunch, don't say "I'll get this"; instead of arguing, say thoughtfully and with appreciation, "Thank you, that's really kind." And see what it feels like to let someone else take control. If you always drive to meetings or school functions, let someone else take the wheel and see how difficult it is to stay quiet as a passenger.

3. The Adventurer

You love excitement, you'll take on any new adventure, or you're happy to go to a party and meet new people. You're not sure why people have to be so serious and caught up in details of minutiae when there is so much to see and do. You don't have to plan out every detail; just go for it and it will work out fine. You don't want to limit your chances of a new experience, and sometimes your ideas can vastly outweigh the actual follow-through.

Greatest fear: Fear of loss or deprivation, fear of missing out (FOMO) on experiences; because you'll feel that you are missing something, you fear the void rather than being present in the moment where you are.

Birth of your personality: You had a lack of something when you were young, maybe you were poor, maybe there weren't any intellectual challenges. With all your energy you found a way to get around those issues, to defend against being deprived. When you were young, the only way to keep from being rejected was to be entertaining; you learned early on that to have value you had to be the life of the party.

Compulsion: Saying yes to everything, to avoid FOMO.

Strategy & Exercise: **Take in all your feelings, good or bad, with curiosity and you'll never feel trapped or want to escape; your sense of wonder and amazement for life will inspire others.** If you normally go out every weekend, pick the next weekend or two and reserve Saturday night for deprivation night. Shut off your phone and all contact with the world; read a good book or watch a movie. Realize that you can be happy and enjoy being alone and missing whatever happens to be going on that night. If you want a bonus, the next day write a journal entry that starts out "What I learned about myself was . . ."

4. The Detective

You solve mysteries; this means you've got to come up with complex ideas and theories, but you're independent and innovative so it's easy for you to do that. You can see the world in a much different and pioneering way than others can. You'll never do a job half-assed; you're determined to do it right.

Greatest fear: Fear of being incompetent or inadequate, the fear of not being great at something, and a fear of failure in other's eyes.

Birth of your personality: The Fear Frontier most often associated with the Detective personality is humiliation as a child, or trauma caused by not being able to do something at an expert level. Kids who are asked to come up in front of the whole class to recite a poem or solve a math problem and then fail are a classic example.

Compulsion: Believing that there is a right way and a wrong way and wanting to keep working until something is perfect.

Strategy & Exercise: **You need to look at decisions as a series of routes like the results of Google Maps; each choice can get you where you want to go; they are just paths and seldom is one "right" and one "wrong."** Pick an activity that you know you are bad at and invite a couple of your friends to join you for a social night out. It could be bowling, karaoke, whatever gets you nervous at the thought of just trying it. Then have a relaxing and light-hearted time with your friends, admitting that you aren't an expert at what you are doing and being OK with that admission and your eventual performance.

5. Law & Order

You're here to right the wrongs and make order of chaos. The world is an imperfect place, so you're the guy who is going to set things straight. You're searching out the truth and you always do things right, no shortcuts. When your Law & Order personality amygdala activates, it is almost in a fight response.

Greatest fear: Fear of being evil or corrupt, or being wrong or making a decision that will lead to catastrophic results.

Birth of your personality: As a child you might have been the one taking on the role of parent or adult because your initial Fear Frontier was when something bad happened by not following the rules or by some traumatic event taking place because something wasn't perfect. (I've worked with CEOs who made a terrible choice as a child that stayed with them—one let the family dog loose on a busy street and the dog was killed by a car.) The defense mechanism you developed was becoming an idealist who creates order out of chaos and you became a very serious person.

Compulsion: Using achievement, work, or workouts to provide value. Workaholics are common in the Law & Order personality.

Strategy & Exercise: **You can be an inspiration for the greater good just the way you are. Skip working late two nights a week to have dinner with family or friends, or skip a morning workout to sleep in once a week.** Find fun in being wrong.

6. The Mediator

You help things operate smoothly; you'll do your best to avoid conflict and stay connected with everybody. You like to be in touch with other people and your own spirituality. You'll even give up your own agenda and desires for other people if it makes everyone happy. You can often see things in a bigger picture beyond what is simply evident to most people. When you're mad you don't let people know; you're better at keeping it to yourself.

Greatest fear: Fear of loss or separation, fear of not being able to take care of your tribe, fear of someone else getting upset or angry with you.

Birth of your personality: You might have been overwhelmed by a parent or dominating sibling, so your defense mechanism became to stay out of the way. Keeping your mouth shut and head low kept you out of trouble but also led you to think you were affecting others' moods. If you reached out to your parent or teacher you might have ended up feeling rejected or bullied; this left you lonely and looking for a way to numb yourself out, maybe by watching TV or going online.

Compulsion: Bottling up everything inside and blowing up when it becomes too much to bear.

Strategy & Exercise: **You must learn to stay in the moment, no matter how uncomfortable that might be; if you can, you'll help others around you feel truly valued and peaceful.** Once a day, work on blurting out a feeling or opinion right at the time it hits you. Engage aggressively one day at work or with your family; try to come up with strong opinions and express them immediately when you think of them—right then in the moment. Even something as simple as when someone asks, "Where do you want to go for lunch?" Your typical answer might be, "I don't care, what do you feel like?" Do just the opposite: when asked, pick a spot, even if it doesn't feel genuine; say, "Let's get sushi."

7. The Giver

You are a people pleaser. You love to feel needed and often can be generous to a fault. You've got buckets of patience and are always ready to lend a hand. Sometimes that might just mean reminding others of their best qualities. You get joy out of helping and are extremely empathetic to other people; some people might even say you're maternal.

Greatest fear: Feeling unappreciated, not belonging to anyone or any group, being unloved.

Birth of your personality: Your Fear Frontier likely developed from a loss; a parent or friend may have left you in some manner when you were young and you therefore believed that if you did something to show you deserved to be kept in the tribe others may not abandon you, and you will never feel unloved again. You are likely to be the one helping to clean up after a party or have a bowl of candy on your desk—not for yourself but for others.

Compulsion: Being motivated by recognition; being unrecognized can lead you to do things to make sure you are noticed.

Strategy & Exercise: **Take care of yourself and you can take care of the world; think about what you need first.** Since recognition is so critical to you when doing something for others, it's time to do some anonymous giving. Choose three opportunities during the day when you can do something nice without any attribution. Even something as simple as randomly putting money in parking meters will work. But the key is that you must keep the three things you do to yourself and not tell anyone.

8. The Competitor

You are ambitious, good at what you do, and highly energetic. You can be charming, and because you're good-looking you are success-fully diplomatic and poised. One thing everyone agrees to is that you're competitive. You usually don't show a lot of emotion, unless it's celebrating a win.

Greatest fear: Failure and humiliation; having no worth or role in society.

Birth of your personality: As a child you may have been rejected from your tribe for doing something poorly or showing a lot of emotion; this may have even led to a humiliating event. Your defense mechanism then was to focus on what other people—parents, teachers, and friends—found valuable and you got really good at that skill since it would get you plenty of praise.

Compulsion: The need to win can drive an addictive behavior like having four or five drinks every night or going shopping three or four times a week.

Strategy & Exercise: **You have to believe you have great value just being yourself. Life is precious; do your part to make it better for everyone.** Limit yourself to two drinks a night, or one day of shopping a month. Do a volunteer day someplace where doing so will not help you toward a goal or ambition. Learn to do something just for the sake of seeing what it's like without being great at it, or without winning. Go out bowling, or play a video game with your kids, or join the office Final Four pool without any emotion attached to winning; in fact, be pleased if you come in last.

9. The Innovator

You are creative and unique in your approach to life. You appreciate art and beauty and like to have beautiful things around you. You spend a lot of time understanding your feelings and getting to the truth of your life and existence, but can't be bothered with logic or facts and figures.

Greatest fear: Fear of being insignificant or abandoned; fear of being flawed.

Birth of your personality: Many innovators are second-born so they want to do something to be unique and not a copy of older siblings. The times in their childhood when they were overlooked or left out of the picture drove them to create a defense mechanism that would surely get them noticed.

Compulsion: To be the victim, and constantly search out a hero to fight your villain.

Strategy & Exercise: **Take the time to be grateful and see the beauty of every moment; don't think you have to build the next great thing to be happy or impactful.** Write out four times in the past when you were the victim of some injustice or were hurt by someone. Then crumple or tear up the paper and let those feelings go, so you don't carry them with you today. An alternative exercise is to dress as normally and conservatively one day at work as you possibly can—plain white shirt, plain pants or skirt, simple shoes. Don't do anything unique and see if people still value and care for you even without a unique identity.

To get to the greatest version of our selves we have to first attack the low-level fears that the prefrontal cortex is constantly dealing with. It's tough work, even though it's not major trauma or stress. That means things might be uncomfortable for a while.

Sometimes it is difficult to break away from inclinations of our personality. We might be committed to playing the role of victim; it might be easier to sit on the couch and drink beer than go for a run, or keep our opinion to ourselves rather than share the truth at work because it might upset someone. We can blame circumstances rather than take accountability for our health, or happiness, or success. With consistent behavior comes a feeling of safety, so staying in the same loop where you never try a new approach will stunt your growth. Growth is what we all need for gratitude and happiness. Avoiding fear can be as simple as staying at work late rather than face a wife looking for more intimacy, or a child with a learning disability. It can be hiding behind a veil of success and never taking risks again because you are afraid you might fail and lose your identity. You know that drinking, eating, sex, exercise, shopping, and work can all be mechanisms to numb an activated amygdala; when there is low-level cortisol coursing through your body causing anxiety—when you start doing things like eating just to relieve anxiety—that's when the behaviors become compulsive.

Forty-Five Days of Elimination

Sounds like a new diet, but it's not, unless you consider it nutrition for your personality. Each one of the nine personalities has a "Greatest Fear," but in the end, as you know from the last chapter, it all comes down to the root of all fear—creating free energy. Free energy, that space between what your mind's database can logically comprehend and predict and what your senses are telling you, is the driver of fear. Your compulsive behaviors are just trying to limit free energy, so we're going to take forty-five days and actively try to create specific fears that test those compulsions.

Expanding your database of Prior Beliefs and increasing the potential outcomes you can imagine are the key, so now we'll challenge those outcomes you have come to expect and add new possible outcomes to your Prior Beliefs. Your next goal is to eliminate all the things that you are doing to numb your anxieties (like excessive drinking, eating, shopping, getting online constantly, overworking, claiming you need to edit it one more time, etc.). Choose your three most common compulsive behaviors (behaviors you engage in to numb anxiety) and eliminate or reduce them for forty-five days. You are going to build the belief that you can be just as happy going for a walk with your dog as finding 70 percent off a Kate Spade bag. You have to commit to breaking the cycle of compulsion, and the only way to do that is to embrace the fear and do it.

Go back to the personality above that seemed closest to you, take one of the suggestions in the personality profile, and commit to doing it at least once a week, ideally more. Many people make the mistake of saying, "I'll take on that challenge when I build up my courage." That's victim thinking. If you are going to be the producer of an amazing life, you must trust the truth—*after I do it* my courage will grow. Action builds courage; courage cannot create action.

Replace a compulsion with a substitute. Try to notice what sets you off on compulsive behavior, and when you sense that cue then replace your normal action with something different. If you usually start drinking when the kids go off to bed, replace the glass of wine with a walk around the neighborhood. Take a risk to try something new and you'll feel the weight of compulsion lifted; because of a simple action you took, you'll build a little bit of courage each day. When the moment is over take ten minutes to write in a journal what it felt like to let go of that compulsion. Find the good in the act (I made myself healthier, I burned some calories, I saved some money, etc.) and give yourself props for replacing the compulsion with a healthier behavior. The writing is your reward for the new behavior. When you write, do it with a pen and paper—there's a connection that is more emotional when writing by hand rather than on a keyboard. Start your journal entry by writing, "I am more powerful today because I . . ."

Since change is never easy, now is the perfect time to see what the latest neuroscience says about change, how fear can keep you from getting the life you want, or how it can be the ultimate fuel to elevate you quickly to live the life of your dreams.

6

⌒

Scare Yourself

Success is never final. Failure is never fatal. It's courage that counts.

—John Wooden

1.

The wind blew gently across Mercer County Lake, a stone's throw from the ivy-covered brickwork of Princeton University. A frigid winter slowly released its grip on the Northeast; spring was sneaking in after the thaw. The first tulips pushed shoots of green and yellow through the soil, dotting the shoreline with color in stark contrast to the lake's icy blackness. Tall men with sculpted bodies lumbered about in one-piece Lycra tank-top suits, reminiscent of 1920's bathing suits. Each man carefully surveyed the lake, checking the wind direction and deciding which lane would have the best conditions. Six blood-red trails of surveyor-straight plastic buoys floated parallel to each other out to a vanishing point. They converged on the horizon about a mile and a quarter, or exactly 2,000 meters, farther down the lake. It was the 1992 Olympic rowing trials.

I had been training specifically in the single scull (one-man boat) for over a year. Last season I won a gold medal and silver medal during the US Olympic festival, marking my first attempt at competitive sculling. The switch to using two oars in the boat instead of just one oar (as I had done through college) was relatively easy for me.[1] During the Olympic Festival I won in the quad, or four-man sculling boat, but now for these Olympic trials I was racing alone. Since college graduation I left/got fired from my job, earned a try-out with the US Training Center, and abandoned any sense of normalcy to push myself for more than two years as a full-time athlete. I was doing well in training. I felt good in my boat. This would be my Cinderella story: "Blue-collar kid out of the University of New Hampshire shocks the sporting world to win the US Olympic trials." I had labored six to eight hours each day in Tampa, Florida, in the months prior, solely preparing for these April trials. I rowed twice a day, and went to the gym between rowing sessions. Other than that I worked hard at napping. Continual suffering and pushing my body were in anticipation of this moment.

My mom and dad drove down from New Hampshire to watch. I had a small cadre of friends on hand to support me as I battled for the lone spot on the Olympic team. There were thirty-six other athletes invited to the trials, each with the same idea in mind. We all wanted to be *that* guy.

As I tugged off my warm-up jacket I felt my sphincter giving way like an over-filled water balloon, and ran for a porta-potty. Entombed in the small plastic cave, I evacuated every last bit of whatever was in my bowels. As I rose from the seat, my legs buckled slightly; they made an unworthy pedestal for my knotted stomach. I left that evil porta-john, weak in the knees, and trudged back to my boat. Then they showed up.

I didn't feel butterflies in my stomach; I felt bats. Big, angry vampire bats slamming against the walls of my sensitive tummy, trying to squeeze up my throat.

Fighting to regain my breathing, I lowered my racing shell into the water and locked in each oar, my eyes darting around frantically but not really seeing. My coach didn't say much and I don't even remember if friends or family wished me luck. I was wallowing in a state of near-nausea. I noticed my hands trembling as I pushed away from the safety of the dock. *What the hell is going on with me?*

I had to stop twice during my warm-up as my stomach heaved. I was about to blow chunks all over the sleek carbon fiber racing shell. Luckily I didn't, but the sensation seemed to be stuck on a repeat cycle in my core. I shouldn't be out here, I thought. At the starting line it got worse. I remember thinking how much bigger that guy from Harvard looked, and the other guy who won a national championship at the University of Pennsylvania was a giant. Everyone else looked stronger; their expensive German-engineered boats looked faster. I couldn't even keep my bow pointed straight down the course during the lineup. When the official finally gave the traditional French command to start, *"Partez!,"* I yanked on the oars with all my might. Frantically I bobbled side to side like a drunk jettisoning the last floating hope of survival from the *Titanic*. My right oar was half buried, ripping through the water, which veered the boat thirty degrees off course to starboard. I quickly found myself dead last. That's where I stayed. The next race that afternoon, my second chance, wasn't much better. I finished the 1992 Olympic trials in fourteenth place. Snap! Back to reality.

Why did I feel so out of control of my own destiny? What was so frightening during the race that hadn't been there during practices? Fear had completely taken over despite months of practice. I felt an emotional pain that tore into my core. I felt cloaked in failure.

As I packed up after the last race underneath clouds of melancholy, my mom and dad added a little extra baggage by dropping off a sack of "we-told-you-this-was-a-bad-idea" and a big box of "nice-couple-of-years-playing-on-the-water." In other words, son, you need to behave like a grown-up—get a nine-to-five job and start a family like everyone else in your clan. Join the softball team at work if you feel like playing outside. The message was clear—time to stop "dodging reality."

That was my thought too: time to face reality. After the race I grew enraged about my performance. I directed my pain at other people who caused it. My coach did a terrible job, the US Rowing Association was rigged, my parents hurt my chances. So many people were fighting against me. It wasn't my fault, it was things I couldn't control, I told myself. I was the *victim*.

I also knew I could do better; I just didn't know how. A nine-to-five job sounded like purgatory; there was something else burning inside me that I needed to find and explore. My reality about life was obviously different from my parents' reality. That difference ended up being my saving grace. However, no matter how independent you are from your mom and dad, it's intimidating to fight directly contradictorily to the rules and ideas they pounded into your head your whole childhood (and unbeknownst to me populated my brain's hard drive with). I knew I wasn't going to do nine-to-five yet. I wanted to get fast. I had to find respect and confidence somewhere—rowing seemed like the place I could be held in esteem. It worked in college. I was afraid socially, and didn't feel like I fit in until I started rowing. After the '92 trials, I never wanted to feel so scared and out of control on the water again, mostly because I knew how good it felt to give it my best and become one with the shell, totally in the moment, completely in flow. Plus, I reveled in the accolades when we brought back that national championship trophy in college—a huge party, a big story in the school paper. I felt valued. I sensed that there were many secrets of life hidden from me that could only be unearthed staying on my Olympic journey.

After a few weeks of soul searching and replaying the races in my mind, I started to let go of the idea that I was a victim and everyone else was fighting me. The prefrontal cortex, my rational mind, started to take over. I still felt powerless against the feeling of emotional pain, but I knew that if I were going to move on I had to face the situation and accept responsibility, then act. As I thought about another four years and what I could change I started to figure out it wasn't my coach, it wasn't my parents, it wasn't a lack of will or a lack of skill—it was fear. At the time I felt that I couldn't control many areas of my life, but the fact that in the single scull we all started at the same place and time, and the first one across the line was the winner, gave me comfort. I had felt peak performance on the water and it was incredible. The purity of rowing was appealing. I vowed to take a different approach. I decided it was up to me, and when I decided I felt empowered to make things better. The definitive act of choosing that makes things better also fueled a release of things that, while they may affect me, I could not control.

I began to believe that I could take charge of this one aspect of my life that seemed so perfectly suited to me. Intellectually, I knew it did not matter where you went to school, how much money your parents had, or how tall you were; it didn't even matter if you had an expensive yellow German racing shell. Intellectually, I knew those things, but emotionally I still blamed a lot of villains in my life. What I didn't realize until years later is that fear is like a mute button on your intuition, stuffing a big pillow over the mouth of your gut feelings. We drown out intuition because an area of our brain called the working memory (think of it like the random access memory [RAM] in your laptop) takes information you need at the moment, and leaves the rest on your hard drive for later. The working memory is like a smartphone—it has access to thousands of apps and data but can only have one app active at a time.

The amygdala, and our survival brain, always wants that app to be the fight, flight, or freeze response. Job one is pass our genes along to the next generation, so it doesn't care how much emotional pain we experience. The working memory can completely fill up with information just to execute survival reactions when your amygdala is activated. This doesn't leave any room for the subtleties of sensing your gut feelings, or listening to your instinct, or playing what-if scenarios; it leaves no room for optimal actions; all you do is fight or flee. To listen to those quiet but wise voices of reflection, you need to be able to access your prefrontal cortex (PFC), clear out the working memory, and provide some adult supervision for the amygdala. I felt like a victim after the trials because my amygdala was in control and wanted to fight. I needed to shift from feeling pain to living with the power of self-accountability. Without a well-trained PFC to pick up the subtle cues of intuition or insight, it meant that I was deaf to the wisdom that my heart and gut knew to be truths. I had to go from being a victim to producing the dominating, successful racing career I wanted. I just didn't know how.

Yes or No, can I reach my dream? I flushed out the first key ingredient to success and expertise in that simple first step. Which one was it? Questioning my future, standing off directly with the man in the mirror, an answer was written within the DNA of every cell in my body. I realized that I actually might have the yes—a genuine belief that I could make my Olympic dream a reality. I believed in myself on the water. And the belief that you can do something amazing is not just a requirement for greatness; it is a powerful motivator. The moment you understand how difficult something is going to be, but you still believe in yourself, is the moment your perspective changes. Your view goes from "Can I do it?" to "What is the first step?"

Your belief is your reality, even if others think your reality is the craziest thing they've ever heard. I just needed to find my own rowing Yoda to help me put it all together and help me understand what happened at the 1992 trials so I could learn from it and never have to experience it again. Placing so far back was devastating, and that devastation was my new motivation.

2.

During the 1992 Olympic Trials I was not just afraid of the embarrassment of losing, or of failure; I was afraid of fear. I created an anxiety loop that blanketed cowardice over my entire life like volcanic ash settling on neighboring mountains. When I felt the parts of my body changing due to fear and my amygdala activation, I became more scared. More dread made fear feel more powerful, which led to getting more scared. This nightmare hamster wheel of anguish ensured my fourteenth-place finish in the trials. Round and round I went. Jane, stop this crazy thing! (That's a *Jetsons* reference, for all you Millennials.)

If I had reflected long enough to ask myself how the cycle of fear felt familiar (which I didn't), I may have been able to recall my first Fear Frontier and how I felt walking into Logan Airport as a six-year-old kid. The same physical reactions were present before the Olympic Trials that I felt recalling that 1970s plane crash. My fear tells were triggered by my Fear Frontier, the point where my PFC stopped making the decisions and the amygdala took over. The stronger the amygdala engagement level and the hippocampus involvement, the stronger our memories are written.

Your Fear Frontier and an early traumatic event, or series of events, can spread through your life and stay with you until death. If you never do anything to change your emotional memories associated with those original fears as a youth, the emotions stay with you in a destructive way. You build defense mechanisms to battle that trauma and see every threat in the same light. Imagine you're living in a Looney Tunes cartoon and a piano drops from five stories up and explodes on the sidewalk right in front of you. The shock of that event elicits a survival reaction from the amygdala. That moment is written in different places simultaneously in your brain—the amygdala, the neocortex, and the hippocampus all play a role; there may be even more locations as well that we're just discovering. There are literally electric fields of potential that are activating in a wave motion all across your brain. Your Fear Frontier creates a looping video along those same neural pathways and waves—the synapses for a specific memory (walking along the sidewalk on Main Street) and the associated emotional memories (might get squashed) have been firing together for so long if left unabated, they become wired together. The semantic memory of what happened and the emotional memory you created (fear, empathy, pain, death) become the equivalent of a path leading from a parking lot down to a sandy beach, a well-worn trail between sharp green beach grass. This means any sidewalk becomes scary and soon you are afraid to go out of the house. The more worn that path is, the more easily those terrible feelings appear; that's why if we have a specific fear (in my case a fear of flying) we can't help but think of it along with the horrific emotional feelings of death, pain, suffering, etc. Unless we take control over our Fear Frontier and learn how to hold off an amygdala hijacking, the outcome we watch in our mind will always be a horror movie. I gave a keynote speech in Las Vegas and asked audience members for traumatic events they experienced before they were ten that stayed with them; one big tough guy answered that he had been working for years to overcome a fear of the dark. His Fear Frontier was planted, remembered vividly, when his mother was tucking him into bed and joked that a new clothes hamper in his room looked like a monster hiding in the corner. She thought it was funny and light-hearted, yet it created a Fear Frontier that stayed with him for more than twenty years.

It's not easy to process these fearful memories created in our youth; they stay in our gut longer than they should. When we become overwhelmed by emotional memories, it's difficult to realize that we are the producers of our life and that if we can produce a horror film, we can just as easily produce an adventure or a love story or a comedy. It's our film; we can own it. The problem is that we've had so much practice watching horror movies and catastrophes in our mind, we're really good at producing the bad stuff. To get good at creating a comedy, an adventure, or the happy-ending love story takes focused hard work, but the payoff is astounding.

Just as we can create connections that are strongly wired together, those same old sandy paths can eventually grow over and you can create a new way to go. That's called neuroplasticity; it means that we can develop new beliefs, skills, emotions, and actions at any age. Like blazing a new path in the grass, it takes a lot of trips across the dunes. The good news is the trips can be real or imagined; to your mind it doesn't matter. We'll talk about how to hack your emotional memory in the next section.

The year after the 1992 trials I started down a new path and found my Yoda. He wasn't much taller than the *Star Wars* character and had a similar sense of humor. His name was Allen Rosenberg

IMAGINATION, NOT RED BULL, GIVES YOU WINGS

The man with no imagination has no wings.

—Muhammad Ali

"The Greatest" was famous for his eloquent prefight predictions that came true: "Archie Moore, you're going down in four." How could he do that? He used fear to fuel his belief that he was the greatest boxer of all time. He could visualize outcomes in his mind before they happened.

The neurons and synapses that fire when something happens are the same neurons that fire when you imagine something happening; that's why visualization practice works so well and so many athletes use it as a training tool. The only difference between an actual event and one that you visualize is the force of the charge along the memory pathways that create emotions. You should try it. The electrical current that connects the brain's synapses, called synaptic transmissions, becomes stronger when more senses and emotions are activated. The more input from senses, the more neurotransmitters are released from presynaptic neurons. There is a long-lasting increase in the ease of synaptic transmission with visualization. In other words, it's the same reality as if it were really happening—just a little bit watered down.

and he had been retired for a few years when I tracked him down. He won Olympic gold medals—both as a coxswain (the little guy who sits in back and steers the boat) and as a coach. After he committed to helping me (which took a lot of convincing) he went to work on me right away, and despite muscle-burning training sessions and radical overhauls of technique, his focused effort was really on my head. Coach Rosenberg was day in and day out helping me build the mind of a champion. He wanted me to face everything and accept 100 percent responsibility for the outcome. He helped me realize that the only person who could change my speed on the water was me. Trainers could help, but they were not heroes. Opponents could challenge me, but they were not villains. To face reality meant more racing. A lot more racing. Rosenberg thought that racing was the best way to face my fear head-on, and that I should do it every day. He sensed that I had a fear of failure, a fear of inadequacy, a fear of rejection and abandonment. Since I

CREATING THE GREATEST OLYMPIAN EVER

Medication or tough love, which path would you take for your child? Michael Phelps had crazy energy as a child. At nine he was diagnosed with ADHD. Like many kids in the USA the doctors were quick to medicate him. His mom, Debbie, adopted an additional strategy; she had him playing lacrosse, soccer, baseball and swimming. Michael loved lacrosse more than swimming. Although he was afraid to put his face in the water, his mom insisted he learn to swim for safety reasons. She told him he could learn backstroke to keep his kisser dry. Even though he loved lacrosse he was getting really good at swimming, and saw all the fun his sister was having going to swim meets. At eleven he was winning medals in swim meets—real medals for podium finishes, not participation medals for tenth place.

His swim coach, Bob Bowman, sat him down and said basically; you suck at lacrosse and baseball but you're a really good swimmer. Tough to hear for a kid, but entirely honest. Bowman said if we work together, you can make the Olympic team in four years. He showed belief and a clearly envisioned future. Phelps too believed, so he asked his mom if he could stop taking ADHD medicine and train for the Olympics. She said yes. He wrote his goals out on a sheet of paper and went to work. He didn't miss a single day of swim practice for the next five years—even on Christmas. The rest is Olympic history.

Trophies and medals belong to those on the podium. Everyone else should be rewarded with the truth.

couldn't actually race every day, that meant I needed another way to face those fears when I wasn't actually on the water racing. Not surprisingly, the answer was the first thing Michael Phelps told me he gained the most benefit from as well.

I learned The Way from psychologists at the US Olympic Training Center. When I went to Colorado Springs in the winter of 1993 to get physiologically tested, plan my training for the year, and rub shoulders with other athletes I met Dr. Shane Murphy. Dr. Murphy was in charge of the psychology team at the training center. It didn't take long for a Murphy and a Sweeney to be spending time together spinning stories, but uncharacteristically this wasn't in the pub over Guinness as you might expect; it was in an egg—a giant human-sized egg where I ended up getting exactly what I needed to save my rowing career and eventually my life.

In the shadow of Pike's Peak and the Garden of the Gods, I spent an hour or two of every day with the top sports psychologists in the world. Dr. Murphy and his team tucked me into a white egg-shaped apparatus a little smaller than a Volkswagen Bug. Imagine an egg split in half top to bottom, then tilted back at forty-five degrees like some giant version of an art-deco Herman Miller chair. Inside was cozy plush padding that felt as close as you can imagine to the inside of your mother's womb, of course without the gooey placenta and umbilical mess. Hidden around the top where my head was cradled was a series of crystal-clear speakers.

My first session in the egg was weird to say the least. I lay back and felt support all around my body—no pressure points, no need to flex a muscle. The voice of one of the psychologists swirled softly around my head and interlaced with music from a soft Indian flute. His steady baritone voice guided me through the first stages of breathing and deep relaxation exercises. It was soothing, and after a few minutes it was too soothing and I fell asleep. He woke me and we started again. Every day we did breathing, relaxation, and focused exercises. It was all new to me, and like any new skill I was improving quickly. What I didn't know was that this was basically planting the seeds to grow beach grass where I wanted it and blaze a path where it would do me the most good. I was about to start fooling my brain and my memory with a new reality.

In the first week of mental training the docs started narrating a movie for me to watch in my mind's eye. Each day I settled into the egg. As the doctor started to get me deeper, I let thoughts fly into my mind, then just as quickly let them fly out until I was focusing just on my breathing. I imagined walking down a flight of stairs, counting backward from ten with each step. With each lower step, I got more and more relaxed. Finally, I opened a mystical door at the bottom of the stairs, unveiling a special screening room. A single plush lounge chair was anchored in front of a giant surround screen like an iMax theater, with an entire black galaxy behind the screen that looked into infinity. Once I slid into the lounge chair, I would watch myself racing in the biggest races possible, the World Cup, Elite Championships, Olympic Trials. I was racing every day. In my mind.

Along with the physical training on weights or the rowing machine, my mental training got more and more intense by the day. After the first ten days I was getting down to the magical screening room at the bottom of the stairs with less and less effort, and actually felt my self independently of my body. It felt as if I were hovering above my body. This was after just ten days of practice. This hypnosis or visualization was taking root in my neural network. That's when the fun really started.

As I was visualizing the races in what seemed like ultra-sharp reality, shit started to go sideways. The psychologist who was my in-egg narrator started creating nightmare scenarios. As I was watching the race I'd be jolted by him telling me I just hit a buoy, an official's boat sent a huge wake crashing over my gunwales, a piece of driftwood was inches under the surface and ripped off my skeg. Face everything, accept responsibility. That's what he made me do. See the worst things that could happen in a race and watch yourself handle them. It felt real, too. As he described each catastrophe, initially I could feel my heart racing and start to lose my focus on my breathing and rowing. By the fourth session of the disasters, I was actually looking forward to what he'd come up with during each session. This training is the exact opposite of pretending no problems exists. I was doing what the stoics called premeditation of evil: imagining the worst that could go wrong and then picturing what I'd do when it did.

Even though I wasn't on the water, the neurons connecting my prefrontal cortex to my amygdala didn't know the difference. I was scaring myself every day with visualization. I would go through a set routine of breathing, then progressively relax each muscle in my body, before I played a movie in my mind. Something was always going wrong during the biggest race in the world. At first the psychologist was talking in my head, helping me recover from the impending disasters while staying in a deep relaxed and suggestive mind-state. He was coaching me through the recovery with phrases such as "You got this. Take a breath and drop the blades in the water with surgical precision. Now accelerate the shell forward. Yes! Now we're moving again." Soon I was able to handle everything that came at me. I'd breathe, assess the situation rationally, smile, and then execute my plan. After the third week it was my own voice in my head coaching me; occasionally he'd repeat a phrase he wanted me to fall back on, such as "I got this." Or "Push through this pain." This is how I learned to really use self-talk to keep my mind focused and keep my amygdala from creeping in and taking over.

The truth is that I, like you, always had the capability to handle anything, but I needed to learn how to develop the mental skills to change my reality. All people, unless they have a birth defect, have the capability to change their reality. All people have the capability to change their mindset. Reality in itself does not exist; it's only our personal reality that exists, so don't run from what you now think is fear—find more and see yourself using it as fuel.

During Olympic training I was scaring myself all the time, in real life and in my imagination through visualization. It wasn't long before my mind shifted from cowardice and constantly worrying about what *might happen* to being able to just focus on rowing. In actual on-the-water races I finally let go of all the thoughts, emotions, clutter, and cross talk that had been sucking my mind's energy. I saw the truth of the world: that I could only control making my own strokes perfect. I was in control of just me. I couldn't control situations, only the way I reacted to them.

I literally laughed during a World Cup race in Lucerne, Switzerland, when I drew an outside lane for the first race and, starting a crucial sprint with five hundred meters to go, got hit with a wake from an official's launch boat, upsetting my balance and spraying water in my shell. I laughed because it was déjà vu; I knew just what to do. The reality I was experiencing kept getting closer and closer to the reality I was envisioning in my mental training sessions. This meant I wasn't producing free energy. I wasn't scared. What a difference mental training made!

At the 1996 Olympic Trials I placed second of all the best rowers in the United States. Training my mind changed my life; just knowing how to get my mind in a relaxed state and adding to my prior beliefs by visualizing various outcomes was like suddenly putting a wide-angle lens on my reality; I saw there was much more to experience. I still got bats in my stomach before the race, but now I had those bats flying in the same direction toward the finish line and I started to notice a power that I'd never experienced before. I would have never imagined I would later use these mental visualization skills to save my life.

> One true way to get in control of your life is to find more fear. Scare yourself at least once a week, every day if you can, and soon you will learn what you control and what you don't.

Your decision to scare yourself has to be final and firm. You have to believe that the only safe place, the only true "getting away from everything" doesn't come from drinking, eating, shopping, gambling, traveling, or even hugging your blanket; finding peace and power comes by searching within yourself, facing everything, accepting responsibility, and taking action. The change in mindset is the key. You can choose to go from being powerless because other influences are causing you pain to being empowered because you realize what you can control and what you can't.

If you want unshakable confidence, you must learn what it is like to find more fear and make a rock-solid commitment not to avoid it. Just the act of committing to search out more fearful moments will change the movie you play in your mind. Taking responsibility will help you recognize when you fall back to a victim mindset. When you let someone else produce your movie, you relinquish control of your success, happiness, and fulfillment. Start talking to yourself in the voice of your hero-self, your movie star persona. What would he or she say in a moment of terror?

There is a monumental difference after you make the commitment to scare yourself, because you know you are feeling fear because you *want to feel it*. It's your choice. Every time you feel your fear tells, you have a chance to act with courage. Before each of my speeches I remind myself that the great actor Henry Fonda never lost his fear tell of nausea before a live stage performance; he was tossing his cookies in his seventies, yet had learned over an Academy Award–winning career to use his fear as fuel. You can, too.

3.

If you can scare yourself every day, do it; you will see results that much faster. Even going through visualization counts; you don't have to jump out of a plane to feel your physiology changing.

There are three reasons for finding more fear:

1. **Awareness and Observation**—learn to determine your body's fear tells. Awareness of changing physiology gives you insight of the amygdala activating the survival response and trying to hijack your working memory. The survival system causes us to react and make snap decisions. Being proactive (not reactive) lets you make optimal decisions. It's also this survival system that, if we know the secrets to harnessing it, can give us superpowers. Keep in mind that the software running the amygdala is two million years old and only

cares about survival and passing your DNA on to the next generation. That only-survive process is what you must override. You have
the ability to pause the movie at the exact moment between the
survival response and the reaction, but only if you recognize that
you are about to make a survival response.

To avoid bad decisions and to optimize choices that result in peak
performance, you must learn to recognize and control your survival
network. When the amygdala hijacks the working memory, it tries
to get you to play that fight or flee app because all it cares about is
survival. You can only have that one app activated in the working
memory, so you have to learn to push that fight or flight app out of
the picture. You've got to learn to control the reaction of fighting or
fleeing and learn to observe the situation and imagine the outcome
of your actions.

Observation will help you determine where you and others are
on the curiosity vs. judgmental spectrum. The more curiosity people show, the more honest they are with others (and themselves),
the less they are likely to be threatened by people unlike them or
their tribe. That's the type of diversity that makes for successful
companies. When hiring people, curiosity is one of the primary
traits I seek out. If my employees sit next to a plumber on a long
flight, I would expect they know the toughest part of his job or the
newest innovation in plumbing by the time they land.

Neurologically the more curious you are the more brainpower
you require, because you can't use shortcuts. Fearful people who
are close-minded let the amygdala hijack their behavior and this
results in shortcut choices that are made in the subconscious mind.
Judgment literally uses just half of your brain.

2. **Belief and Orientation**—To rewrite your traumatic memories and
   reframe your mindset you must develop the unfaltering belief that
   you can accomplish what you set your mind to. Even before you
   become truly courageous you must act as if you are already there.
   Courage is a choice and a change in your body's electric wiring and
   wireless communication. You change those two fields of energy by
   changing the paths in your mind that you are firing—that's why it is
   so important to get out of your comfort zone since that is the result
   of using the same continual paths in your brain. This means letting
   go of judgments and limits that were likely imposed on you as a
   child when you were too young and undeveloped to push back on
   them. Remember, for most of our life someone else populated our
   subconscious database for us by choosing where we were born, what
   language we spoke, and so on. If you believe in yourself, your level
   of curiosity goes up exponentially and you don't feel the need to
   prove yourself or appear smart. Rather than feel threatened, you can

ask questions. Curiosity takes courage and reframing every interaction as a situation you created so you could learn something will dramatically increase the speed of your understanding and success.

Understanding the differences in personality types can be particularly effective in career settings because you can seek out people who coalesce big-picture thinking with detail-oriented action, feeling, or intuitive communication, and a logical or creative mindset. You can balance your team for high performance if you are curious and courageous. It's diversity that can change the orientation you have before making critical decisions, because different subconscious hard drives look at problems from different perspectives.

3. **Action and Peak Performance**—Finding fear will activate your survival response and boost your nervous system to react as quickly as possible. Don't react (unless of course you're getting out of the way of a speeding train or falling piano). Taking a moment to plan action, then gathering new information after the action and starting the process over again with the result of your action is critical. There are only two ways to make decisions; one is out of fear, the other is out of opportunity. The goal of *Fear Is Fuel* is to get you to activate your survival system and then take control of your working memory with curiosity and a diverse orientation. This creates moments of peak performance. Our body is designed to perform best under stress; we need to use that stress response when it is created. Or we need to create it—sometimes by finding fear, sometimes by exercising or fasting, sometimes by abstaining from sex or drinking alcohol, sometimes by doing high-intensity intervals. Stress is good.

If you apply the principles in this book, all your critical choices in life, the ones that would naturally have you elicit a survival response, can be made so optimally it's like hitting it out of the park in the ninth inning of the World Series game seven (for the Red Sox of course).

Now that you've scared yourself to find your tells, you've added a few lunch hours replacing judgment with curiosity, you're ready for the Olympic training of fearlessness. But first let's a take a quick review of what happens so you have a good image in your mind.

Left unabated, the amygdala will drive your body to react like a wild animal. The reaction for people who live in a state of fear is shown in figure 6.1.

Letting the amygdala drive us immediately to a reaction of Anger, Disgust, Sadness, and Fear not only cannibalizes our happiness and success but shows the rest of the world and colleagues our

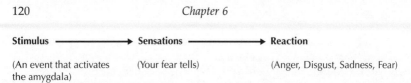

Figure 6.1.   Fear as a Reaction

emotional immaturity. No one wants to follow a leader who lets his life be controlled by someone else. People do not want to work for a person with a victim mentality unless they too are committed to being a victim with their boss. If you short-circuit the amygdala's activation to fearful emotions, you can replace those reactions with curiosity and love.

Even if you don't physically do something that's scary (like sing karaoke in front of your boss or jump out of a plane), now that you have identified your fear tells, you can start to use them every day. When you start to feel a physical change, you can notice a typical reaction (dread, anxiety, anger, etc.), but now you have some experience changing the reaction from a survival reaction into a conscious action. You can stop to use the moment between your subconscious reacting and consciously deciding whether you will execute that reaction. The moment between your subconscious database making the choice and you acting on that choice, you have a split second to hit pause—that notion is called volitional control. You can focus on your choices. Etch it in your soul that you have to stop and realize you always have a choice. The primary outcome you should to move toward is *curiosity*. Every time you stop and realize you have a choice to proceed or not, tell yourself—*be curious* (see figure 6.2).

You may not have access to a giant egg, as I did at the Olympic Training Center, but the truth is you don't need one. Find a quiet spot where you won't be bothered for twenty minutes and let's bring up some memories. You've got all the power to do what famed Stoic leader Marcus Aurelius would do; premeditate on some evil. Like me during the Olympic training sessions, the first five to ten times will be just learning how to control your breath and get your body and mind open to suggestion. You are literally getting ready

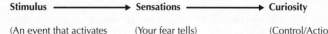

Figure 6.2.   Curiosity as a Reaction

to rewire your neural networks and fields of potential into a course of courage. This is the exact same protocol I used to become one of the top athletes in the world, and later to save my life when I was at Hopkins with one foot in the grave and another on a banana peel.

Step 1—Graduated Breathing

Start breathing in for a count of four, hold it for four, and release for four. Then inhale for an eight count, hold it for eight, and let it out for a count of eight, then do a sixteen count the same way. After the first sixteen count, breathe in for a second sixteen count, hold it for sixteen, and then release the entire breath at once. After that just focus on steady breaths filling the bottom of your lungs, the middle, then the top. Exhale in reverse order and make sure you are pulling your belly button toward your spine. It should look like this: 4-4-4, 8-8-8, 16-16-16, 16-16-Big Exhale.

Step 2—Progressive Relaxation

Starting at the top of your head, focus and feel every detail; scan down muscle by muscle and body part by body part. Relax your forehead, then feel your eyes soften, ears, jaws, and so on. Feel each body part getting warm, heavy, and relaxed. Go all the way down to your toes. If you are having trouble with this skill, you can start by tensing up one body part at a time for a few seconds, then feeling the relaxation when you release the tension.

Step 3—Descending the Relaxation Stairs

Once you have scanned your entire body, time to go even deeper. Imagine ten steps leading down to a giant door. Slowly descend, counting backward from ten, getting warmer, heavier, and more re-laxed with each step. Try to imagine things that relax like your body and see it flattening into the earth—imagine butter melting on a hot stove, water seeping into the sand, and so on.

Step 4—Your iMax Theater

Once you are down the stairs, open the door and walk into the most high-tech iMax theater you can imagine. When you are fully relaxed take your place in your comfy chair in front of the iMax screen and you can do one of the two following visualizations.

Visualization 1 — Victim to Creator

Take a few moments now to recall moments that epitomize your reaction to the amygdala dumping that fear cocktail through your body. Try to recall your fear tells in full swing. Feel the sweaty palms, the fast-beating heart—all your tells. Smell the fear. When you can recall a specific and detailed moment of unbridled anger, complete disgust, tremendous sadness, and the most terrifying fear, answer the questions in table 6.1.

Choose one of the most vivid moments, or ideally one of the earliest and vivid memories of fear, you can recall. You're trying to recall any traumatic event that created one of the four emotions.

Try to find a situation where you had a reaction like the following:

Your boss sends you an email that makes you **angry**—your reaction is to prove you are right, so you argue.

Your boss sends you an email that **disgusts** you—your reaction is to judge her and feel superior.

Your boss sends you an email that makes you **sad**—your reaction makes you ashamed.

Your boss sends you an email that makes you **scared**—your reaction is to stop doing anything new, creative, or bold and live in fear of being fired.

Those are examples of you reacting, and letting fear drive your decisions. Think of a time when it was clear that you did not control your mind and soul and clearly were not the creator of your life. You were allowing someone else to influence your life. This is a time

Table 6.1.   Fear Responses

When I feel:	I sense my	and my	After one minute I feel	An hour later I feel
Anger				
Disgust				
Sadness				
Fear				

when you let life happen to you. You gave permission for someone or something to write the story of your life.

Whatever that event was that followed that script is the premise we are going to change.

Time to change what happened with control of your mind and soul. Whatever the scenario you chose, your premise, you should have a change that is clear and easy to visualize.

For instance, using the above premise:

Your boss sends you an email that makes you **angry**—first wonder why you are upset. What is it that hit one of your triggers? What about getting angry at that trigger seems familiar; when have you had similar reaction in the past? Pretend the email came from someone you really loved and cared about; would you have the same reaction? If not, why not?

Your boss sends you an email that **disgusts** you—get curious as to whether this disgusts her or other people. Consider that something that your culture thinks is disgusting might be perfectly acceptable in another culture. If your boss thought it was disgusting, what might her motivation be for sharing it?

Your boss sends you an email that makes you **sad**—consider the nature of attachment, does holding on to things create sadness? When else have you felt sorrow similar to the way you are feeling it now? Where does sorrow show up in your body? What are you attached to and what can you think of that is not permanent?

Your boss sends you an email that makes you **scared**—you should easily recognize where you feel this by your tells, so look for the feelings; try to really focus on the change in your body. Think about time and what is happening right now in the present. How is your health, the lives of ones you love right now? How safe are you at the moment? Once you are present, try to realize that you can use your survival response to form an optimal response, plan your next steps, you just need to free that working memory first. Do a four-by-four breathing exercise, assess the situation, smile, and then focus on your body.

That creates the adaptation that changes the framing of your premise.

The commitment to feeling your fear, facing everything, and accepting responsibility starts with recognizing those moments as they arise. Because you can't control how often they happen in your day, you've often got to make them happen to practice responding to them. You must train those neurons and peptides and synapses to get to work on your courage highway. So every day take twenty minutes, choose a premise, watch it unfolding, and then hit the "pause button" on your visualization. Decide consciously on a course of action that aligns with your soul—that feeds your purpose—then play it out. See the change in you, and also see the change in other people involved in the visualization when you get curious.

As you get in touch with your body, you begin to recognize the subtle changes you are chipping away at, that giant boulder of fear that blocks the vault of all your wisdom and courage. Part of chipping away at the boulder is shifting those physical feelings to a new mindset; you are gradually changing from having a mindset of things being threatening to things being a challenge that you are ready to face. You can use self-talk as you chip away at the boulder, telling yourself all this hard work will pay off.

Visualization 2—Wimp to Peak Performer

Try to find one of your fears and then choose where it might sit on the Terror Triangle (physical side, instinctual side, or emotional side) and do the preparation walking down to your virtual iMax theater. Once you get into your visualization chair and can start to imagine an event; make it one that scares you the most.

As you lie in the chair watching your iMax movie, try to feel your tells ramping up in intensity—try to hit all your senses. Feel the wind on your face, and the sweat seeping down your armpits, smell the fear, hear the sounds of whatever is happening, and so on. Make it as real as possible.

Now shift.

As you feel your tells and start to get scared, the first thing you need to do is move your eyes. Imagine you are watching a tennis match; shift your eyes left to right quickly, while keeping them closed.

This eye movement hack was first discovered in 1990 by a psychologist named Francine Shapiro, but it wasn't until 2018 that a group of researchers from New York University led by Linda de Voogd determined that eye movement activates a dorsal frontoparietal network and briefly shuts off the amygdala, basically disassociating the fear from the actual memory.

Now you can change your mindset to recognize those symptoms of fear and symptoms of excitement, anticipation of something great happening. See yourself smiling and getting pumped up to get it on. Shift your mindset from threat to challenge. You want to have the same attitude as a championship fighter right before the bell rings—bouncing effortlessly on your toes ready to get it on. Bring on what ever could happen and see a courageous you.

The goal of *Fear Is Fuel* is to use your fight, flight, or freeze response to get to peak performance. One of the foundations of peak performance is the belief that those feelings give you a superhuman boost. Scaring yourself is a critical step to learning to use fear as fuel and unlocking the superhuman potential inside yourself.

7

$\backsim$

The BASE Method

Control your own destiny or someone else will.

—Jack Welch

1.

Now is the time for you to find something that scares you. If I simply walked you through this powerful framework you're about to learn, it would be about as effective as feeling what making love is like based on the pictures and diagrams your eighth grade teacher showed you during SexEd. It won't work because only you can have the reaction you are going to have. Only you know what would happen with your mind and emotions. Only you know your tells, your senses, your reality. What follows is your guidebook to acting with courage. Some guidebooks give you advice on the best route or the specifics of a climb or ski. This one gives you a guide to your mind, but it is completely interactive; there's no point in studying it or thinking about it, you've got to use it in the real world. Time to take the leap.

Find an activity out of your comfort zone and make a plan to do it in the next week. Move courageously forward using the BASE framework, as you start to feel your tells. Keep in mind that there really is one root of all fear—that's the creation of free energy that comes when we can't handle uncertainty, surprise, or the unknown. That free energy, which might sound good because it's free, is really pretty bad for you because it is energy for the amygdala. Our survival brain, running that two-million-year-old software, gets stronger when it's fueled by free energy. Remind yourself that you don't have to worry about the unknown; you just have to deal with the present, deal with the now. Remind yourself that you are in control, then deploy the BASE method and it will change your life. You can handle whatever comes your way. Using this simple framework and steadily pushing out your Fear Frontier will rewrite your subconscious database and reeducate your survival system as to what to fear. Every day, if you try to find something that is a little more out of your comfort zone, you'll experience phenomenal changes in your life. Soon you will expect courage. Time to stop worrying about fear and start mastering it. The only way to make both your dreams come true and your nightmares end is to wake up. This is your wake-up call.

2.

"You went shark diving in South Africa? No way!"

"Yup, at first I *really* didn't want to go. I guess I was afraid more than anything. I actually thought, 'there's no way he'll get me near a great white shark.'"

"How did you like it?"

"It was incredible, absolutely breathtaking. I wouldn't have believed it.

"As soon as I saw one of the sharks, and this thing was over fifteen feet long, I totally lost my fear and was mesmerized by its grace and elegance. I remember every detail like a photograph."

"Really, you weren't scared?"

"It was weirdly calming, maybe because they were so beautiful and I was in a cage but if anyone described that sensation to me before I got on the boat I would never have believed them. I felt like I was part of the ocean. At one point I almost forgot to breathe."

I've been diving hundreds of times, a few dozen times with my wife, and I would never have described seeing a sixteen-foot great white tearing into fish guts as calming. But that's the point. She did.

When Christen, my wife, was explaining to one of her good friends what shark diving was like, I was amazed how different her experience was from mine. Everyone reacts in different ways to the same experience, yet what is universally true is that the most astounding experiences in life are always after you cross over your Fear Frontier and still have the courage to stay in control. You'll never know the amazing experiences open to you until you try.

Shark diving was my wife's most impactful experience with the BASE method, and she has used it countless times since then. Knowing it's the unknown, the uncertainty—the free energy—that causes every fear has helped her make her decisions based on opportunity now, not out of fear. She's used the BASE method at school meetings when our kids were in trouble and we had to see the principal; she used it during rock climbs that were outside her comfort zone, before presentations she did to the hockey club, during obstacle races, when she was tired and soaked in any scary situation to make sure her amygdala wasn't in charge and free energy didn't fuel the demons in her mind.

Once you create awareness of your fear tells, you need a strategy for getting control of your amygdala as soon as it jumps into action. When you (not your survival network) are in charge, you can change your mindset from your feelings indicating an impending disaster to the excitement that your body has changed to get the maximum performance. One hundred thousand years ago, your pupils dilated, your heartbeat increased, and digestion and other unnecessary things like empathy stopped. Those reactions might have saved you from the saber-toothed tiger or whatever the hell was alive back then that wanted you for lunch. Job one was for you to live and continue your primary focus of procreation; that meant taking as few risks as possible. Since we don't have packs of tigers running around the mean streets of New York, or Boston, or London, or most other places for that matter, it's time to reframe your survival response to help create success in today's world.

The framework that I teach has both the combination of thousands of years of proof with the breathing, and the latest cutting-edge research into the neurological changes with the smiling and shortcut elimination. It's simple and it's easy to remember. It's not always easy, especially if you haven't learned to detach yourself from a situation, but you can do it. I know you can. I call it the BASE method. It's an acronym for the four things you should do as soon as you start to feel your fear tells.

A FERRARI'S WORTH OF FEAR

Ever had a real financial roller coaster day? Fear can help you end up on top if you take the time to use it. After selling an investment property in Colorado and making a great profit I found out how fear can fuel financial returns as well. My business had a particularly good year and the icing on the cake was a few angel investments that were paying back capital and significant returns. With big windfalls it's easy to forget the tax obligations that carve into them. However, I figured with deductions, charitable giving, and planning it would be a sizable number.

My accountant finally shot me an email—the PDF was attached, and I could use the last four digits of my Social Security number to reveal the secure documents Uncle Sam was about to get that showed exactly what I owed for the previous year. When I hit the return button, the first thing I focused on was a payment due of nearly $200,000. Kapow! That sent my amygdala into high gear. Immediate fear of loss. I saw the new renovation we had planned going up in smoke, and a couple of big climbing and biking expeditions drying up as well. I was on the way to the gym when I got that email and I decided I should stop at the closest bar. I needed a drink.

That was my knee-jerk reaction—a shot or three of whiskey will make this very bad news go away. I got ahold of my senses and thought OK, time to use this reaction beyond what it was designed to do: help me not just survive but thrive. I pulled over to breathe a few four-by-fours. I said aloud, "this tax bill is my threat." What's my solution, what's my opportunity? I closed my eyes and focused.

I asked myself, what are all my possible paths to take? I kept the long steady breaths. Then it hit me like a ton of bricks, all the other investments over the past couple of years that went bad were finally going to bring me some benefit. I never took a deduction on any of the companies I invested in that had failed! I could write off all those worthless ones now. A couple of hours going through old hard drives and my accountant had some new info. Twenty-four hours later I had a $70,000 tax bill due. Enough savings to buy a new Ferrari—or pay for our renovation. Guess which I did?

Breathe

There are entire books written on the power of the breath. It's the key to existence. When you've taken your last breath you know you've only got a few minutes left before you're done in this life. Yogis, mystics, and monks all know the importance of proper breathing technique. Sadly, many people in the Western world had forgotten about breathing until recently. The good news for data-driven skeptics is that there is mounting scientific research and data around breathing techniques used in yoga, tai chi, and other ancient practices as being effective treatments against anxiety, depression, and post-traumatic stress disorder (PTSD), as well as for building up the immune system and even changing the body's core temperature.

At the Olympic training center and during my athletic career I learned visualization to imagine every possible outcome and see myself coming through and winning. I used the same technique to save my life when I was at Johns Hopkins with a rare form of leukemia. Now I use it every day to envision the life of my dreams. When you are scared and your amygdala is trying to hijack your actions, it's time for a different kind of breathing. Now you're going to ninja warrior training for breath.

As you increase the air coming into your body, the amount of CO_2 in your blood and arteries will drop and your blood becomes more alkaline. An increase in alkaline pH increases the hemoglobin's ability to bind oxygen, meaning that you will have more fuel going to your muscles and most importantly to your brain. Normal shallow breathing gets about 32 percent of the oxygen in the lungs to the muscles. With breathing techniques, you can double the oxygen in your body; add exercise and the muscle oxygen can increase to more than 75 percent. Steady and deep breathing also changes the type of heartbeat you experience when you are scared, angry, or under anxiety. Heart rate variability is how often and with how much force your heart beats. If your heart is beating at 120 beats per minute and you are scared there is a dramatically different heartbeat than if your heart is beating at 120 beats per minute and you are in the zone. An EKG of the two types of heartbeats—an erratic, scared heartbeat and a coherent, controlled heartbeat—can be seen in figure 7.1.

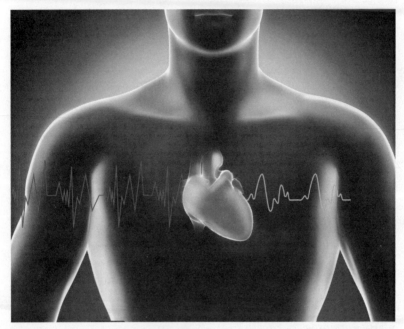

Figure 7.1. An erratic heartbeat (left) of a scared person and a coherent heartbeat (right) of someone focused and in the zone

The method I teach is called a four-by-four. The four-by-four method is centuries old and everyone from Navy SEALs to 103-year-old tai chi masters have used it. It's a simple 4-4-4-4 pattern:

Inhale to a slow count of four.

Hold lungs full of air for a count of four.

Exhale to a count of four.

Hold empty lungs for a count of four.

A key visual to keep in mind is that the air going in starts filling up the bottom of your lungs, and your stomach should push out, then fill up the top of your lungs, and lastly try to picture the back of your shoulders and neck filling up with that last bit of air. Empty the reverse way and end by squeezing your stomach in and holding your belly button close to your spine. Studies have shown that in as little as three breaths the heartbeat will change. In five to ten breaths you can completely shut off the amygdala if you are trained in using this technique.

That's the B—*Breathe* using the four-by-four.

Assess the Situation

Focusing on the moment as an observer is how you accurately assess what is happening. We increase uncertainty and free energy by trying to imagine the future. When the amygdala is in charge of the movie projector, what we see in the future is disaster, doom, and gloom. Staying in the present, asking yourself if you are safe and if there is a good opportunity to learn, will help you build courage and make the right decisions.

Assessing the situation can only be done with a focus on the here and now, and a detachment most people have not practiced in their lives. This is why developing a hunger in your soul, a true intention and commitment to be curious helps so much. If you wonder about the state of things immediately in the moment—not what they might be like in five seconds, five minutes, or five hours, but right now, you will be able to alleviate 90 percent of your fears and start to formulate a course of action. As you breathe a few four-by-fours, take the time to observe outside of yourself first, then inside your emotions. Now is the best time to adopt the mindset of a producer of your own destiny and work really hard to get rid of the victim mindset. Everything is your creation.

After working with more than five hundred CEOs and presidents of major companies, I've found that even many high-performing, materially successful people don't know when they are sabotaging their happiness and growth by maintaining a victim mindset and not being able to assess a situation impartially. There are dead giveaways—usually with relationships when people say things like "If only my partner would change and stop this behavior, I'd be happy" or "He's 50 percent of this marriage; it's time for him to change" or "My boss makes me so angry because he expects me to be an expert on this new app." The truth of the matter is that if you want any happy relationship at work or at home you have to realize you are 100 percent (not 50 percent) responsible for the feelings and actions you take, and that no one can make you sad or angry or upset except you. You are responsible and you are there to learn. Every action you take should add positively to your database of knowledge, so keeping in mind that you are learning (not blaming) when you take 100 percent accountability is critical to healthy growth.

As you orient yourself to the event that caused a fear response, keep in mind that most humans really suck at understanding probabilities. We are programmed to avoid even the smallest bit of risk. If we had a good grasp on odds, no one would be afraid to fly in a commercial airliner or swim in the ocean. You might be one of the millions of people in the world who are afraid to fly, so you get it. The reason is that the human brain processes probabilities in a very coarse manner that makes it nearly impossible for us to distinguish between one in a thousand likelihood, one in a million, or one in a billion. We are much more apt to look at things in a more rudimentary way. We usually divide risk into four or five buckets—that will never happen, that seems unlikely, I'd give it a fifty-fifty chance, it's pretty likely, or that's going to happen for sure. This analysis of risk, of course, misses out on an infinite number of subtleties. However, our coarse assessment becomes important when considering an extremely low probability event that could have catastrophic consequences. The fact that some force might wipe out our entire family or office building or town doesn't mean we should put any resources toward something that has a one in ten million chance of happening. From a leadership perspective, being able to assess a situation in the moment, develop a solid understanding of the risk and impact, and then create a course of action is what separates an Elon Musk from a Jeff Thorlander. Jeff (not his real name) was a rising investment banking star on his way to running an entire division for Morgan Stanley when 9/11 hit. Since that day in 2001 he has not gotten on an airplane. He lost his job, his house, and his future. He's a manager for a bank in Rhode Island now, and his two teenage children have never flown anywhere either. If he could assess risk and tame his fear, he would be making millions changing businesses all over the world and giving his family the gift of seeing the world, experiencing other cultures, and studying different languages.

You might not want to be Elon Musk, but if you do want to lead people you need to learn courage and risk vs. fear. Assessing the situation lets you see that you are really in control. You are the only one who can choose how you act in any situation. If you remember the that root of all fear is the uncertainty, the unknown, that measure called Free Energy, you can step back and observe life from the point of view of how you plan your action. You, and no one else, control your feelings. No one can make you feel scared, worthless, stupid, ugly, or anything else unless you give them permission. And why would you ever do that?

That's the A—*Assess* the situation from the role of an outside observer.

Smile and Shift Your Eyes

What do you say to a one-legged hitchhiker?

Hop in. Ha! Did you laugh? The act of flexing the forty-three muscles that require you to smile has an immediate effect on your central nervous system. It turns out the old adage "grin and bear it" is grounded in sound science. When you smile, even if it is fake or forced (one experiment had participants clench chopsticks in their teeth to activate the facial muscles so they didn't think happy thoughts that might have changed the outcome)[1] you create a chain reaction that helps the brain produce something called neuropeptides. These cause your sympathetic nervous system to loosen its grip on your body. The neuropeptides help you regain control of your working memory. Even forcing a fake smile when you are in a high-stress state—when there is anxiety or uncertainty or free energy—can reduce cortisol, the stress hormone, by up to 80 percent. Keep in mind that working memory is like a smartphone—thousands of apps can be stored on it, but only one app can be up on the screen at any one time. When the amygdala tried to hijack your actions, the only app it puts up on your working memory is fight, flight, or freeze. That almost always results in poor choices, because they are emotionally reactive. With a smile and the release of neuropeptides other changes take place, the levels of cortisol fall, and your working memory can be used to focus on the present moment and take proactive action. You can think in layers of decisions and outcomes, not just fight or flight.

The other S (Shift) reminds you to shift your eyes back and forth, side to side as you process a situation, like you're watching a couple of Chinese Olympians playing table tennis. There is an interesting field of psychology for treating anxiety that uses eye movement therapy; it's called EMDR (eye movement desensitization and reprocessing). The idea is that we have unprocessed memories that cause us to behave as if we were in a traumatic situation every time we get in a situation where that memory or environment is recalled. Neuroscientists haven't quite figured out why, but for some reason when you think of a traumatic memory and start shifting your eyes left to right, and then think of something pleasant, the trauma associated with this memory decreases. That's a bit of a simplification, but the truth is that it works and you can use it the same way Francine Shapiro, PhD, the woman who created the therapy, discovered it. She was walking through Central Park in 1987 with some things weighing

EMPTYING YOUR WORKING MEMORY

The lateral prefrontal cortex houses the key to one of our biggest allies or enemies—the working memory. This is like the RAM drive on a computer—it can only hold a little bit of information compared to the vast hard drive that makes up other parts of memory. Dr. Earl Miller at MIT has shown that most people can hold a maximum of four things in the working memory at once. When the amygdala is activated, working memory is filled up with reactionary survival actions and plans. Evolution has made us very efficient at figuring out how to fight or flee, and that takes up most of our working memory and hijacks the sympathetic nervous system. To use fear as fuel we have to clear the working memory of survival reactions and make a well-planned and successful decision. This requires being in the present and assessing the situation right now. Learning to breathe in the four-by-four method I lay out with the BASE method will clear space in the working memory for you. Once it does, you observe completely, orient yourself, and then make a decision. Breathing, consciously being curious, and suspending judgment allows you to use fear as fuel. Think about the feeling you want to feel—like courage. Think also of sending courage and peace to whomever or whatever has activated your amygdala. Tom Brady practices emptying the working memory by spending an hour a few times a week in a sensory-depriving float tank. His mind can focus on being in the present because fighting gravity and taking in sensation comes to a stop; you should give the practice a try either in a float tank or just whenever you need to be present.

heavily on her mind when she started watching things move quickly side to side like a fan watching Pete Sampras play Rafael Nadal and suddenly she felt better.[2] This began her lifelong pursuit of a protocol and method for using eye movement to treat PTSD and depression; it has been widely proven to be as, if not more, effective than traditional therapies like cognitive behavioral therapy.[3] Some scientists think moving our eyes and recalling trauma is a waking version of rapid eye movement sleep where we process all the memories from the day and consolidate them into our hard drive. Think of the process like saving a word document and its data off your laptop's RAM chip before you shut down your computer; it's off the RAM onto the hard drive. Same idea—that's how our memories are stored and processed, but we aren't quite sure of the mechanisms yet. Either way, it's a good hack to have in your toolbox of stress reducing techniques and it's fun to look at another person and do.

That's the S—*Smile* and shift your eyes back and forth.

Eliminate Your Mind's Shortcuts

E is to eliminate the efficient survival shortcuts we have created over a lifetime of living. The B, A, and S will have severed the grip the amygdala has on your working memory; the first three steps are a way of getting rid of the free energy that causes our bodily signals and internal perceptions to be out of whack. The B, A, and S will get you to a point where you can evolve from looking at things as a threat and being out of your control to seeing most things that happen in life as a challenge and an opportunity to learn and grow. The E, however, is what will change everything.

Eliminating shortcuts is all about analyzing possible actions and making multilevel choices. The actions you take when you get to the point of being able to stop yourself from reacting or knowing will make this the most critical juncture in your personal development.

With your fear cocktail still coursing through your body, you are set to be stronger and smarter than at any other time. First you need to remind yourself when you feel the excitement and the buzz of fear that you are in the best possible mind frame to act—your body is primed for performance and you are pumping with excitement. This reframing of your mindset is critical. The more you use self-talk at this stage (especially the same self-talk you used during visualization) the bigger the benefit from the fear cocktail pumping through your body.

A note on self-talk: like any great athlete you need to talk to yourself all the time. People who become great, who lead the life of their dreams, always use self-talk. When you are trying to eliminate shortcuts this habit is crucial: asking yourself "What is happening right now?" to keep yourself in the role of observer.

The first thing to do is lay out the options. Ask yourself, "What is likely to happen if I make Choice A, then Choice B, then Choice C?" Then tell yourself you are in control of making the best choice for your future success. Self-talk in this way has to become a habit; in fact researchers in Germany and the United States[4] found that people who engaged in self-talk didn't get the benefit from it until after about a month of practicing. In one study subjects were put in an fMRI machine and shown terrifying pictures; their amygdala activated at the image of a man getting stabbed or a house burning down. The subjects were told to use self-talk to say "I'm just looking at pictures" or "I'm safe in a university lab." Scientists called this a reality check that, once practiced for several weeks, showed dramatic downregulation of the amygdala and the emotions created by an amygdala hijacking. In fear as fuel terms, it allowed someone to use that fear cocktail after they realized they were being hijacked by the amygdala, clear out their working memory, and get the prefrontal cortex in charge. The subjects reduced the Free Energy, engaged the sgACC part of their brain for courage, and changed their frame of things. Anyone can do that. You can do that.

The only catch is that when, at the end of a month, they asked the control group who were not using the reality check for the first four weeks to try the same self-talk, there was no dramatic improvement. In other words, self-talk takes practice and a few weeks to really learn how to control the amygdala.[5]

Now you're ready to Eliminate the shortcuts that are created by emotional valence. The first thing to do is tell yourself to STOP, before you react using that survival, free-energy-fueled fear. Once you stop the reaction, you can analyze all the possible choices you have. Curiosity should be the emotion you try with all your being to activate. Don't get me wrong; the harder your amygdala was activated the tougher it is to get curious and look at things as an observer. You can do it. As soon as you stopped that survival reaction and can think of more than one alternative, that's the sign that you will use as much of your brain's processing power as possible.

The mistake many people make, especially in business, is just analyzing a single, current choice, the choice most likely to present itself in the fight, flight, or freeze response. You have to think of each choice sprouting a branch in an entire tree of possible alternatives. Then you must look farther out on the branches of that tree to see the outcome of the first and then second choice.

Two essential components of uber-successful decision makers and leaders are that they question, with radical curiosity, every significant choice presented to them. The neuroscience reason for doing this is to eliminate the valence shortcuts our brain tries so hard to use. Those shortcuts have evolved over surviving for our lifetime (and our ancestors' lifetimes), so our survival brain thinks that since they worked so well we should use them over and over again. If we allow our past to write our future we will only survive; we will never thrive.

Valence enables your subconscious to choose how to make you act right now—the choice is based on your subconscious hard drive. Valence is the fastest and easiest way to make a survival reaction—but in the real world this means a suboptimal decision. What most people do, especially those trapped in a world of mediocrity, is let their subconscious decide using valence and then recall their own biases to justify that course of action.

Open and unemotional curiosity is the first step to eliminating valence. The second step is sprouting the branches of a decision tree out to the next couple of choices and then the follow-on effect of each choice. It requires confidence and courage because we are biased to our subconscious choices and we try to use those biases as justifications. We must create additional choices and follow them to an envisioned future. See figure 7.2.

Valence Elimination

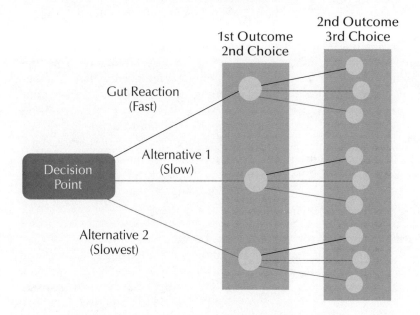

Stop! Think of two other possible courses of action, then investigate follow-on results and opportunities

Figure 7.2. Valence Elimination

Courage and confidence drive some of the most famous individuals to make radically better choices than average people. Buzz Aldrin, the legendary astronaut and the second man on the moon, was a fighter pilot in Germany when he first heard about the astronaut training program. One of the principal requirements for application was that the astronauts be experienced test pilots. Aldrin wasn't a test pilot. Not surprisingly, Aldrin applied and not surprisingly given the strictness of the military in following procedures, he was rejected. He could have responded by telling them to kiss his ass, or going out and getting drunk. He was a winner, though; he was a producer of his own life. Military personnel are trained to follow rules and stay in line so, one would think that after being told he was not astronaut material he would have stayed a fighter pilot, become an instructor, returned to the Military Academy to bring up the next generation, or any one of the opportunities that were open to him as a decorated combat-proven pilot. Instead, he went back to NASA again and reapplied. He didn't blame the military for stupid rules, he didn't say it was someone else's fault he didn't get it. He rewrote the application and convinced them that he should be accepted. He controlled what he could control. Aldrin says he never thought he'd be one of the first guys on the moon. This time he was accepted. He wasn't even on the original crew that would go to the moon; he and Neil Armstrong were on the backup crew that got their shot when the primary crew was killed in a freak on-the-ground testing accident months before the launch.

Another easy way to think about eliminating the valence shortcuts when you think you are right is, as Ray Dalio famously learned, ask yourself *why* you are right (see chapter 10). This forces the same type of thorough analysis on your course of action that will not let shortcuts slip through.

Breathe, Assess, Smile and shift, and Eliminate shortcuts (BASE)—that's an easy to remember, neuroscience-based method of putting fear to work for you. Try it next time you are feeling anxious. I used it last year and it saved me $125,000 and a bad hangover. I shit you not, it works. If it helps, repeat the mantra "having courage takes fear" as you breathe. I guarantee BASE will get you back to a position to realize only you can control how you feel, only you can create courage, and eventually, just maybe, you will be cool enough to get curious as to why you got so worked up in the first place.

3.

Just have one more try, it's dead easy to die. It's the keeping on living that's hard.

—Robert Service

It was minus thirty-five degrees and the Australian explorer Douglas Mawson kept repeating that mantra in his head. He was 350 miles from his mother ship on the Antarctic and one of his two partners had just plummeted with his sled and six dogs through a snow bridge and fallen 150 feet to his death. He didn't just lose a close friend; he lost all his food and his tent as well.

One hundred years ago we had stress. The BASE method is designed to make the most of the newest, most intelligent part of our brain (the prefrontal cortex) to make life happier, more fulfilling, more uplifting and impactful. The BASE method teaches us how to get away from the primal survival network in our brain and focus on thriving, not just surviving. But we need the survival part for health, longevity, and strength. We need to push out of our comfort zone and realize how much more each one of us can do. Some people realize this and try to replicate the efforts of Mawson, by doing endurance races or obstacle courses, but not enough of us. His story shows what humans can endure and what we should try to get a taste of in our life.

Douglas Mawson was the commander of an audacious expedition. In 1912 the Australian sailed his boat into the windiest harbor in the world with the goal of creating a survey of 2,000 miles of Antarctic coast a year after the famous Scott and Shackleton expeditions. It was May 1912, one of the coldest and darkest months of the year. The average—not maximum—*average* wind speed was sixty-one miles per hour. To be most efficient mapping the massive coast, he split his crew up into teams that would branch out like spokes in a wheel to map the continent. He took two of the toughest men, Belgrave Ninnis and Xavier Mertz (a Swiss ski champion and the fittest man on the expedition) with him to tackle the most treacherous geography. Each man had a dog team and sled. The trio set off south to map the course from their ship to the point where Scott had landed his expedition the year before.

The cold was not the biggest threat; the wind was not the biggest threat; the crevasses were. The team crossed countless crevasses.

The youngest man, Ninnis, was given the best dog team with all the food, tents, and supplies that were critical to survival. Mawson assumed that the last sled would be the safest, since the first two would have fallen through any hidden snow bridges first. Consequently, the third guy in line would carry the most important supplies and to stay safe he'd just have to stay in the tracks of his teammates. He was wrong. The first to perish was the last sled; Ninnis and his team were in the rear. He fell to his death while Mawson and his partner looked on in horror. Mawson and Mertz knew they had to return to the mother ship or starve to death. In an effort to skirt the deadly glaciers, they added a hundred extra miles to their return trip. Mawson's second partner began to lose his mind. In one documented incident Mawson tried to sit on him to control his outbursts. The pair had less than a week's rations left and the knowledge that it would take more than six weeks in the bitter cold to return to base camp.

Amazingly, Mawson kept recording information and compass headings in his journal. His intent was to map the continent and his soul was committed to doing that for all humanity. He wanted to leave a legacy. You can endure tremendous suffering if your soul is invested and your motivation is beyond personal gain. All Mawson could do was focus on the present moment and do his job, and try to keep Mertz from going completely insane. He knew they were likely to starve or freeze to death but he took strength from the knowledge that if he could safely cache his journal somewhere it might be recovered; more than 1,500 miles of Antarctic land would be mapped. This was ten times what already existed.

It wasn't long before the starving duo began killing dogs; one every couple of days to feed themselves and the remaining dogs. Several weeks after they lost Ninnis they killed the last dog. The pair was burning an estimated three thousand calories a day and taking in less than one thousand. They were, by now, pulling the sleds themselves and inching along in the shattering cold and wind. Science now tells us that they had developed so much brown fat around their spines and organs that they were adapted to the cold, burning much more efficient fat and producing incredibly high levels of glutathione, a powerful antioxidant.

Tragically, Mertz perished just twenty miles from the mother ship, but at long last Mawson made it back. His equipment, nutrition, and training all would be laughed at in our ultra-high-tech Gore-Tex, PolarFleece, PowerBar-eating world. But the truth of the matter is that that's why we are here and the wooly mammoth isn't. Mawson's incredible tale of survival, will, and adaptation reminds us how amazing the human body is. Homo sapiens have survived because of our unique ability to adapt. Our bodies are designed to defend against stress. We need stress to keep our immune system in tiptop shape. The sole reason we are the top of the food chain is our ability to adapt to changing conditions and still thrive.

The world now, however, is as dangerously cushy as it's ever been—moving walkways glide us along, sliding carry-on bags fitted with wheels; escalators bring us up flights too short for an elevator; bikes have electric motors; people take elevators up two floors to their hotel rooms. Our urban architects are designing the death of not only the physical effort that is so important to keeping us prepared for any of life's eventualities; we're taking stress away from our immune system. This environmental stress elimination is even worse—we can press a button to turn on a hot plate under our ass like we are cheese on a raclette cooker, or pack a down jacket developed for a minus one hundred degrees Everest summit for a trip to our son's football game. In the summer, walking a charity 5K, participants wear frozen gel necklaces to relieve the morning heat. Our bodies are not being stressed by physical effort or environmental challenges. With a lack of stress, the system will adapt and conserve resources, thus assuming our immune system is not required because it is not being strained. No need to produce highly efficient antioxidants like glutathione and adiponectin because there is no signal of oxidation stress, so shut down that well of youthful vitality. Adiponectin is a protein that reduces obesity and decreases heart disease.[6] Making it worse is a constant barrage of high-sugar items and highly processed foods. Rather than ever get to fat-burning efficiency, we've been trained to gas up the furnace on Snickers, and replenish the little glucose stove inside our belly every hour or so. Our body was designed to hunt or forage, eat a lot, and then wait for the next kill. That could be days. We have become so far removed from the original stresses we were designed for that the only hard-evidence proof for extending our life is by calorie restriction, or fasting. That means the average person gets to eat so much, has so much readily available food, that we are overburdening our bodies digesting it all and the only way to live longer is to eat less.[7]

Why have we allowed ourselves to get to this passive state of satiated existence? Because it's easy to be numb, and it creeps in on us. It takes little or no effort to follow the herd, and if you don't do what everyone else does people might think you're a freak! Most people never learn how to use fear as fuel; that means most choices they make in life are out of fear.

There are two ways to make decisions in your life: out of fear or out of opportunity. Making decisions based on fear will almost always lead to regret. Making choices based on opportunity is often scary—should you quit your high-paying corporate job and start your own company? Should you move overseas and learn a new language? Fear is the easy and much less rewarding way to decide what to do with your life. Two things are quite clear from terabytes and terabytes of scientific study over the past decade:

1. We need to get comfortable with fear, know it's only our survival mechanism, and learn how to use fear optimally when we make decisions in our life. We must look at life as a challenge and not a threat if we want to live the best life possible, be happy, fulfilled, and in loving relationships.
2. We need to take the comfort out of our daily life and get back to stressing the body with exercise, cold exposure, intermittent fasting, and out-of-our-comfort-zone physical adventures, and then fuel it naturally with no processed foods and very limited sugar and carbohydrates.

Go stress your body and mind and use your fear as fuel; you'll feel amazing every time you do.

II

COURAGE

8

∽

The Courage Conundrum

The courageous man withstands and fears those things which it is necessary [to fear and withstand].

—Aristotle

1.

The single engine droned optimistically on. Diamonds of light twinkled brilliantly in the moonless night. The blackness that created an astronomical bonanza brought with it a perception nightmare from five thousand feet in the air: the impossible challenge of separating the sky's end from the ground's beginning. It's called a hidden horizon. This optical challenge has caused many a pilot to spin into a vertigo-induced death spiral. In 1933 there were no air traffic controllers, no radar, and no sophisticated instruments to safely guide pilots through such perils as hidden horizons in rural Africa. A single-engine plane and lonely pilot had to toil along, steering the straightest line possible between waypoints. They had a blurry, bouncy, dashboard-mounted compass to guide them. Strapping into the cockpit came with the knowledge that one failure of judgment or equipment would suck both plane and pilot into an eons-old cycle of life and death on the Dark Continent. This night's particular mission started with the noble intent of saving a life. Now the odds were approaching even that it might end up costing two.

The mining camp should have drifted into sight as a ship crests over a featureless horizon, yet not even a glimmer of light broke the black ahead. But you can't give up hope; it's all you have.

The 350-mile range of the small plane was being tested. Anxiety combined with the constant calculations of the pilot, blending into a unique alchemy of laser-like focus. It wasn't just sight that was limited, but sound as well. Only two reverberations penetrated the night air; the pilot's dutiful and magnified heartbeat and the drone of the eight cylinders; pap-pap-pap-pap-pap-pap-pap-papping along. Both pilot and engine guarded the knowledge that this could be their final flight. And both proceeded unwaveringly with an outcome unknown.

2.

I left Gold's Gym on a flawless seventy-degree Indian-summer day. The sky was a uniform wash of cobalt blue. The world's most badass truck, a 1999 Hummer H1, made famous by Arnold Schwarzenegger, waited for me in the corner of the parking lot. It was gloss black with the ServerVault logo faux-riveted on each side. The truck was impossible to miss. It was conversation stopping, a rolling billboard for the secure cloud computing company I had started two years earlier. As I mounted the driver's side entry, firmly wrapping my fingers around the door frame handle, I paused. The morning was good. My muscles were pumped. I was energized. The same feeling followed most early-morning workouts. I felt strong and light with heightened senses. I didn't know it at the time, but my pituitary gland responded to the stress of working out by secreting hormones and making my senses sharper. I bathed in the perfect temperature, the cloudless sky, and a caressing breeze. What a flawless day to stay outside. However, duty called. With the realization of my workday ahead, a familiar feeling of anxiety began clawing at my stomach. I was headed to a 10:00 meeting at the Pentagon in Arlington, Virginia, to meet a potential client. Time to roll. Could I win them over? What did they want to hear? I worried as I drove.

Heading along the Beltway toward DC, I caught site of the Potomac River—as a longtime oarsman my instinct is to assess any water's calmness and suitability for rowing. I do it instinctively, with a glance. The Hummer rumbled off the Beltway and onto the

George Washington Parkway. Peering down, it was easy to see the reflection of a lonely cloud and green trees along the edge mirrored in the glassy-smooth water. I muted the thumping Kid Rock CD, and punched the keys on my Blackberry, dialing my wife to see if she could meet later for lunch. But the call didn't go through. On the second try, the phone didn't even ring.

The DC region has a radio station famous for "traffic and weather on the eights" so Kid Rock gave way to WTOP. Roaring down the GW Parkway, a quick check of traffic was in order in case there were any issues. Then the world stopped. The first words I heard boom across the airwaves were "New York is under attack."

I listened to the newscaster's frantic narration. Two planes had torpedoed into the Twin Towers and, according to the radio, both towers were engulfed in flames, the government was grounding every plane in the air, fighter jets were being scrambled, and the president was calling it an attack on American soil. Instinct told me just to pull over to the side of the busy parkway. My stomach flipped up and folded over, trying to squeeze up my throat. I was overloaded trying to drive and process this at the same time. My hands were shaking and my palms began to sweat. I looked around blindly for answers.

Do you remember where you were when you heard about 9/11? Do you remember what you did or how you felt?

I didn't focus on it at the time, but a low-flying plane passed on my left, following the normal approach pattern down the Potomac River toward Reagan National Airport. My mind's autopilot steered the truck along as my thoughts raced about, not knowing what to think. Then, at 9:40 that morning I was seized with a level of terror unfelt before in my life when a mushroom cloud sprouted up in front of me. It couldn't be real. Watching the scene just a few miles from the Pentagon, I assumed it had been bombed.

I tried futilely to call my wife. I couldn't think. In a panic I turned the truck away from the Pentagon and fled for the closest, safest place I could think of—our local Irish Bar. Ireland's Four Courts was just a few miles in the other direction, in Arlington, Virginia, and a mile and a half from our house. I fled. Seventeen years later and after dozens of interviews with world-class neuroscientists and psychologists I finally figured out what happened to me, and many other Americans, that day.

If you wonder about fear there are countless answers—petabytes of data and research from the world's top universities and researchers. Paradoxically, courage is uncharted territory. September 11, 2001, ushered in a generation of fear and worry that has bound our nation in a straitjacket of anxiety for almost two decades. Fear is still fed and exploited by politicians, media, and marketers for their own gain.

There were hundreds of thousands of people like me fleeing, a population of scared citizens running away from fear that chased us like a relentless shadow. A couple of years later, the effects of being in a near constant state of dread almost killed me. The rare form of leukemia that sent me to Johns Hopkins in 2004 and led me down the path to facing down my own death taught me that bravery is a choice and running from fear is the least effective way to deal with it, and in fact makes fear and its corrosive effects even stronger.

The African pilot in 1933 made a very different choice about life than I had made in 2001.

Lesson 1 is simple: courage is a choice you can make if you want and you really try—an option I didn't consider during 9/11 when I might have helped others. An option I didn't know how to cultivate in myself during my efforts to build my first start-up company.

Lesson 2 is less obvious but more impactful: people who work on long-term courage have more positive relationships with others, can learn personal mastery and autonomy, and foster a feeling of purpose and meaning in life. This is referred to as a state of psychological well-being and also shows strong correlation to better health.[1] Maybe even more importantly, a study published in January 2019 in the *Social Psychiatry and Psychiatric Epidemiology* journal by Abdonas Tamosiunas and colleagues showed that having psychological well-being is an important predictor of longevity. As if living a happy, fulfilling life weren't enough, the conclusion of this study should provide some incentive to work on becoming brave—courageous people live longer.[2]

The main reason people who can be truly open-minded and curious are able to find out what their ultimate life looks like is that they have the courage to explore. The same attitude will foster the courage to execute on their dream life and make the most of their opportunities.

COURAGE OR FEARLESSNESS

Courage means doing something while you are scared, or have anxiety, or are in a panic. Free energy fuels your amygdala, but you stay in control. Fearlessness means you aren't in one of those agitated states, your physiology hasn't changed, and you are not trying to avoid a situation. You don't produce free energy. A great example of fearlessness is the real-life Spider-Man named Alex Honnold. Honnold is the only person to ever free solo Yosemite's legendary El Capitan's three-thousand-foot sheer granite face. Free soloing is climbing without the safety of ropes or equipment as backup in case you fall. He is famous for his fearlessness. Honnold has the ability to completely deactivate his amygdala. What most of the public doesn't know is that when he free solos a route, he has usually done the climb so many times with the safety and backup of ropes that he literally knows every single move on the route. This high-level repetitive training, combined with an extremely elevated level of confidence and mental control, eliminates his fear and anxiety. That's fearlessness.

One courageous climbing act he has admitted to is when he free soloed a legendary Yosemite climb called Astroman. He didn't do the same level of preparation he had done for his other free solos. One thousand feet up on the cliff, he came to a puzzling section and froze. He wondered what the hell to do—navigate a tricky boulder move requiring 100 percent commitment, basically a jump that if he missed he'd die, or go around and find an easier way. He chose to go around, but admitted to being scared the entire time. That was courage. He's also managed to find courage when he found his new girlfriend because he told *Alpinist Magazine* in an interview, "I don't know what made me strong mentally, if I even am. You should see me around hot ladies. Terrified."[1]

Note

1. "Solo, Part 1: Alex Honnold," *Alpinist*, June 25, 2008, http://www.alpinist.com/doc/web08x/wfeature-solo-honnold.

I didn't know it at the time, but it turns out that courage is one of my superpowers; it was hidden under a blanket of lies created by fear. You need to learn the truth too and uncover your courage. We all have the capability to do so. Our lives change for the better in every way when we do.

It's easier to choose bravery if you understand the difference between fast and slow courage because one will change your life forever, as a friendly little snake taught the world of science.

3.

If you picture the Grinch as an older man, with a slight paunch, wrinkled eyes circled by large round glasses, and a mop of curly white hair, you'd have a pretty good image of the guy in front of you. He's about to slide a brightly colored, four-foot-long snake toward your face and watch you wage mental war with yourself. If you're seeing this man then you're likely in the coffin-like tube of an fMRI machine so you can't exactly flee, either. The snake handler's name is Dr. Yadin Dudai. He's a world-renowned Israeli neuroscientist and neurobiologist. If you could think clearly you might even notice a slightly impish grin as he passes the snake toward you and wonder if he is enjoying his role testing your courage a little too much.

There are literally thousands of peer-reviewed studies on fear, from many different perspectives; neuroscience, neurobiology, psychology. You name it; fear has been studied for it. As one of my neuroscience resources from Georgetown University, Dr. Abigail Marsh, pointed out, "most human fear/anxiety research that is clinically oriented is focused on reducing subjective and physiological symptoms of fear and anxiety [what I call your fear tells], rather than teaching people to move forward despite their anxiety."[3]

It is important to understand the difference between fearlessness and courage (see sidebar). The process of building resistance to a fear is called habituation or extinction, as opposed to employing courage and being able to use fear as fuel. The goal of most fear studies is to get subjects closer to fearlessness or extinction. Many studies focus on learning what happens to the brain when we get scared and process trauma. Few studies make it a goal to find courage. That's a monumental mistake for courage seekers like you.

Courage enables you to learn how to use fear as fuel—you will make radically better decisions under pressure because your mind and body are prepped for superhuman performance. The more you practice the more you learn the kind of mental control and mindfulness that allows you to be courageous in any situation and always perform at your peak. You will obtain one of the most important virtues that make up a fulfilling life. Bottom line is you will use your fear rather than your fear using you.

There is a point when getting used to fear, where after repeated exposure to the same fear, you get more and more used to that specific threat and your body stops creating a physiological reaction (see figure 8.1). This change happens even though the senses are receiving the same information, but because you are habituated and the amygdala doesn't activate and try to take over, you don't interpret the same inputs as a threat anymore. The fear cocktail your body produces is what allows you to perform at your ultimate capability. Your fear tells notify you that your body has started pumping out adrenaline, cortisol, dehydroepiandrosterone (DHEA), and norepinephrine, to help you survive. Using the techniques in the BASE method will create neurobiological changes to those initial secretions that convert to performance-enhancing, pleasure-producing enzymes such as dopamine, endorphins, anandamide, serotonin, and oxytocin. That's the root of using fear as fuel. When your body stops making the fear cocktail and you no longer feel your fear tells, it's a sign you have stopped excreting those same compounds because you no longer feel the need to avoid that source of fear. That point (right of the vertical bar in figure 8.1) is when you become

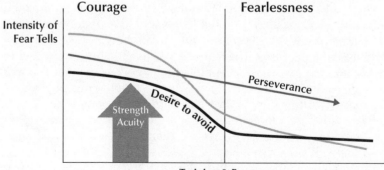

Figure 8.1. The Transition to Fearlessness

fearless in a specific situation. There are some situations, like flying on a commercial jetliner, where you probably want to be fearless, and others, like piloting a stunt plane in an aerobatics competition, where you want the benefit of the peak-performance neurobiological changes that athletes and special forces veterans often describe as a state of flow.

A notable example of extinction and becoming fearless is the scourge of six-year-olds everywhere: riding the bus to school. The first few times mounting those four giant steps into the abyss of bullies, nose pickers, and booger flickers tests the limits of childhood courage. Fortunately, in that instance most kids are getting some coaching from a parent and sometimes the driver. In many cases, this is one of the first instances when they begin pushing out their fear frontier. Miraculously, after a week or two it isn't so bad. In fact, if you have a few good friends on the bus, the same terrifying situation has probably changed into something fun that you might even look forward to. If you take the role of an observer, watching a movie of your life, you will see that nothing about the events is any different—same yellow bus, same four steps, same nose pickers— what's changed is your perception or orientation to the situation. The story you tell yourself has changed. Your self-talk has changed. Your expectations have changed. It takes courage, however, to get on the bus the first time because you are acting against your will in the face of fear.

When you were scared getting on the bus, you mustered superkid powers to keep going. Some parents have fingernail scars on their arms that prove how surpassingly strong their kids became as they fought to stay off the bus. Your body was producing that fear cocktail and changing your physiology to fight or flee. You could see better, hear better, and think better (but likely you were not in control of your actions because your prefrontal cortex was only just beginning to develop). That's when you could use fear as fuel to really tear away from your mom. Once you overcome that fear and become habituated to the bus, you won't get those same physiological changes from getting on the bus.

Eliminating the emotional memories of fear, or what neuroscientists refer to as extinction misses the chance to harness a vast array of untapped human potential. The closer we get to fearlessness through repeated exposure and additional training the less our fear tells manifest with those physiological changes. It is exactly those bodily changes we can use to our benefit. Our superhuman potential only comes with courage; when you cross the line to fearlessness you can lose much of those physiological advantages. We need courage in our life for peak performance, but there is a benefit to learning how to habituate or extinguish fear as well.

Many people who are very good at a specific skill have the similar neurological processes as trained monks like Matthieu Ricard, whom you met in chapter 1. There is a second stage of control, after you learn to use fear as fuel, that allows you to activate a similar fear cocktail and create laser-like focus when needed, as Alex Honnold does on his fifteenth or twentieth time free solo climbing the side of a mountain cliff. His mind crosses over into fearlessness, but his body has been trained for perfection and consequently he has the courage and confidence to never doubt himself. This is what many athletes refer to as being in the zone, and most recently has been popularized as a state of flow. The term *flow* comes from a book of the same name by a psychologist named Mihaly Csikszentmihalyi that I first read in 1993 on the recommendation of the US Olympic Training Center psychologist. Flow is the point when any person can change his or her mind into a state of what neuroscientists call hypofrontality. Basically it means shutting off all the chatter and voices in our head and just being in the present, focused on the task at hand. It is literally the feeling of perfection when time seems to stand still, things appear super clear, often in slow motion. If we learn how to use fear as fuel, and how to take advantage of biological changes in our mind and body, we can accomplish amazing things, first using fear as fuel and second quicker access to a state of flow. The conundrum is that in order to have courage we need to have fear first—courage is the overcoming of fear to action.

There may be times when you want to just get to fearlessness and access flow. There are people who have mental defects (lesions on the amygdala for instance) that make them fearless. They literally don't have a fear response to anything, which can be quite dangerous at times. There are a number of other drawbacks to this condition, but one is that they miss the chance of superhuman performance, because their body does not respond with a survival response of increasing strength and intelligence. Your goal should be control of your body and mind with the ability to release some of your performance-enhancing hormones and enzymes. You can think of Fear as Fuel and then Fear as Flow.

Rock climber Alex Honnold has such a command over his mental imagery and execution, he can visualize every move perfectly (out of hundreds) and then his body executes each flawless movement. By training himself to a point of fearlessness he may have lost that initial shock of fear most of the time, but he has trained his physiology to perform in the moment; in a very complex way he has trained his body to produce the benefit of the fear cocktail on demand and jump right into the Fear as Flow state.

To live a completely balanced life we have to go back and look at all three sides of the Terror Triangle. Honnold has mastered accessing Fear as Fuel and using Fear as Flow for rock climbing. He has achieved this ultimate elite level for one side of the Terror Triangle, physical fear. However, in the Academy Award–winning National Geographic movie *Free Solo*, he talks openly about his fear and awkwardness in social situations. He is a rank amateur on that side of the Terror Triangle because he had not put the kind of focused and purposeful practice he did on the wall into being in a group setting being sociable. He is not nearly as emotionally courageous as he is physically courageous and fearless. Most of us have a similar imbalance. While we may not be Captain Courageous on the physical side, we might spend more time practicing that than working on emotional issues, or we might have become fascinated by snakes as a child and overcome instinctual fears. Balance takes work, but it pays huge dividends. We're only beginning to understand how courage can show up in one area but not others.

Courage research is a barren landscape compared to the bountiful studies on fear; the global library of scientific research on courage has the equivalent of a few wrinkled magazines sitting on the coffee table of your therapist's waiting room. The lack of research doesn't mean courage is not important; it means it is more elusive.

Countless times each day the average person wages a mental war between making a courageous choice or a fearful decision. The more often you succumb to (or avoid) your fears, the less likely your subconscious is to even give quarter to the regiment of courage available for your personal battles; you'll surrender. Fear emerges victorious; you freeze your actions like a soldier caught in a minefield; you fret, you worry, and eventually you run. Then boom! That fear-based decision eventually comes back to bite you in the ass. This can be in something as simple as meeting with your child's middle school teacher, giving an interview to the press, or presenting at a big industry conference. If you don't have some courage—if you can't shut out that negative talk in your head and replace it with positive affirmations—you'll be destined to fail.

Courage is a precious commodity that does not occur naturally. Just the fact that we are not all imbued with courage from birth[4] is one of the things that makes bravery such a desirable and sought-after character trait. Every superhero movie from *Captain America* to *Black Panther* to *Wonder Woman* comes down to the hero's journey finding courage and acting assertively in the face of fear.

Philosophers from Plato and Socrates to Seneca and Marcus Aurelius have fought to cultivate courage as a foundational character trait of a worthy life. Most of them say it is *the* most important trait. There are a handful of psychological studies on courage using behavior of military men, but not until 2010 with Dr. Dudai's snake study did we have an inkling of what was happening inside the brain, neurologically, when it comes to acting courageously.

Dr. Dudai's study helped peer inside our heads and answer several burning questions such as could we learn courage or are people just born courageous? Do they only act with courage when the need arises or are there courageous actors all the time? Does the amygdala change inside the head of someone with courage or is there a separate neural network of bravery that heroes access? The good news is that neuroscientists are shifting the battleground from an all-out war on fear to a curious dissection of courage. So far they have focused on proving how to construct courage and what I consider the two different types of courage—fast and slow.

Dr. Dudai and his colleagues at Tel Aviv University convinced a group of people who were admittedly afraid of snakes to lie down in the tube of an fMRI machine and bring a four-foot-long corn snake as close to their head as possible. The subjects had control of a conveyor belt that rolled the snake toward their own heads (showing courage) or could push it farther away (succumbing to their fears). Their expectations of that moment determined whether they were courageous or truly wimps. As they experienced the choice, Dudai and his team watched real-time activity in their brains. The people in the study were specifically selected because they were afraid of snakes. Dudai evaluated the test subjects on two key behaviors—physiological change by how much their skin conductivity changed (a typical fear tell measuring perspiration) and if the subject attempted to further avoid the snakes (a flee response).

What Dudai found gives hope for everyone in need of courage; simply adopting a courageous attitude can make you courageous. "Fake it until you make it" not only applies to coaching your son's hockey team but also to courage. That's the construction of fast courage; it's an immediate choice. It is accepting the gap in the unknown between what might happen and what is happening now. If you can remove yourself from being the person this is happening to and become an observer to watch from afar and assess the situation (the BASE method from chapter 7), you can see the movement unfolding and you can picture or imagine yourself acting with courage. If you can imagine and see it happening, you can adopt that brave reaction from your imagination into the real world. If you can bring the positive emotions of feeling strong and courageous to that vision you will change the expected or predicted state and actually draw that positive outcome toward you and increase its probability. I never knew how to do this, so going back to 9/11 in front of the Pentagon, I had the ability to neither assess the situation nor imagine myself as courageous. I had no idea what was happening in my mind and I had no willingness to choose courage. I was in dire need of fast courage.

Constructing fast courage uses the physics of our brain by setting an expectation of the worst-case scenario. First, you calculate the likelihood of the worst outcome happening, then you figure out how to mitigate that bad outcome, and finally you assign a value to a successful outcome. This mental algorithm allows you to move forward with action. Fast courage is really an algorithm we choose to run in an instant.[5] The only requirement is that you must be able to observe your situation to first run the algorithm. Acting in the face of danger (real or perceived) transpires when you can assess the situation properly by calculating the outcomes of choice, which inspires enough confidence in your choices to overcome the amygdala hijacking. It takes work, though, and practice. The principle of physics that best proves this is called the Free Energy Principle, which also helps construct long-lasting Slow Courage. (Review chapter 4 for the details of the Free Energy Principle.)

Fast courage means you must override the amygdala instead of letting the amygdala hijack you. If you recall from chapter 6, the working memory in the prefrontal cortex (which I said was like a computer's RAM drive) is the adult supervision of your brain; it's the area that can make informed, intelligent choices. What you need to remember from a neuroscience perspective is that working memory is like a smartphone—it can hold all the information in the world; thousands and thousands of apps; but you can only have one app on the screen working at any time.

The amygdala wants you to run for your life, so it tries pulling up the "Run Like Hell" app on your working memory.

The flee app came up and stayed up for me on 9/11 until I was in a safe place. Other times that little almond-shaped gland wants you to fight—so it pulls up the "Scream, Yell, and Win this Battle at All Costs" app. You get into a screaming match with your kids to get in bed, and you lose sight of the fact that your screaming is just activating their amygdala and no one wins. With the fear as fuel system you've learned how to shut off the amygdala's app and fill your working memory's screen with your ultimate decision-making app. I wish I could tell you it's easy, but it's not; your amygdala never tires of entering the octagon for a few rounds of drama. It will try to get back to a fight, flight, or freeze app and it will almost always sneak up on you—driving in the car, hearing a colleague's comment, or misinterpreting an email. Fast courage means for one instance you wrestle control of the working memory from the amygdala and act bravely.

Courage has the equivalent of chemical training wheels as well. If you produce a little squirt of oxytocin, that chemical can jump-start courage. Oxytocin is a neurotransmitter and a hormone that is produced in the hypothalamus and moved through your pituitary gland. If you do something good to help someone else out, you'll produce more than good karma; you produce the feel-good hormone oxytocin. What Dr. Marsh found from her watershed experiments at Georgetown was that after conditioning mice to a ringing tone and then a shock (stimulus & response) the mice would soon freeze in terror upon hearing the noise. Fright covered them like the lava from Vesuvius, locking them in place in an instant. The amygdala hijacked the working memory with a "freeze app." The mice found courage, however, when the mother mouse saw her babies in an adjacent cage that needed to be opened to get them out of harm's way. When the terrifying sound was played while she was in the presence of her offspring, the mother mouse's brain produced a shot of oxytocin, helping spur on her courage to release her babies from the painful predicament. She was able to shut off her freeze response and activate a courage response. And, unlike me at the Pentagon, she didn't flee or freeze.

Mommy mouse shows what happens when the future of her tribe might be in jeopardy. This is an altruistic behavior. It is the most powerful variable that would have changed my behavior of September 11—if my wife or one of my friends was at the Pentagon in need of help. If you ever wonder about the science behind corporate ropes courses or adventure falls, this is it—practicing stressful moments with a team will help engender trust in that team and loyalty and belonging because oxytocin is released to keep you acting courageously. It is one of the two primary catalysts of fast courage. Another is altruism.

Altruism does not always have to indicate sacrifice or pain. In Dr. Marsh's book *The Fear Factor*, she focuses on people who perform altruistic actions because of a sense of fulfillment; they can get as much pleasure out of helping someone as they can out of making money or having career success. Marsh uses the ultimate altruists as an example: people who anonymously donate a kidney to someone they never did, and never will, meet. When asked why they underwent this painful operation, the consensus is that someone may die if they don't. Not only are these altruists happier, but they are more courageous as well. They have better insight into people and can recognize fearful expressions in other people's faces more quickly than a normal person. They also have an amygdala that is 8 percent larger, on average, than a normal person. Compare this with sociopaths and psychopaths that Marsh and her colleagues studied, whose amygdala were up to 20 percent smaller than normal people; they could not recognize the look of fear in people's faces no matter how hard they tried.[6] The good news is neuroplasticity proves that with normal healthy biology we can change our brains and become more altruistic and thus more fulfilled and happy in our own lives. It is one way to build courage that benefits all of society.

The second important ingredient in fast courage is seeing the situation as an observer. If you can talk to yourself in the moment and can explain the situation, you are more likely to be able to maintain control of your working memory. For example, in an argument with your coworker if your amygdala is trying to install the fight app to your working memory, you can talk to yourself to try and get control back. Just saying something as simple as "step back" silently in your head will lead to a much better outcome. Self-talk will help you assess the situation the more direct you can become. Try to tell yourself "don't let the fight app start running" or "pull up the curious app and let's try to figure out why she's dug in her heels" or "what are my goals and how can I best reach them?" Just taking the position of an observer opens the pathway to the root of all courage—the subgenual anterior cingulate cortex or sgACC—because you are trying to figure out details of emotions, pay-off, alternatives. That's why the BASE method has A or "assess the situation as an observer would" as the second step to using fear as fuel.

4.

If the amygdala is the Wicked Witch of the West turning us into cowardly, selfish, or angry survivors, the sgACC is our courageous Glinda the Good Witch, who convinces us that courage comes from within and we all have it and need to find it in order to thrive and not just survive. The sgACC is the part of the brain the Lion eventually found after his journey through Oz. It is what we all need to find to change our lives with long lasting Slow Courage.

One of the biggest hurdles to building courage is our subconscious. We can all observe visual, auditory, and other sensory data, but we are actually only taking 10 percent of the data in consciously; everything else comes into our subconscious mind. For instance, if you were focused in the present moment while visiting Dr. Dudai's lab you might see the snake just sitting in its box sampling the smell of the lab with a flicking tongue, lethargically swaying its head side to side, perhaps contentedly ready to curl up and take a nap. But this is where your subconscious will try to play a trick on you again— you've got to be ready for it. Your amygdala ignores that present reality because it already saw the deadly-looking snake ready to strike out in an instant, imagining razor-sharp fangs that will pierce deep to your nervous system, instantly killing you as it spits fire and snorts smoke. That instinctual fear fuels your imagination and commands you to take flight action and get as far away as possible. Your subconscious limbic survival network places a much higher probability on death by snake than actually exists because that instinctual fear is hardwired in your brain; because you are uncertain how this might happen you produce free energy and feel the fear. In essence, your body involuntary gets you (or the snake) away. Survival trumps courage and your control over the amygdala has been lost. That's cowardice in action. You are trying to flush out free

WHY COURAGE IS SEXY

Biologically there are significant differences between men and women; that's just a fact of how we are made. Those variances affect the chemical changes in our mind during an amygdala hijacking. In 1988 researchers found that men enjoyed a horror film more if they were with a female companion who showed distress during the film. Conversely, the women said they enjoyed the film more if their male companion stayed calm and unmoved.

The real reason, however, you guys should ask your next date to a horror movie is because men who showed courage during a horror film were rated as more attractive than men who didn't show courage. Want to be seen more like Cruise and less like DeVito? Take your next date to a scary movie and stay cool![1]

Note

1. G. G. Sparks, "The Relationship between Distress and Delight in Males' and Females' Reactions to Frightening Films," *Human Communication Research* 17, no. 4 (1991), 625–37.

energy by getting back to a known safe state. Can you remember a time when your amygdala created an imaginary reality that caused you to act like a wimp, and later you realized how ridiculous your behavior was? It's not all about the amygdala, however.

When the amygdala takes charge of the nervous system and hijacks the working memory, it factors in sensory inputs like items on a Chinese buffet; however, it selectively uses whatever information it thinks it needs to keep you alive. If it smells smoke, for instance, it will often ignore other less important data and just focus on that threat.

When Dudai and his team analyzed the brains of those courageous subjects who brought the snake closer to themselves, they saw the amygdala switch off and noticed significant activity in the sgACC. The sgACC is one of the emotional seats of our brain; it's so powerful, in fact, that people with severe depression can be helped just by stimulating the sgACC to improve the neurological connection to the rest of their brain.[7] When suicidal patients receive an increase in the functional connectivity from the sgACC to other parts of the brain (the communication lines improved) they report feeling less helpless and more courageous and in control. The sgACC is also the foundation of the network that helps process big risk and reward along with emotions. Think of it as the hub that connects the various emotional spokes in your mind.

The implication for your own courage journey is that anyone can turn off the amygdala hijacking and instead choose to engage the sgACC. It's like saying no to that pizza and ordering a salad instead. It might be a tougher choice, but it's the better choice in the long run. You can choose to be courageous; all it requires is a belief that you can do it. The more self-confidence you have, the easier it is to choose courage. That is the only thing that separates courageous people from your once-wimpy author who fled from the Pentagon.

When you make the choice to be courageous, you start a process in your brain that takes energy. By activating and using all the action potential between neurons and synapses within the various sgACC networks, you exhibit courage. Initially, this takes a lot of energy—like choosing a salad for the first time instead of the pizza. The laws of physics tell us that any living being wants to use as little energy as possible to function, and if more energy is needed the organism doesn't like it. This means Fast Courage is possible when you decide, but because the activity connected between the sgACC, the amygdala, the sensory gathering and learning networks (like the basal ganglia) is so new and unused it takes a lot of energy to be courageous the first few times. There is also an entire wireless network of communication that must coordinate all of this and hum across the specific regions of your brain to enable this communication. There are no shortcuts and it's not easy, but it's simple to decide to be brave.

Fast Courage is a rare occurrence because it doesn't happen often so the courage networks are not accustomed to firing together. They certainly haven't been wired together yet. Flight, running away, may be your default when it comes to standing up for yourself at work, avoiding speaking in public, taking a trip to a strange place, going to the doctor, or even flying (like me). People often combat these weaknesses with "liquid courage." It took me four or five beers to become lubricated enough to drag myself onto a plane before I decided to be brave, and before I found my superpower of courage. Even if you are afraid to fly, can't ask a girl out, or run from a spider, one day you may see a stranger with a flat tire on the shoulder of a dangerous highway and put yourself at risk to help him out and execute one single, courageous act. That's Fast Courage that happened because of empathy and altruism; it takes many more actions like that to wire your courage network together into Slow Courage. If the neural networks aren't yet wired together it takes an extraordinary amount of energy to make them fire together. That's why long-lasting courage takes practice, confidence, and belief to become the default. Those are the ingredients of Slow Courage and becoming a courageous person and changing your life. Just like the people in the snake study, you can make the choice to become courageous and it literally turns on a new part of your brain and shuts off the amygdala.

The way to engage the sgACC and to increase courage is to increase the connectivity to that network within the brain. Because of neuroplasticity our brains can change at any age. Remember that we can construct the brain's equivalent of a hyperloop between areas that we use a lot to make those actions more efficient. Courage, like other specific knowledge, can be grown, and the part of your brain that it requires will grow along with it. Neuroplasticity proves that any neural network that fires together enough will wire together.

One of the early breakthrough proofs of neuroplasticity was when researchers from the University College London scanned the brains of seventy-nine would-be London taxi drivers who were attempting to memorize every street in London to pass their taxi driver license test (some of them had to take the test twelve times to pass, and in the end only half actually were able to commit all 25,000 streets to memory and pass). The researchers (using an imaging technique called voxel-based morphometry developed by the author of Free Energy Principle, Karl Friston) found that the subjects' hippocampus area was significantly larger than the thirty-one control subjects, who were of a similar age group and demographic but not studying to take the exam. While the successful taxi drivers did indeed create more grey matter in their brains via neuroplasticity (they were not born that way), once they retired and no longer needed to use that road information daily, the hippocampus eventually shrunk back to normal. The hippocampus does a lot of things in the mind; to streamline our discussion say it handles directions and maps. The equivalent area for courage is the sgACC—so if you want true lasting courage, something that may allow you to, by choice, put your very existence on the line, then you need to train that sgACC. That's Slow Courage. There's no hack for that. I can't tell you a shortcut, there's no courage pill—like one of the most courageous men of our generation, Arnold Schwarzenegger, has always said, to get good at anything worthwhile takes repetitions; reps, reps, reps. So you need to practice being courageous. The good news is that deciding to pick up the phone and call someone you've been avoiding, speaking up at a meeting, refusing that piece of pizza, getting on a plane alone to a strange place, or jumping in the water all can be courageous acts with great results. While *The Wizard of Oz* was just a movie, the world is full of Good Witches like Glinda and evil Wicked Witches of the West. Anyone, good or evil, can use the same principles to make courage one of their superpowers, and realize what the Lion figured

A VERY SPARTAN SWIM

After leg four of a six-part adventure race on Nantucket Island, Joe DeSena dropped a forty-pound sandbag he had just humped several miles down a sandy beach. He was supposed to tag his partner, who would swim across the inlet toward the finish. As he came into the transition area other swimmers were hesitating and saying "no way— if they spotted a shark, I'm not going in." DeSena, terrified of sharks since seeing the movie *Jaws* as a child, passed his partner and jumped into the water.

DeSena was a successful Wall Street stock trader who took his life savings and started a series of obstacle course races designed to push people out of their comfort zone. This led to the wildly popular Spartan Races. DeSena finds courage by not giving himself time to flinch when he feels his fear tells trying to take control. Every time he senses fear creeping in, he has a commitment to lean into that fear and (assuming there isn't a very high probability of death) do that thing that made him scared. He says facing his fears always leads to great outcomes.

That race in Nantucket, facing his fear of sharks and using that fear as fuel for his swim, led to one the most important discoveries of his life. On the other side of the beach, when he finally made landfall he met a beautiful competitor. Soon they were on a date. It wasn't long before she became Joe's wife; the woman he calls Supermom. She was literally on the other side of his fears and has been the best part of his life for sixteen years. As DeSena told me, "I just had to get past the sharks to get the prize—which is almost always the case in life—it's where the magic happens."

out at the end of the movie – your capacity for courage is already there, you just need to decide to use it.

"Our results propose . . . the ability to carry out a voluntary action opposite to that promoted by ongoing fear, namely courage," Dr. Dudai said during an interview after his study in 2010. "Specifically, our findings delineate the importance of maintaining high sgACC activity in successful efforts to overcome ongoing fear and point to the possibility of manipulating sgACC activity in therapeutic intervention [or training] in disorders involving a failure to overcome fear."[8]

What that means to you is that if you practice finding fear as often as you can, and learn how to keep making opportunity-based decisions using that fear as fuel, you will engage your sgACC. The opposite is also true; if you succumb to fear and run away you close the connection to the sgACC. It's almost as if the sgACC can use the same free energy your amygdala uses, but to fuel courage. The trick is to believe that the expected outcome can be good and courage can be activated. Every time you face your fear, imagine a small LED path lighting up just behind your eyes where the courage center is located. Soon you will enjoy the changes in your body, embrace the butterflies in your stomach, get excited about the dry mouth and sweaty palms, and use fear as fuel. The more you can light that path up, the more the neurons will wire together and the easier it becomes to be courageous each time you are faced with a frightening choice. The neurons that fire together soon enough will wire together and you will learn slow courage, just like one of the most famous woman aviators of all time.

5.

Now it's your turn to commit to finding courage. Tell yourself "I will find courage every day. When I wake up in the morning, I am going to tell myself to be courageous today." It helps if you can look at yourself from afar, as if you were watching a movie of your day—and then coach yourself along the way. Teddy Roosevelt said to first imagine yourself being courageous to see what it would look like, then try to act out that image. Self-talk is one of the best ways to do it. You can talk positively to yourself, and once you understand the neuroscience behind it you've got the tools to literally control your own mind.

Take the opportunity to add courage to your morning routine. If you shower, shave, or get dressed in front of the same mirror every day, put a small note with the word "Courage" on it so you'll be able to lock your courage reminder in with a morning routine. Your life will change dramatically from today forward if you lock in courage in your life.

What will develop if you commit to courage is a gradual change in your actions. First, you'll notice a modification in your decision making. Second, you will note a difference in your confidence. Third, people will start to say they have noticed a change in you.

You make a decision in one of two ways—out of fear or out of opportunity. Fear-based decisions almost always lead to regret. Your decision making can be raised to a much higher level; you don't have to be Bill Gates or Albert Einstein to make smart choices. Great leaders and athletes are a product of their choices in life. Make every choice based on opportunity and accept whatever comes your way. Observing the situation and choosing opportunity will create a courageous mind and your neurons and synapses will change because you train that path to the sgACC and the wireless mesh that directs your neurological traffic that way. You can make faster, bolder, and more effective choices.

The term "analysis paralysis" illustrates a fear-based weakness and a by-product of fear-based decision making that plagues many people. Analysis paralysis, the inability to be decisive, is driven by the fear of making the wrong decisions, fear of failure, fear of judgment—there are many reasons, but if you have enough information and don't act then a fear or dread is at the root of your indecisiveness. Learning bravery will dramatically increase your certainty, and the outcome of every decision can be a breakthrough learning moment. Because you are deciding with courage, the choices come faster and allow you to learn more information with each new decision. Compared to the old you who might be stuck in the paralysis of choices and take days to decide something, the new you can act quickly and courageously and can gain more information and learn with each selection.

Being certain and confident drives grit and perseverance, too. Perseverance in turn makes you more confident. In her book, *Grit*, Angela Duckworth showed that people who don't quit, who keep trying, are significantly more successful than their more intelligent counterparts who give up.[9] A primary reason people give up is fear.

They are fearful that they will fail, they are fearful that they will lose what they already have, they are afraid of rejection for doing something different. They are fearful that they will go beyond what their family or peer group has told them is their limit. If you find the courage to keep making decisions out of opportunity, keep learning from your failures, and not succumb to fear, then you will become a great leader within your company, your communities, and your world.

Courage is one of the greatest predictors of success in life, principally because it is the foundation for doing innovative things, trying untested solutions, risking failures, and creating great triumphs. You need courage to take risks. As Teddy Roosevelt so famously preached, the ability to courageously stave off nay-sayers and spur yourself on through failure and defeat is what ensures that your fate will never be with those timid souls who know neither victory nor defeat. If you cultivate courage and use fear as fuel you will be able to confront all of the challenges life has to offer. If you don't cultivate courage you open yourself to being manipulated by marketers, politicians, peers, and competitors who use fear to manipulate and influence your actions.

It's easy to think that people like Abraham Lincoln, Neil Armstrong, Christopher Columbus, Charles Lindbergh, and Beryl Markham (who you are about to read about) were all extraordinary people cut from a different cloth than you and I were, but they were not. They were ordinary people, and in fact it wasn't until many of them had nothing to lose that they became courageous. When Nelson Mandela was shipped off to Robben Island, he lost everything including his right to look up and see a blue sky or hear a chirping bird; he lost everything, that is, except his cause and his belief that men deserve equality. That is the final key to courage; in order to truly be able to rid yourself of fear-based decisions you have to have something beyond yourself as a motivating cause.

Accountability is an easy way to track your courage and altruism. At our house we have a list on our refrigerator for all the actions our three teenagers do; the left column is good karma points, the right column is bad karma points, and all of their rewards (new phones, sleep-overs, new hockey sticks) are based on the ratio of good to bad. This system of tracking altruism has had a dramatic effect on the lives of our children. If you don't have a mentor or someone who can act as a courage coach and keep you accountable in your daily life, then you need to find one.

You can even find guidance in your imagination. Pick a hero or a set of heroes that you can bring to life. After I recovered from leukemia and was back to the RFID company I founded, people noticed a dramatic change. The courage halo effect was arching over everything I did. Employees and customers both noticed the change in me and several said something. When they did I told them it came from my meetings with Teddy and George. When I was recovering from leukemia, I read dozens of books but a few that stood out for me were about Teddy Roosevelt and George Patton—so much so that I began to read as much about the two men as I could get my hands on. On my drive in to work each morning I'd go over the tasks and challenges of the day, and I'd pretend that I had one of those great leaders sitting next to me. I'd play out different situations in my head, I'd recount military strategy and try to apply it opportunistically to our business conundrums. My decisiveness grew and I would often remind myself that a "good plan violently executed right now is far better than a perfect plan executed next week," as Patton was famous for saying. I began to see that in accepting and welcoming these challenges I was getting a much bigger sense of victory and success in the present. It wasn't about the big exit or sale as it had been; rather it was about success in the present and being in the arena, as Roosevelt's "Strenuous Life" essay so eloquently puts it. I was having fun doing the same thing that had made me miserable. I also had a clearer vision for balance in my life because of this courage.

Eventually, if you are thoughtful about your choices, when you come to make a choice you will engage both hemispheres of your brain. If you practice enough conscious courageous decision making a choice can become your cue to let a habit take over. The cue tells your brain to use the courage pathway to the sgACC to make this decision to the best of your ability. You get excited, your amygdala activates, but doesn't control the prefrontal cortex and your brain goes into the routine. The routine you will have formed is defining the fear-based choices and the opportunity-based choices and then picking one of the opportunity-based choices. This becomes your fix. Courage becomes a habit.

This habitual neuroscience all relies on a golf ball–sized area of the brain called the basal ganglia. When you've wired the brain into a habit then things work on autopilot. The basal ganglia offloads the action from the prefrontal cortex (where you have to consciously think about doing something) and you can execute the act of courage without having to toil over it. When you make courage a habit, the choices you make in life will start to seem lucky. If you are open to it and you practice courage, the universe will become a very friendly place and good things will happen spontaneously, just as a little girl from England found out in the remotest stretches of Africa.

6.

On the horizon the faintest dot of orange dissolved a hole in the African darkness. Beryl Markham squeezed her eyes shut tight, making seams in her leathery face and then popped them wide open in what someone might think was a look of shocked amazement, all in an effort to clear her tired eyes of any illusions of the mining camp. As she flew on, and gradually saw another orange speck, then another, she realized they weren't glimmers of African fireflies but rather the mining camp she had feared she might never find. She sucked in her first full breath of the cool night air in what seemed like forever and let her shoulders drop and jaw relax. She would soon be safe. The primitive orange torches glowed like two rows of neatly lined embers pulled from a fire. Three hundred feet above those life-guiding lights, the plane circled the dry and dusty strip of land bordered by the twenty or so lanterns on each side. A single buffalo, a kudu, or even a hyena could mean certain death for the pilot and the plane as it settled out of the ink-black sky, so a reconnoiter flyby was the first order of business. On the second circle around, the natives on the ground watched slack-jawed as the plane dove toward the end of the makeshift runway, and suddenly pulled up, as if following the line of God's own hockey stick. The silence of the Serengeti night was broken by the boisterous engine wheezing its relief as the Avian rolled to a stop.

As the pilot pulled off a hat and goggle combination, her long hair cascaded like a waterfall across her shoulders. It was 1942 and Beryl Markham was trying to save a man's life by bringing a bottle of oxygen from Nairobi, Kenya, to this remote mining camp three hundred miles south. The cry for help had been sent by foot thirty hours earlier and Markham, knowing all the dangers of flying on a moonless night over Africa with a single-engine plane, decided to take off anyway. That choice, one made not out of fear but rather out of the opportunity of saving a stranger's life, was an altruistic decision that had become an ingrained habit for a girl who had developed that kind of lasting courage as a child, that made her one of the most famous women of her era, despite living thousands of miles away from the typical limelight.

Markham's life was a wonderful example of how a timid, "proper" girl from the English aristocracy could slowly develop an incredible level of courage and use it not only to set world records and many "world firsts" but also to become a courageous and fulfilled person living her passion even while wading in a sea of machismo devoid of any other women in colonial east Africa. In her beautifully written autobiography (in my top twenty-five book list) called *West With the Night*, Markham tells her tale of growing up in East Africa,[10] and shares incredible stories that when pieced together make the perfect tapestry for learning to be courageous. She exudes extraordinary courage in her ability to break down barriers, go against long-standing traditions, and set new standards. Beryl learned how to channel her fear into fuel, and then she learned to call upon courage whenever she needed it. If you want to know the details of how she created courage, follow the steps in chapter 11.

9

~

Share Together
or Fear Apart

Let us not emphasize all on which we differ but all we have in common.
Let us consider not what we fear separately but what we share together.

—John F. Kennedy

Clouds of dust swirled around naked legs as peasants in worn dark togas swarmed through the market. Floating from columns of shadow into rods of sunshine, the dust particles glittered amid people and produce. The wheels and legs of a sturdy wooden cart sat among animals, excrement, and food. Cattle, chickens, and sheep cried above voices of vendors, creating a cacophony of market sounds. Two boys scrambled behind their father. Each boy carried a small lamb close to his chest. Both balls of fluff baaaed up at a mother ewe held across the father's broad shoulders, his right hand gripping both front legs to his chest and his left hand clutching the rear legs against his other breast. Suddenly the father dropped to a knee and gushed reverent words of thanks to a man who looked, by all outward appearances, to be a peasant. He had the sturdy build of someone who worked the fields, and a roadwork of veins mapped across his forearms; the sinewy lines of his shoulder muscles rippled as he adjusted his plain toga pulla, the normal attire of a common laborer. He smiled down at the genuflecting father. His bare feet and muscled calves were caked with the golden-grey dust eddying around the marketplace. The father bowing to this common-looking man was thanking the senator for saving his family farm. The senator was Marcus Porcius Cato Uticensis, simply known as Cato the Younger. Cato saved the man's farm after a local territorial battle. Most other leaders at that time in Rome would have kept it as a spoil to be plied for political favor or given the farm to their soldiers. Cato believed that commandeering property as a spoil was wrong. He knew corruption and that sort of greed were ruining the Roman Republic.

Near the end of the Roman Republic, the only enemy of Julius Caesar whom Caesar refused to pardon was Cato. Cato lived by a philosophy called Stoicism, which meant putting his virtue and morals above all else, including his own life. He fought for what was right, just, and often unpopular. His adherence to a code of courage and righteousness made him an anomaly among men at this stage of the Roman Republic. These same qualities and his honorable death made him the inspiration for the most powerful nation of all time.

Cato overcame the root of all fears and realized that courage was the key to a life well lived. He was able to cultivate such a strong mental fortitude that not even one of the most powerful men to ever live, Julius Caesar, could influence him with fear or threats. The fact that Cato was able to learn the kind of courage that made him impervious to political influence, impervious to outside pressure, gives hope to all of us in a modern age where the principal weapon of politicians is fear. Not surprisingly, anxiety effects at least 25 percent of our population.

Fear as a political tool certainly wasn't exclusive to the Roman Republic. In the United States, we may have perfected fear as a political tool in the past twenty-five years, but we are certainly not alone. That's no way to live. In fact, our founding fathers envisioned a republic that stood for something more, a nation cultivating similar ideals to those that Cato was willing to die for. If you don't think you are up to Cato's standard, think again; we all have it in us. It's a choice we can make.

If we go back to that Roman marketplace you might wonder why Cato the senator looked indistinguishable from a common laborer, and why he eschewed the colorful and pretentious robes of his station. He did so because he wanted to experience the worst-case scenario. Treading along barefoot, instead of wearing the ornate leather footwear the aristocracy flaunted, helped him imagine what it would be like if he lost his wealth and prestige. He wanted to know what it would feel like to lose everything, to become a common soldier or peasant, so that as he made choices in the Senate his actions would not be influenced by fear of losing his wealth or status. Limiting free energy was not his goal most likely, but that was the outcome. He wanted to know what it felt like to be a soldier, a commoner, a farmer, and live the bad outcome. It helped him take risks. He added another perspective to orient himself in the world.

What you have right now in your cranium is biologically the exact same things as Cato, except perhaps for well-defined values and a sense of purpose. It's up to each of us to lead a life of virtue and set an example for the rest of the world. It's a choice. First, you need to define your values; integrity, honor, valor, independence, duty, curiosity, selflessness, and loyalty are a few that might be important to you. Second, you must commit to courage, which means never giving up, staying resilient.

Living by the virtue of courage like Cato could be a single choice that dramatically impacts the rest of your life—it drives happiness, health, and longevity. Cato wasn't alone; countless other people have taken the Stoics' ideals and used them to change the world; they did this by sharing the philosophy together, and triumphing over their separate fears.

George Washington, our nation's premier founding father, lived by the philosophy of Stoicism and its high moral standard in an effort to create a harmonious life. Washington, despite never attending college, studied philosophy. Many Washingtonian scholars believe that because of his relationship with his wealthy neighbor, Lord

THE SECRET BEHIND WASHINGTON'S LONG, COURAGEOUS LIFE

George Washington was one of the most courageous men in history—putting his life on the line and fighting against all odds to create a new nation. He was living in an era when the average life expectancy was thirty-six years.

Despite harsh wartime conditions, horrific battles, and barbaric medical practices, Washington lived to the ripe old age of sixty-seven. One reason he lived so long, according to the latest research, is that he was courageous. Courage is highly correlated to psychological well-being, happiness, and longevity. In addition to living a better life, if you choose courage you'll have more time to enjoy it!

Fairfax, he had access to a nearly unlimited supply of books and plays. His favorite play was Joseph Addison's *Cato: Liberty on the Stage*. Washington even used Cato's story to turn the tide of the war for independence, just when the patriots needed it most.

The frigid campaign at Valley Forge drove Washington's troops to the point of desperation. Yet the new nation's existence hinged on victory. Over the long winter 2,500 of his 12,000 troops died of exposure. It was at the end of that struggle, with good men dying like dogs left in the cold, when Washington ordered his favorite play, *Cato*, to be performed for the troops. It was an unusual choice to many who initially learn that in the play (and in his life) Cato stoically falls on his sword during the battle of Utica rather than surrender and compromise his political ideals and virtues to live under Julius Caesar. The tragedy is that he learns, just before he dies, that a fleet of allied reinforcements arrived at Utica and that "were Cato at their head, once more might Rome assert her rights, and claim her liberty."[1] Instead Caesar consolidated power and created a tainted empire where once stood a proud republic. Washington's troops got the message. The soldiers kept fighting in the face of death, because they knew they had something worth fighting for. They fought in horrendous conditions. They lived and died, never giving up until reinforcements could arrive and they could take the day. Then they did.

Valley Forge was the tip of an influential iceberg that Cato's legacy calved as the most powerful nation of all time was formed, the United States of America. In phrases that every US schoolchild learns early on in history class, Cato's influence resounds:

- "Give me liberty or give me death!" shouted Patrick Henry in a famous address at the Second Virginia Convention in 1775. His inspiration likely was Addison's play: Act II, Scene 4: *"It is not now time to talk of aught/But chains or conquest, liberty or death."*
- "I only regret that I have but one life to give for my country": the last words of Nathan Hale, a US patriot who was hanged on September 22, 1776, by the British for being a spy. From Addison's play: Act IV, Scene 4: *"What a pity it is/That we can die but once to serve our country."*

Principle is power. A single principled person can be the inspiration for an entire nation, an entire company, or even a neighborhood.

Cato chose to die, in a gut-wrenching way, rather than live under a tyrant. His principles gave him the courage to take his own life. His strength was the inspiration for the founding fathers of the United States, and countless others.

Cato well knew the inevitability of death, that every person's life ends the same way. It is how he lived and how he died that created a life well lived. If you truly love the feeling of freedom, of courage and confidence, and realize it is power, and it was a state your old self only achieved occasionally, then you have the chance to change your life. Abandon your old self for a new, more powerful you. Learning and adopting just three primary ideals can change your brain and change your life. Spending a few minutes each morning contemplating three things can set every day up for a day that fills you with power, because of your principles.

Cato's ideals of living have faded in recent generations; their disappearance has allowed the birth of a US political system that continues to have a bigger and more devastating wedge driven between the two parties. Gone is the connection between parties that courageously allowed for understanding and compromise. Gone is the collaborative nature that allowed for progress. Each of you has the power to change not just your life, but the world as well. It starts with one person. It starts with principles.

Here are three very simple ideals. They are not easy to adopt. One reason these are the most powerful of virtues is that all three are grounded in recent scientific research. They take practice and actually will change the structure of the brain. Neuroscience provides evidence that these behaviors can literally alter the biology in your mind. Changing from your old self to a new, powerful you takes practice, discipline, and a trust that acting with virtue results in a long-term, fulfilling life. There is no doubt the philosophy works if you make it a habit to practice. Start your day with the following three actions:

Prepare for the worst, love your neighbor, and imagine your death.

Those are three cornerstones of Cato's philosophy that can change your life. Only in the last five years has neuroscience demonstrated why doing those three actions make people happier, more fulfilled, and more successful than people who do not adopt those same practices. After a few weeks of implementing this morning routine, you

JUST THREE DAYS TO THRIVE

Think you can change your life in just three days? You can with the right approach. The sgACC is a primary brain region responsible for courage and emotion. The amygdala and limbic network can override the sgACC and obliterate feelings of courage if the uncertainty, or free energy, exceeds our capacity to imagine the outcome. So you need to imagine more! Like other parts of the brain, the sgACC is trainable. Premeditation of evil, visualization, and even just relaxing meditation all can start to change the wiring of your brain in just three days.

A 2015 study by Dr. Adrienne Taren at the University of Pittsburgh proved "mindfulness meditation training promotes functional neuroplastic changes, suggesting an amygdala-sgACC pathway for stress reduction effects." In just three days.

The study had a control group relax for three days and the study group practice mindfulness meditation. The subjects sat down every morning meditating on the worst things to happen in their day and how they can learn from everything they face, even just for a few days. It changed their lives and can change yours, especially if you make it part of a daily routine.

will notice that you're making radically better choices in your life, because fear is less and less of a motivator. You can stop reacting, and you don't have to feel powerless ever again.

Important Message for Chronic Depression and Anxiety Patients: The three practices based on Stoic philosophy should not be adopted by persons diagnosed with general anxiety disorder, social anxiety disorder, or certain phobias. The requirement for adopting these three actions is that you have a firm grasp of what you can control and what you cannot control. If you have significant difficulty letting go of things you cannot control and envision nothing but negativity and disaster in the future, you should seek therapeutic assistance before starting the routine presented here.

Visualization, simply sitting and imagining the future and seeing the worst case, was what Stoics called Premeditatio Malorum, the premeditation of evil. Cato took it one step further and lived it out by wearing a laborer's clothing in public. The Stoics believed that courage was one of the four primary virtues every person should cultivate (the other three were wisdom, morality, and moderation). Their way of building courage was to plan for the worst-case scenario, and actually see it happening in their mind. They would sit quietly, breathe deeply, and try to imagine a future where everything went terribly wrong, and then see themselves responding courageously in that situation, acting on what they could control. This visualization was how Stoics trained to be brave. In order to act with valor, they imagined the worst possible outcomes to any given scenario. With the worst image in mind, they methodically imagined each different outcome and how they would mitigate the negative. If you are a modern-day Stoic, sit for fifteen or twenty minutes in the morning and imagine your PowerPoint slides having a font that didn't load on your host computer, the client saying he or she just saw a better version of what you are selling, or your key employee coming in and telling you he wants to code naked at his cubicle. Then imagine how you will deal with the scenarios that pop up today.

I didn't realize it at the time, but the US Olympic psychologists had me doing Premeditatio Malorum for my regattas. I started out just imagining the race, then things progressively became more challenging. The visualization they led me through, picturing my rowing races, where my boat was swamped by a wake or I hit a buoy, is why eventually nothing came as a surprise to me on the water. I went from having a limited database of prior beliefs to a much more encompassing perspective; this nearly eliminated the possibility of creating free energy during a race because nothing could surprise me short of the Loch Ness Monster rearing up to swallow a competitor. The visualization training is how I embraced the fear of competition and turned it into excitement. It's how I kept my cool on the racecourse and evaluated my options with lightning speed. Having the power of knowing you can imagine every possible scenario allows you great freedom, because you can make any choice you want without hesitation. Remember, there are only two ways to make a decision: out of fear or out of opportunity. Fear-based decisions almost always lead to regret. Opportunity-based decisions lead to growth.

After I got out of Hopkins and beat leukemia, I truly felt the truth that we never know when death will come knocking. Seeing my own death right at that moment made me feel that I had many things to say to many people. I hadn't said them because I was afraid. I decided to overcome that fear of vulnerability. I started imagining every time I travel, or even leave the house, that it was the last time I would see my wife. When I see my parents, I ask myself what if they die today, have I thanked them for everything, do I have anything I want to say to them? If one of my kids were suddenly kidnapped, am I confident I have let them know how I feel? If I die this afternoon do I want to spend the day with someone who complains all the time or is constantly a victim? Thinking about bad outcomes throughout the day is a simple adoption of premeditating the worst, and it's a quick way to build courage to overcome internal fears like rejection or abandonment.

If you meditated on every possible bad outcome before big, scary decisions like quitting your job to start a company, or getting married, or writing a book, you can eliminate fear-based decisions because you will have a plan for all outcomes. If you consider the worst aftermath of your current dilemma, you can also think about what you'd do after that happened, and after the next result, and the next. The more layers of choice and outcomes you can work through in your mind (or on paper), the more power you will have over your actions and the more you will be free to make a brave choice. The key to courage, as you will soon realize, is taking away the surprise and uncertainty.

Cato continuously acted with courage, and what he learned as he meditated on the worst and acted with courage was that seldom, if ever, did his worst nightmares come true. The reason he acted with courage was his drive and passion—he put the highest value on exemplifying honor and virtue. Cato valued bravery above wealth and his purpose was to lead the people of Rome fairly. With a family history that rose and fell like a spring tide, it would have been easy for him to stay stuck in the past, complaining about this event or that. He never did. He knew ruminating on regrets of the past only creates suffering in the present.

How often do you fret over things that have already happened? How often do you worry about things in the future? Cato seldom worried about building tomorrow's legacy; he focused on being the most virtuous version of himself in the present. He made sure he lived fully and died honorably.

Premeditatio Malorum and the act of premeditating horrible outcomes is effective because it leverages neuroscience. It helps you hack the root of all fear using the anxiety networks within the brain. The mind's primary goal is to eliminate prediction error (neuroscientists call it PEM for prediction error minimization). Our mind doesn't like surprises; anything unexpected is seen as a threat to survival. Threats elicit the fight, flight, or freeze response and will force us into fear-based actions. Our mind's goal is to minimize the difference between its *predictions* about the sensory input and the *actual* sensory input. That chasm between your expectations and your sensory input is called Free Energy, which is the root of all fear I covered in detail in chapter 4.

Fear inhibits sympathy. Sympathy provides great information and Stoics practiced understanding the way others feel; they understood sympathy and its value in society. Marcus Aurelius said in his meditations,

> *Accept the things to which fate binds you, and love the people with whom fate brings you together, but do so with all your heart.*

If you love the people around you with all your heart, you will find that courage comes with much less thought and self-pity is left for those who waste their precious time worrying. If you accept fate and love in the present there is no room for worry. This takes courage.

Sympathy and empathy, while different, both get the wave of cranial energy firing toward the courage center in the sgACC. Imagine walking out your front door and seeing flames lashing out of a second-story window in a neighbor's house, and then hearing a scream. If we can imagine what it would be like to be a small child, or our small child, suffocating in a sea of thick smoke, helpless to her fate, we would be more likely to act courageously to save that child. Engaging our imagination in that way activates a neurological network that can override the amygdala's default self-preservation settings.

Every time you imagine doing courageous actions, you will slowly change the wiring in your brain. This change is neuroplasticity. It's what allows London cabbies to famously learn the city's 25,000 streets that make up "The Knowledge." When studying to pass their qualification exam, the successful candidates actually increase part of their gray matter. They need so many neurons to fire together that they wire together entire new sections of brain. If courage rather than geographical prowess is your goal you must keep wiring the courage networks together, keep using them, keep engaging the sgACC, the network responsible for courage. But first you need to build the road to courage.

When Israeli neuroscientist Dr. Yadin Dudai recruited people who were afraid of snakes and then put the subjects in an MRI, they had a choice. They could wait and see what happened (be courageous) or they could give in and let fear win (push the button that moved the snake farther away). No one can make you courageous; no one can give you confidence. You have to find it yourself. Once you do, you must keep finding it, over and over again until it becomes a default. It's simple, but not easy. It's a choice.

Understanding how someone feels and sharing their pain can help you be more courageous. The Stoic philosophers from 300 BC knew this neuroscience secret though it wasn't proven until 2015 by Dr. Abigail Marsh and her team at Georgetown University. Sympathy fuels courage. That courage comes after you make a choice. You don't have to be a coward. Cowardice is simply a higher value placed on self-preservation than on a loftier, external motivation such as virtue or sympathy. Sympathy or empathy and understanding how others are suffering can help you build courage.

What happens to someone behaving cowardly is that their current existence is too far removed from their expectation of reality, or simply what they're accustomed to. This new, unexpected state of being activates the limbic system, specifically the amygdala, to flee or fight, to get things back within expectations. Your body wants to eliminate the Free Energy that going outside expectations created. What happened to me on 9/11 when I turned off the George Washington Parkway after trying to rationalize the mushroom cloud that sprouted up a mile in front of me at the Pentagon was a lot of free energy. My future vision of reality had no expectation of a bomb in it, or a plane, or an attack, so when it happened I was stunned into a stupor. The free energy gap was massive. Having never practiced dealing with a gap in prediction error like that, my only reaction was to flee in terror. The fleeing was trying to get my reality back to the range where I expected it to be. With enough training anyone can stop free energy from creating a cowardly reaction; then if you feel what other people are experiencing, and can share their suffering, it will even help your brain to route the current thought toward a courageous network instead of your fear network. However, there is a catch—you must choose to act and to assess the situation first.

When the amygdala hijacks the working memory, it bypasses conscious thought. People who are not used to that physiological state of fear (scientifically called arousal) may not realize that they can take control consciously of the working memory. This is using our volition or will power. If I had stopped to think about the people suffering at the Pentagon, I might have taken a different course of action. If I could see people in pain, feel them suffering, and witness their courage I might have chosen a more noble path, because my brain would have released dopamine and made a connection to my sgACC—the courage network. If prior to that point I had scared myself more often I would have been comfortable with that discomfort. If I consciously took my working memory back, I could have thought about the people who needed help.

Dr. George Bonanno from Columbia University has done groundbreaking research on resilience that proved nearly everyone has the tools to learn courage and grit. Perseverance, follow-through, and resilience are the building blocks of grit if you have a goal to go after. That means that if you want to become brave, you have to scare yourself often so you can act in the face of fear, then persevere through it. When that network fires together it wires together into long-lasting courage.

Courage can only happen in the presence of fear, and fear comes in three different components that make up the Terror Triangle shown in chapter 2—Instinctual Fears, Physical Fears, and Emotional Fears. If you have adopted the philosophy of this book you will welcome the changes in your biology that take place as your amygdala triggers the fear response (your tells), and you'll take the time to assess the situation and clear out your working memory to take control over your decision making and actions. You'll find that acting with courage is easier in specific areas and more difficult in others, and that's why it's important to keep practicing scaring yourself on all sides of the Terror Triangle. Leaving part of the Terror Triangle unexplored and untrained is like a football player leaving his legs untrained while he lifts weights to strengthen his upper body day in and day out; he'll soon look like a giant light bulb that would topple over with the slightest push because his untrained legs would be so weak. Balance all three types of fear and you'll live big.

The first two principles, Premeditatio Malorum and Sympathy, are easy to implement and conceptually simple to understand. You can start that practice now by going to chapter 6 and following the visualization method I learned at the Olympic Training Center. The last principle, however, is the most challenging, because it is what the father of Stoicism, Epictetus, called the source of cowardice:

> *the source of all human evils, and of mean-spiritedness and cowardice, is not death, but rather the fear of death.*

The last principle is to learn how to die well, to live with the reality that the Angel of Death can demand your body, which she loaned you, to be returned to the earth at any moment. Memento Mori is to think about the pinnacle of evil outcomes—your own death. If you take accountability for your own death, you can never be held prisoner by anyone, and never be a victim at someone else's hand. You can love fully, engage genuinely, and live life to the fullest.

Let's expose a bit of nonsense you've probably heard: if you are scared or have anxiety, go to your "safe place" or "your happy place." The thinking goes that you should imagine someplace that makes you feel safe and happy and everything will be right in the world. If I were giving someone an ideal recipe to create a life of anxiety, depression, and failure, the advice I would give is to pretend problems don't exist or get someone else to deal with them. Maybe I'd suggest you go put on soft music and leave your troubles behind, or spark up a joint and float away into never-never land. From a neurological perspective what you are purposely doing is increasing free energy by not meditating on all possible outcomes. You would actually increase surprise and uncertainty. The bottom line is that reality won't change when you come back from hiding—your deadline will still be there, you'll still be with the same partner, you will be in the same body. The obstacle doesn't move until you learn the lesson it was put there to teach you. Whatever you are running from will always catch back up with you. Increasing free energy, the difference between reality and perception, has the exact opposite effect of making someone feel better, or helping someone act to change the reality. Since free energy is the root of all fear, going to your safe place, not thinking about all possible states of reality, just makes suffering worse. It gives power to fear. It strips courage from you and delays action.

Avoiding anxiety habituates your brain to running away from fear. Soon the simple idea of something fearful, not an actual traumatic event like being fired from a job, but just the thought of being fired, triggers your amygdala into trying to take over. This changes the way you act. When the amygdala tries to take over, you steer a fear-based course of action. Next you get anxious about becoming scared, and of course that causes you to get more anxious and make more fear-based decisions. To make courage-based choices you need to know you can control your thoughts.

The key to practicing control lies in something called volitional control. It means you gain agency over your thoughts when you want to. We can all do this. Volition is the idea that you choose when to act, what to focus on, and how to create a solution. New research from MIT suggests that we control thoughts using wireless pulses to direct traffic in our brains. Dr. Earl Miller at MIT has even gone so far as to redefine the working memory part of the prefrontal cortex as the spot where volition lives and the wireless communication within the brain is how volition is created.[2] You can think of this as our free will being driven by wireless remote control.

There are those who believe that humans have no free will, that we only act upon biologically evolved desires. It's true that simple creatures just react to their environment; animals will move in a reflexive way to stimuli, like cockroaches scurrying away from bright light. Many of the no-free-will zealots point to an experiment done in the 1980s by a scientist named Benjamin Libet. Libet connected subjects to EEG machines that could read brain activity and asked the participants to push a button and say verbally when they decided to push the button. He tried to prove that the mind's subconscious activity was registering on the EEG before the subjects said they decided to push it. His reasoning was that subconsciously he could record an action that they had already decided to push the button and then justified the timing to stay consistent with their thought. However, while subconscious decisions are responsible for 75 percent or more of our daily choices, unquestioned actions only happen because we let them go unquestioned. It's a choice not to choose.

What do you do when you walk into Starbucks? Or when you pull up the Starbucks app? If we stopped to consider wanting whole milk in our coffee, we could make the effort to consciously question our choice and consider alternatives. Why not soy or almond? What about just black? But it's not that important to our happiness and health, so we let the subconscious drive. To say that all choices are made without us knowing it is an oversimplification of how the mind works.

We develop theories or our own ideas about what's going on in the world; that's part of volition. To exercise volition, we must *choose* when to act and what to focus on. When we free up the working memory to consider our choices, we engage cortical mechanisms that create a rhythmic interplay; think of it as a constant humming in your brain. We start wireless waves rolling at the same frequency between different parts of our brain, using energy in big gulps. When we don't choose with thought and exercise our volition, the subconscious stays in charge. The subconscious has a very well-defined map of what our view on the world should be. That view is based on all the things that have gone into our subconscious mind throughout our lifetime. It's the thoughtless ordering of whole milk. One of the most interesting ways that we can prove that everything we take into our subconscious mind affects us is to look at overcoming phobias.

The subconscious mind controls most of our world, but the point of this chapter is that we can control it in many ways, and thereby get as much control over our world as we choose. In a fascinating study led by Dr. Bradley Peterson at the Children's Hospital in Los Angeles, two groups of kids participated in a test to overcome fear of spiders. The researchers had a group of kids who were afraid of spiders and another control group that was not afraid. They had three images put on a screen while the kids were having their brain activity measured in an fMRI machine: first, a one-millisecond exposure of a tarantula that's so quick you wouldn't know it happened; second, a ten-second exposure to the same tarantula; last, a one-millisecond exposure to a flower. The ten-second exposure caused all the kids' brains to react in some manner or another; however, only the kids who were afraid of spiders had brain activity when the one-millisecond, subliminal flash of the tarantula took place. Strangely enough, the researchers found that after the subliminal flash of the spider the kids were less afraid of spiders. The subconscious database added a new item to its database and that item had no negative valence, or negative fearful emotion associated with it, so when the kids' conscious mind retrieved an image of spiders there was less fear than prior to the experience.[3] This is why trying and experiencing new things is so important to our happiness and success; even subconscious data can reduce our free energy.

There are myriad more examples that prove we can be the architects of our desires; we can literally rewrite our subconscious hard drive to make decisions before our conscious mind decides what to do, consciously or in the case of getting over phobias subconsciously. Monks and yogis know that with practice we can control ourselves beyond simple evolutionary desires. Alcoholics who don't drink anymore, prisoners like Bobby Sands who have died in self-imposed hunger strikes, are additional examples of humans who exert dominion over their chemical makeup. We do this through volition and a very complex set of wireless communication. We have the will to live (in most cases), the will to learn and grow wisdom, and the will to create and communicate through language.

Many scientists do not like the idea of a creationist God who gets credit for things, so they refute the possibility that there may be more to conscious existence than we currently know, or more accurately more about humans that we do not have the technology to measure. This myopic view, akin to the greatest minds at the time believing the earth was flat or the sun revolved around the earth, will eventually be disproved when we create the technology to measure an unknown phenomenon like consciousness. Without tools to measure the soul or a self, some scientists have swung far in the opposite direction of curiosity to a place of knowing and judging something that we do not have the technology or equipment to measure. In defending a lifetime of work, they become afraid rather than curiously embracing the possibility of new discovery. No one yet knows where the human soul comes from and where it goes. That doesn't mean we'll never find out. Without the curiosity that a soul can exist and persist outside a body, scientists are only left to determine that existence is just a biological soup, with actions and outcomes determined by chemical interactions. One action that does not always make sense chemically is courage.

Courage usually only occurs naturally in protecting our offspring, seldom in other instances, because it does little to help our genes pass on to the next generation. Courageous behavior often gets an organism (like a human) off balance. History shows that we can build valor and courage—it is not preordained by biological evolution or even epigenetics (traits being passed down by your parents).

The wireless oscillations in our cranium, the brain waves, are what we need to engage to live by Cato's three principles. It's that humming started in the working memory that is correlated with conscious thought and our ability to make choices. For fifty years the focus in studying the brain was on the individual neuron's action potential, one cell's ability to shoot chemicals across the synapses to another cell, enabling communication. Brainwaves didn't fit into that model. The brain oscillations used to be thought of as a by-product of the synapses firing back and forth; like a car's vibration coming off the motor because cylinders are firing up and down, it doesn't do anything; it just happens. In 2018 a team of researchers at MIT proved that the humming of the brain is actually a form of wireless connectivity critical to the communication, not a result of it.[4] This is a wireless communication within our own brain that acts like a traffic cop, directing communication from one network to another. Dr. Earl Miller at MIT believes that volitional control is directed by the humming in our brain—when we want to make a choice and plan for the future we use this wireless network to connect different components within the brain. Different populations of neurons will get into oscillations at the same time at the same frequency; these alliances of humming communication are also constantly shifting within the brain. This humming is how our brain regulates communication.

The connections and waves between the working memory and the amygdala can get stronger and stronger the more you use them, so if you are continually enforcing the "fear-to-anxiety-to-greater fear" loop, those neurons that are always firing together will wire together and you are training yourself to be in a constant state of dread and anxiety; you become a free energy factory. That wave from the bleachers will be in constant movement down the horror highway. That's a recipe for growing cowardice and avoidance. Your flight response takes over and you run to your "safe place." You miss out on the opportunity to solve the problem and build courage. You miss out on life.

Here comes the tough love: If you are under thirty years old you're likely part of a generation that got medals for fourteenth place. By now you may have figured out that no one in the real world cares about fourth, fifth, and certainly not fourteenth place. That might have really scared you when you came to this realization or made you angry and want to fight. What Mom and Dad should have been telling you is that if you're not on the podium, train harder and smarter or find another sport you are better suited for. They were afraid to tell you that your reality didn't match up with your results because reality is something children can't handle. Bullshit.

We all have greatness inside us; usually it takes time to find it. Sometimes it takes even longer to mine it. It's worth the effort because finding your genius and what you are great at will change your life. Unfortunately, many of us are too scared to admit that we suck at a lot of things or are afraid to experiment and look foolish in order to find our true talents. If you knew you were going to die in a month, but always wanted to try skydiving or singing on stage but fear held you back, would you do it? I hope so.

False greatness perpetuated by well-meaning parents or coaches can drop a damp blanket over the flame of excellence and drive youth to give up before they uncover their superpowers. It's better to search for greatness and genius than give in to mediocrity. Never stop searching until you find your calling. Can you imagine if Michael Phelps got a trophy for finishing thirteenth in a lacrosse tournament and went through life thinking he was an award-winning lacrosse player? Thankfully his bad-ass mom and a caring, no BS coach gave him an uncommon dose of tough love, telling him his lacrosse skills were mediocre at best, but as a swimmer he really was special. Now Baltimore can lay claim to the greatest Olympian of all time.

False greatness passed on to help kids feel good is one problem at the root of many anxieties. Eschewing accountability is another. Possibly the toughest part about starting life in this century is being taught to slide your problems across the table to someone else, like pushing away chalky beets at the dinner table. Offloading problems rather than facing them teaches developing minds that there is always a hero to call on when dealing with a tough situation, which increases the free energy when there is no hero available. Many high schools teach kids to deal with a bully by going to someone else who will confront the scoundrel; the victim just needs to report him to the bully-control officer. That is the opposite of facing everything and accepting responsibility.

Looking for someone else to solve your problems is seeing yourself as a victim; if you are a victim, you always need a hero to save you. Then you are giving your free will over to someone else, that person you need to solve your problems. The truth is that you should stand up to bullies, whether they are bullying you or someone else. We create our own destiny. No one can take away your dignity or power without your permission. It really is that simple; it's an individual's responsibility to do the difficult work and accept that there is some pain and suffering required to stop a bigger pain and longer suffering. Parents, teachers, and counselors can provide support and encouragement but if a child is going to shed the soft exoskeleton of a victim and grow the hardened armor of someone who fights for what they believe in, who seeks courage and truth, who produces their own life, they must learn to do the work. Even having painful or scary experiences without a bully present, or without an immediate threat, is critical to developing confident, courageous adults.

Nearly every culture since the beginning of time has had coming-of-age rituals, tests to prove manhood and often womanhood. The mere existence of a coming-of-age ritual teaches courage and accountability; elders want their youth to learn how to tame fear, because there are scary moments in the real world they will eventually have to face alone. Everyone must face daunting challenges at some point, so we have a responsibility as a culture to teach our youth how to best face the truth. Shying away from the truth, and making children feel good in the moment, does them a tremendous disservice. Pushing children out of their comfort zone and building the courage to have curiosity in our behavior is how we can create accountable and confident cultures. Tribal elders in accountable societies know that kids who have learned to face everything and accept responsibility make better citizens, better leaders, better neighbors.

The opposite of teaching courage is teaching avoidance, which can create a loop of fear-induced paralysis. This is one reason that contemplating our own death is so important to living a big life today. If you thought this was your last day on this earth, would you do what you are doing now? If you knew you were going to die next week and leave your children behind, do you know that you have you taught them lessons that will serve them well, or have you tried to just be their friend? Trying to make life as smooth as possible for children is what I call bulldozer parenting, plowing the path as smoothly as possible. It's not just parents who succumb to threats; it's school administrators as well: "I'll sue if you don't take down the climbing rope at gym class, Johnny's overactive pituitary gland made him too heavy to climb it; plus he is scared of heights. With that rope haunting him he doesn't feel adequate or like a part of his class; he dreads gym." The ropes are gone; Johnny believes he is weak because of a pituitary gland, not the double Starbuck's sugarchino he has every day after school or the fact that he doesn't exercise regularly and now he is conditioned to expect Mommy or Daddy to be there when the road gets rough to smooth it over. The World Health Organization says "anxiety disorder" is the single largest health issue the world faces today. There are biological reasons for anxiety in many people—there always have been—however, the recent growth in the diagnosis seems to be due to other influences. I believe parenting style is the area of most impact.

If you ready yourself for anything, even your death can be an event of note, a part of your legacy. Take time now to imagine your death, contemplate the moment of you actually dying. It might be tomorrow; it might be fifty years from tomorrow; we never know. However, to meet death well, understand what you can control and cannot. You are going to die, that is out of your control, but you can control how you act, what you do, and the wisdom you could gain or share out of dying. How you will behave? Recognize that one of your goals in life should be a great death.

One of the best deaths ever recorded was that of Socrates (sounds funny to read doesn't it?). He was sentenced to death for corrupting the youth with radical ideas and forced to drink a cup of deadly hemlock. Witnesses said that Socrates, as he was drinking the poison, was unfazed, happy, and contemplating not hatred for his persecutors but a sense of sympathy that they were misguided. Phaedo remarked, "his mien and his language were so noble in the hour of his death he seemed blessed and without fear."[5] He believed that mortal men could kill him, but never harm him. He was in control of his own death, even though it was at the timing of someone else. Socrates might be too far in the rear-view mirror to hold any real meaning for you, so let's look at another wonderful death.

Steve Jobs was diagnosed with a rare form of pancreatic cancer in 2003. He spent the ensuing eight years before his death living one of the most amazing, impactful lives imaginable. He died among his family and as he was checking out he uttered one phrase three times, as if in a sense of wonderment: "Oh wow, oh wow, oh wow."[6] But he recognized his death after his first bout with cancer and, like Cato, created a courageous life with that knowledge. Jobs delivered a heartfelt commencement speech to the Stanford University graduating class of 2005. He had beaten a first round of cancer just the year before. He offered the graduating class the same advice that Cato,

Socrates, and the Stoics espoused, the same advice you can put to work right now. Along with having sympathy and love for those around you, and contemplating awful outcomes in the future, he advised students to remember your death. Make your choices out of opportunity, not because of fear, and never look back.

> Remembering that I'll be dead soon is the most important tool I've ever encountered to help me make the big choices in life.
>
> Almost everything—all external expectations, all pride, all fear of embarrassment or failure—these things just fall away in the face of death, leaving only what is truly important.
>
> Remembering that you are going to die is the best way I know to avoid the trap of thinking you have something to lose. You are already naked. There is no reason not to follow your heart.

—Steve Jobs, May 2005

10

⌒

The Best Decision
You'll Never Make

The essence of good is a certain kind of reasoned choice.

—Epictetus

1.

Imagine you are Sarah. Your phone just chimed a tweet notification. You open Twitter and see this:

@SarahKSilverman *CUNT*

Sense your immediate reaction to that. How do you feel right now? Let's make it a little more personal, pretend you are a woman who uses Twitter to help your business and to share your life with friends and fans. OK, now replace Sarah Silverman's handle with your name. How does that make you feel? Would you respond to that person, right now? Most people will react with his or her survival instinct and that would be the worst possible choice, because it only uses half of your brain.

Learning how to use both sides of your brain for communication, and how to connect different neural networks, can not only bring you to peak performance but is one of the best weapons we have to fight for peace and love. To prove how powerful this technique can be, let's hear the rest of the Sarah Silverman story.

That was an actual tweet from one of actress and comedian Sarah Silverman's followers. Sarah was in a Twittersphere dialogue about being open to other political points of view. Responding to her tweets, one of her followers, Jeremy Jamrozy, sent that lone obscenity.

In the instant she saw it Silverman had a choice of possible responses (you've probably already thought of several yourself). She could have fought back. But she didn't. She responded with kindness and connected with the man who wrote it. By not reacting negatively, she engaged both hemispheres of her brain and changed her subconscious database, and eventually changed the world.

You can adopt the same technique she used, and if you practice, it will dramatically change you by rebuilding your brain's hard drive. It could help you change the entire world as well, or at least your corner of it.

What did Silverman do that was so powerful? To understand the answer to that, we have to look at what happens in the brain when you are given stimulus (like someone slandering you) and then you are expected to make a response. From a neurological perspective, before you even think consciously about how you feel, your eye's visual receptors already sent the C-word through an area called the basolateral amygdala, where the neurons encode the data and send it to the right hemisphere of your brain to be processed. You can think of this part of the amygdala as the railroad switch sending the thought down either a good track or a bad track. Subconscious evaluation of good or bad happens for different reasons. Eons ago our brain created shortcuts to make the fastest possible reactions to a stimulus: one shortcut routes good things and one shortcut filters bad things without having to think consciously about the choice. Since reality and dogma are different for different tribes, these shortcuts are built based on our life experiences and genealogy. In the days when the wheel was innovative, the amygdala's shortcuts provided life-saving speed.

Why do we have shortcuts that parse out the good from the evil? Because our brain is designed to be as efficient as possible, it wants to stay in an efficient state of homeostasis and conserve energy, yet always be ready for action. Shortcuts make the brain's work easier and optimize us for survival moments. But not for happiness or success.

Imagine when warring tribes were killing each other for survival. A good mental shortcut was a lifesaver. Being able to instantly recognize if someone is in our tribe, and what their expression says about their mood, could possibly keep you from getting a sharp rock upside the head. Knowing from a young age if the red berries or blue berries are good to eat, or if that guy who lives in the giant cave might be great father to your children, were all important things to know quickly when survival was a daily fight. Routing data quickly happens because we subconsciously take in entire situations in an instant. When we see Fido wagging his tail, we see hundreds of things at once—his ears back in a smile and lopping tongue out, corners of the mouth pulled back easily, and so on. We smile too because that visual data your eyes and ears sensed was immediately routed through a series of networks (wireless and wired) to the left side of our brain where positive data are sent (before we can even consciously think of it). The question of data routing to a good side (left) or bad side (right) of the brain had been under debate for the past century. It took a whole bunch of little white mice, the daughter of a French farmer, and the latest technology to prove the theory, however.

I walked into Café Luna in Kendall Square looking for one of the world's brightest neuroscientists. Dr. Anna Beyeler's research was the talk of the brain world, and I descended on MIT in Cambridge, Massachusetts, to find out why. Looking around the near-empty coffee shop I saw a few guys and one impeccably dressed woman, a blue crepe scarf draped around her slender neck; she had long dark hair pulled up in a messy bun. She saw me walk in and flashed a Mona Lisa smile, her bright blue eyes conveying a passion and excitement for life. Not the image I had in mind of a neuroscientist. The daughter of a farmer, Beyeler grew up in rural France and became fascinated with the brain's workings as a young girl. Bucking the conventions of traditional roles (her parents wanted her to be a chef) she confidently worked her way through the University of Bordeaux before being accepted as a postdoctoral student at MIT, where she joined forces with Dr. Kay Tye in the newly emerging field of optogenetics: using light to control and track neurons. She loves mice, and talks reverently of their intelligence and personality, which is a good thing since she spends most of her day with them. Today Dr. Beyeler is a tenured professor at the French NIH (INSERM) in Bordeaux. And yes, she's an amazing cook.

Credit for the breakthrough also belongs to the little black rodents using their mind's shortcuts. Beyeler and her colleagues injected the mice's brain with a vector containing the gene coding for a special light-sensitive protein called channelrhodopsin, which allows the activation of neurons when stimulated by blue light. Through a tiny optic fiber (the same type used for providing internet to our homes), placed above the injected brain region, this blue light is able to activate neurons with a millisecond precision. This technique developed in 2005 revolutionized the field of neuroscience, per its capability of probing specific neuron populations during mice behaviors. A twin technique, relying on fluorescent sensors of neural activity, peering through a special microscope at an injected mouse brain reveals a bunch of individual neurons glowing in the dark. This new method of observing the brain's activity has allowed scientists to track thousands of neurons at a time (instead of seeing just one neuron fire) and see how the brain reacts in various situations. This detailed look inside a brain wasn't possible just a few years ago. Looking inside a mouse's melon gives us much better knowledge of how humans react.

Once the mice had those proteins expressed into their brains, Beyeler started to train them based on the idea of a Pavlovian response. A specific sound played every time the mice were given sweet water to drink. Imagine hearing a bell ring and then someone hands you a thick and frosty chocolate shake—soon you'd associate the bell ringing with something positive (assuming you like chocolate shakes, and after all who doesn't, besides my daughter?). Then the team played a different sound and gave the mouse a drink laced with quinine, a very bitter tastant. The little guys puckered up and squeaked out an *ewww*. One noise for a positive association; one noise for a negative prediction. That's the idea of stimulus and response.

As the MIT team started watching the neurons respond when they played the two different sounds, they witnessed the eureka moment: they noticed there was a difference between the amygdala network of neurons activated when the blissful noise was played, compared to the network of neurons activated when the negative noise was played.

Those specific neural circuits express what Beyeler calls assigning *emotional valence*. Valence theory suggests that your subconscious mind classifies good from bad and that data sorting determines where the information is processed. Valence is another way to describe the shortcuts. Free energy also comes into play because the shortcuts will assign probabilities (precision) of expected outcomes to limit the free energy and emotional arousal.

Without us ever realizing it, our amygdala subconsciously integrates data inputs—sights, sounds, smells, memories, evolutionary imprints, everything in a moment. We assign either a positive or negative valence to an emotion and sensory input based on all the things integrated into our subconscious database. The shortcut went from theory to fact when Beyeler and Tye were the first researchers to show that the predictor of the bitter taste of quinine will preferentially

CHANGING IS THE HARDEST PART

Our brain's evolutionary memory is a little like the old *Wall Street Journal (WSJ)*. For those of you who remember before computer screens or even Bloomberg terminals, stockbrokers would look at the stock data information in the back pages of the *WSJ*. Publishing stock prices began when the paper was born in 1889. In the 1980s Bloomberg created desktop terminals to electronically access stock information for a monthly fee. Reading day-old quotes on paper was soon to be a thing of the past for brokers.

Soon even an Average Joe had access to real-time stock information. Online brokerages emerged in the 1990s, sharing information on the internet for free. Archaically, the *WSJ* kept publishing printed pages of data. By the new millennium most investors had a computer that could access real-time stock prices, but the *WSJ* couldn't shake the past. They were still printing day-old quotes on paper. It wasn't until 2016—more than thirty years after it was apparent that no one read the quotes in the back of the paper—that they stopped wasting ink and killing trees by printing day-old stock prices. Your brain's instinctual memories (fear of snakes, fear of spiders, fear of loud noises, fear of repeating holes, etc.) take even longer to be eliminated. If adaptation worked really well, we'd be terrified of riding in cars, not seeing a snake. Since it doesn't work all that well to live the best life possible, you have to consciously work on changing instinctual fears to something that serves you as well as your laptop stock picking!

activate one series of neurons and the sound predicting the good taste of sugar preferentially activates a different of neurons.

This lightning-fast sorting valence allows us to make split second survival actions. It enables our brain to use the least amount of energy possible. Valence is what classified the tweet that Sarah Silverman received most likely as negative in your mind, then set you up for the appropriate response. The amygdala's neural circuit of your brain fired when you saw the C-word, before you had time to think about it. Shortcuts, for good or bad, are great for survival but bad for open-mindedness, creativity, innovation, and seeing an unbiased reality. Valence is how our brain (and we) becomes judgmental.

The problem with valence is that it's based on a brain that experienced very different threats thousands of years ago; in other words, it hurts more than helps our chances of success in a modern world. Keep in mind that the amygdala, which directs these shortcuts, is basically running a piece of software that last had an update two million years ago. Valence relies on shortcuts that were useful hundreds of thousands of years ago. Our survival software has only one purpose: survival of the tribe (gene pool). The data and algorithms that software relies on to direct behavior are seldom relevant in today's ultra-safe society. Valence shortcuts leave out the tremendous processing power of a complete mind and allow an entire hemisphere to sit idle. Stepping out in front of a speeding bus will make you appreciate how well these shortcuts work, but most of our amygdala engagements aren't life-or-death reactions like that. Shortcuts are the mental equivalent of using four cylinders of an eight-cylinder Ferrari engine to race around a track and save gas. Shortcuts never use the entire mental intellectual engine; they trust everything that's in historical memories. We bias our thinking based on tribal behavior and primitive threats of bygone eras. If the car's software is designed to burn the least amount of fuel (or in the case of human software to simply survive) then it's doing OK. In life we don't want to save fuel—we want to win the race. We want to feel the shaking of five hundred horsepower vibrating up our spine and let it loose. If you understand a bit about our mental engine you can maximize its performance.

We're about to update our mental software and hack your brain into an entire new reality of growth, innovation, and happiness. If you aren't sure we make prehistoric decisions and still employ survival-based decisions today, think again. For proof you can look at the poor little creature that's had a bad rap since the Garden of Eden days—the snake.

There are, on average, fewer than ten people a year who die from snakebites of the three hundred million people who live in the United States (about the same for spiders). Yet people still harbor an instinctual fear of the cold, slithery ones. In other words, many of our survival mechanisms and fear instincts are not useful in our modern world, but they, like the stock quotes in the back of the WSJ (see sidebar), are damn hard to get rid of. But if we want to live an authentic life of passion, adventure, and excellence, then get rid of them we must. Unleashing the intellectual horsepower that lies within your subconscious mind means you need as many of your neurons and synapses firing and fully engaged as possible. You have to race with the whole engine. Our biology resists using the whole brain because it uses so much energy it brings the brain out of balance. For any big life choices and challenges, you should not rely on your subconscious shortcuts, or the innate desire to maintain a low-energy balance and limit free energy, because our survival mechanisms are not programmed to select opportunity-based choices. Your mind wants to limit the prediction error and that means making a choice based on fear. In fact, if your job involves any kind of creativity or problem solving, these shortcuts are the exact opposite of what will make you successful.

Increasing the connections and engaging more of the brain is the opposite of using your shortcuts. There's a special immune system for the brain that can actually help drive creativity and innovation. Our amygdala takes in data and compares it with our lifetime hard drive data; then we use our shortcuts to elicit a fear response. This is a hyper-efficient reaction. If you order the same extra-hot Caffè Misto at Starbucks every morning, these shortcuts are fine. However, we want the power and control to break these cycles when we need to come up with opportunity-based alternatives. The changes in our physiology because of fear are good because they provide energy for thinking, but we need to change the process so that fear becomes flow.

When our noggin gets out of balance, or uses too much energy, there are special immune cells that ramp up to push the system back to a normal, balanced state. These special cells are secreted by activated leukocytes (white blood cells) at the brain's borders. Your efficient mind thinks ramping up the immune cells wastes energy and costs extra effort (that's what getting out of balance looks like), but in today's low-threat society, doing extra work that might take more time and use more energy is a good thing to stimulate cellular activity and connect different regions of the brain.

Every time you use fear as fuel you build a stronger cranial immune system; when you seek out challenges, your brain's protection system has to keep revved up to meet the potential threat. Flexing your brain isn't a whole lot different from using your muscles. Lounging on the couch conserving energy for the ultimate Armageddon battle will benefit you with a few days of recovery. If months or years go by and you are not training your defenses, then when you wield a sword in battle, you'll feel like *The Simpsons'* Mr. Burns, unable to lift the sword off the rack after years of eating bon-bons and watching cartoons. The flip side is that if you started working out today, just doing one or two pushups a day and adding a couple more repetitions each week, before you know it you will be able to bang out twenty-five pushups without thinking about it. Grabbing that sword like Galahad would be easy as you swagger to the fight. You become stronger and your body works better because of incrementally increasing stress. Your mind is the same. You purposely get outside your expectations creating a free energy moment that pushes your body out of balance and therefore it must compensate to get back to the expected state, or change the expectations. If we can avoid relying on the shortcuts our mind uses, we will end up happier, making better decisions, being more creative, understanding more of the world, and staving off memory and cognitive disorders such as Alzheimer's and dementia. That bucket of benefits comes to us by eliminating valence.

Valence theory states that the two hemispheres of your brain handle different emotions. In other words, data that you receive from your sensory perceptions (sight, hearing, smell, touch) gets processed by the subconscious and quickly labeled. It's that qualification that keeps us from being the best version of ourselves. Many people wrongly believe that they are consciously aware of all their actions. Nearly everyone I've taken through the fear as fuel method is astonished at how much fear puts a hidden governor on our decision-making quality. Combatting hidden fears by building courage is worth the effort because we now have data that says courage makes you happier and more creative and literally helps you live longer.[1]

When it comes to energy and resources, the brain believes that using less is more, so it will take a lot of conscious effort to raise your neural engagement. The brain and our entire being tries to stay within the bounds of what it knows—when it gets out of whack that's when you create free energy or some basic fear because our system alarms are trying to get us back to the expected state of being. The well-used neural circuits that create shortcuts have trodden paths in the forest of your mind that will need to be grown over a little at a time. Eliminating valence will change your life.

Well-worn connections between neurons require less energy to use and the path is quicker to travel. Arcing a new connection or jumping across different, less-used neural circuits requires a lot more energy, depending on the type of connection (what neuroscientists refer to as gating). We are just now starting to understand why mature connections—those well-worn paths or shortcuts—are stronger and faster firing.[2] The connections between neurons can change over time, at any age, not just when the brain is in early development. The ability to change is due to neuroplasticity.

Just a few years ago scientists thought that people's brain structure was mostly fixed after the mid-twenties. That's been proven very wrong. The truth is that your brain is constantly rewiring itself at all ages. Sure, it is easier to revamp your brain when you are younger, but it is possible to do it at any age. The more signals sent between different neurons, the more powerful the specific connections will grow (it's the size of the connection; technically there is an increase in the amplitude of the post-synaptic neuron's response, which is why with each new experience and each remembered event or fact, the brain slightly changes its wiring).

You can think of this wiring process like cross-country skiing in deep powder snow. The first person to ski across a field is working really hard, picking up each ski, pushing down hard into the snow and compressing the snow, setting tracks for the first time. Going beyond a flat field and climbing up a hill requires that first person to make important decisions about how aggressive an angle to climb, and when to create switchbacks and make turns. This conscious decision making, planning while also compressing the loose snow, requires a lot of energy. Our first skier's friend, the guy behind him, is also working hard, especially if the snow is deep, but not nearly as hard as the leader. Most of the decisions and planning work is done. The second person is just further compacting the snow and making it even easier for the third, fourth, and fifth person. A well-compacted and established track means everyone on it now can just cruise along and enjoy the scenery, using much less energy. The problem with this approach in skiing (and in our reactions to events) is that anyone who just follows tracks can't choose where they go. New skiers can't exercise their creativity, innovate, or try different routes. Without the conscious choice to get out of the tracks, a following skier would be stuck in the track even if an avalanche came tumbling down. The ideal option in skiing and in our minds is a well-worn track to use when it's OK for things to be easy and fast, but cultivate an ability to jump out of the tracks and push ourselves—try something new, creative, or different when we decide it's optimal. That's the curiosity path that can change your life. Getting comfortable with being uncomfortable expands your perspective and helps get your mind OK with uncertainty and the unknown, it creates a wider range of possibilities before the free energy principle kicks in. The best way to jump out of the tracks is to be fueled by your fear response and in control.

Through new imaging technologies like optigenetics and fMRI techniques, scientists have proven that distinct sides of the brain process distinct emotions. Up until just a few years ago many researchers believed that there was one location for emotions. This was known as the right-hemisphere hypothesis, which said the right side of our brain section was dominant for processing all emotions regardless of whether it was good or bad, or technically speaking regardless of affective valence. Thanks to Beyeler and Tye and their little white friends, we know that theory is false. We can now watch the good news shortcuts firing over one group of neurons to the left hemisphere and the bad news shortcuts going to the right on a different network.

Your brain works like that snowy ski track—there are millions of well-worn tracks in your mind's neural network. Valance at the subconscious level means you build those tracks in the snow by skiing the same route over and over. The problem with these valance paths is that there isn't a naturally occurring third option for curiosity. There is only good or bad, so you have to change that.

If you are willing to push yourself and don't allow the brain to stay lazy, you can reap tremendous long-term rewards by eliminating valence shortcuts. Cerebral fitness, and developing new connections and waves, can do more than just help you think more creatively, make better decisions, and create new opportunities; broadening your beliefs and experiences is a great way to build your social media reputation too, as you'll soon see.

2.

Imagine Sarah Silverman seeing the tweet. Her brain routes the data to the right hemisphere, where threats are processed. Normally people would react based on that action. Not her. Picture Silverman setting down her phone, taking a few deep breaths, calming her mind, and trying to clear it of any thoughts. However she did it, she wrestled control of her reactions back from the amygdala and the survival network that wanted to fight or flee.

Once she was in control of her emotion and had stopped the creation of free energy uncertainty, she scrolled through the man's

Twitter feed.[3] She wanted to better understand his view of the world, his orientation. Sarah's valence processing would have immediately treated the fact that someone used harsh language in an attempt to verbally attack her as bad, the modern-day equivalent of being pushed off a cliff, away from the safety of her tribe. Her amygdala would have taken in the visual information and activated her fear tells; a fear cocktail would send adrenaline, cortisol, DHEA, and a host of enzymes coursing through her body to prepare for a fight. She would have felt her fear tells, such as an increased heart rate, faster breathing, and heightened sensory perceptions. She would have felt fear inputs and might have had an emotion of dread, anxiety, or anger. The default response would be to fight. Sarah decided to stop and make a choice, use that fear as fuel; not to fight but to question. She found the curiosity path.

As Silverman's body was likely buzzing from that fear cocktail triggered by her amygdala's fight-or-flight response, she cleared out her working memory, changed her perspective from flight or fight to curiosity and positivity. This put things back into balance from a Free Energy perspective and meant she could think rationally. Gaining control of her working memory allowed her to behave proactively, rather than immediately react to her fear inputs. Then she sent out this tweet in response:

> I believe in you. I read ur timeline & I see what ur doing & your rage is thinly veiled pain. But u know that. I know this feeling. Ps My back Fucking sux too. See what happens when u choose love. I see it in you.[4]

"See what happens when you choose love." She tries to teach the same approach and prompts him to eliminate the valence shortcuts that caused him to react to her original tweet. Astonishingly, the man tweeted back to her; the dialogue went on extensively, but how it resolved in the end shows the tremendous power of consciously eliminating our valence process.

Without awareness, we have shortcuts and use them all the time; without the discipline to seek alternatives, the valence process would have activated a fight-or-flight response. Most people would lash out or delete that person's account. The engagement between Silverman and Jamrozy culminated with her paying for some of his medical care. He publicly and sincerely apologized for attacking her, and dozens of media outlets from *Men's Health*[5] to *USA Today* reported on the seemingly miraculous way she engaged with the man. It was a rare bit of positive news and a great use of social media we don't see often enough. It also made news because of how rare it is for someone to have the mental discipline to shut off the survival response and turn hate speech into a moment of loving kindness.

That's an amazing example of what happens when we exercise our mind and don't become mentally lazy, lying on the proverbial couch all day. Sarah was ready to pick up her sword and fight for love and understanding; that's how using fear as fuel can help us create world peace. That's also how you can take more control over your life and not let others control how you feel. What if Silverman's reaction wasn't so unusual? Forty-seven percent of people who have been harassed online keep the battle going and confront the person right back on social media, according to a Pew Center Research study from 2014.[6] What if the responses were based on curiosity, love, and understanding all the time? What a wonderful world it would be!

The untrained subconscious mind keeps us from creating a wonderful world. Most of the history and the data loaded up to the massive hard drive that makes up your subconscious came from what others have fed to you. Our internal hard drive is so complex that neuroscientists aren't really sure how much storage we have. Many researchers believe it's around one thousand terabytes (in 2019 two terabytes is the average hard drive on an Apple MacBook, so your brain has the equivalent storage of five hundred laptops). Because we didn't build the foundation of our subconscious mind, our hidden fears are tougher to uncover. Most people don't realize how much our subconscious impacts our actions. The things that were taught *to* us, or ingrained *in* us, as children are tough to spot because we grew up believing them. We aren't able to choose inputs that create our orientation on the world. The town we grew up in, the color of our skin, the animals we saw all were out of our control. If English is your native language, you probably didn't make that choice—someone else decided they were going to teach you how to speak. Language is a foundation of your subconscious, but there are many other influences. Think about all the other components that create your reality—whether you can swim, what you think of dogs, your attitude toward religion, which way to look before you cross a busy road, how you handle finances—all create your unique perspective in the world. It wasn't until you started to develop your prefrontal cortex as a teen that you could think independently and question things that go into your vast database of knowledge. Those early lessons and memories were stored in many areas of the brain, not just around the amygdala but in other areas deep in your survival brain because the intelligent thinking part (the prefrontal cortex) didn't develop until your twenties. If we really want a clear idea of a bigger reality, a reality where we can be ready for anything and are not thrown off balance by uncertainty and fear (where we don't create Free Energy to fuel the amygdala) we have to try to rewrite some things we were taught when we were young.

If something out of the ordinary happens in your world right now, your amygdala will activate. When you see (or hear, or smell, or touch, or sense) something, your mind wants to classify what you are seeing. Thanks to your mom and dad (and teachers, coaches, friends, and siblings) you have been brought up with certain beliefs and orientations that things are good or bad. The amalgamation of all your history makes up your personal reality and it is unlike anyone else's in the world. That's something to celebrate. You can, and should, work hard to widen your reality by looking below the surface. Opening the aperture on your world to really benefit from the universe being a very friendly place requires faith in what you can't see, and a discipline to question what you think you know.

3.

A cocky thirty-five-year-old stood in front of the US Congress testifying about the emerging global debt crisis. The year was 1982 and the cigarette-smoking, mostly male congress hung on every word of the confident, educated, and experienced stock trader. His credentials (educated at Harvard Business School), and experience in the markets (he correctly predicted Mexico's default on its debt to the United States), earned him an invitation to testify as an expert witness. He promised the worried leaders "with absolute certainty because I know how markets work"[7] that the stock markets were on the verge of a significant drop. It was a huge prediction error on his part; he "knew" the equities markets would go down, yet they shot up. He was dead wrong, and he lost so much money for himself and his clients that he had to shut down his company and let everyone go.

In Ray Dalio's April 2017 TED Talk he exclaimed, "I was such an arrogant jerk!" Jerk that he might have been, he had courage and perseverance. Not willing to give up after his company tanked, Dalio borrowed $4,000 from his father. He made what he called one of the most painful decisions in his life; he chose to start again. What made that opportunity-based choice one of the most valuable learning experiences in his life was relearning how to make decisions. He was already courageous enough to make choices based on opportunity, not on fear, but what he hadn't realized is that his hidden fears, defense mechanisms, and subconscious shortcuts were holding him back. Eliminating the valence of an arrogant jerk wasn't easy, but he stumbled on a process that helped him override the shortcuts he had been using for major actions he took in life. He learned how to add much more processing power to his actions. In fact, he even turned it into an algorithm that drives a software platform at his firm, Bridgewater. What did Dalio do? He eliminated the valence from his decision making.

Dalio took the pain of running out of money and used it as motivation to examine how he got there. His deep self-reflection was what eventually saved him and turned him into the success he is today, not just by material standards but also his impact on the world. He found something simple, but much like the tools in this book, simple doesn't mean easy. In his TED talk he shares the moment when his life and business changed:

"I stopped saying 'I know I'm right' and started asking myself '*How* do I know I'm right?'"[8] This simple shift in mindset helped eliminate the shortcuts he once used to think he was right and started engaging deeper parts of his brain and populating his subconscious with a different orientation, to determine why he might be right, or wrong.

One of the top takeaways from this book is:

> By practicing valence elimination, you will hack your neural circuits to make significantly better decisions and open your mind to a more expansive reality.

Sarah Silverman and Ray Dalio act the same way, curious and open. Always wondering. Fear isn't something they avoid; it's something they use as fuel to look at things differently than someone who only survives. They eliminate shortcuts of the subconscious mind. This takes self-awareness and training.

Time to Change Your Mind

The next section of this chapter will show you how to start your own Valence Elimination Training (or VETing), a highly trainable, simple method of optimizing your brain function. This simple neural hack can have a profound effect on your life, happiness, and success.

Once you adopt the process you will see results in the first few weeks. Understanding valence elimination training is one of those "Aha" moments that, once you catch yourself consciously getting the benefits, you will realize how great leaders and superstar athletes look at the world. You'll optimize your mental function by recruiting more neurons and gray matter even as you age. VETing will enable you to do the same thing entrepreneurs and venture capitalists in Silicon Valley have been trying to do with expensive neurotropic drugs: light up more circuits in the brain for a higher level of mental clarity, and enable you to work better with other people. With my natural method you won't have any of the jittery side effects and stomach erosion you'd get from chugging noxious energy drinks or popping prescription stimulants such as Nuvigil or Adderall. And more importantly, VETing will make you a happier, healthier person and a positive addition to society. You'll attract more people like you, and you'll be luckier because you are less judgmental of things being "bad," and open to more ideas.

When you receive data from any of your body's data input sources (eyes, ears, nose, etc.), that information first goes to the thalamus and then right to the amygdala to determine at the most fundamental level whether you should run like hell or try to mate with the person in front of you. Your lizard brain, which is a by-product of the lowest survival-level DNA inside your body, is trying to either survive or procreate. In a very simple fashion, the lower functioning part of our brains puts everything into a good bucket or a bad bucket. Survival threat—bad; procreation—good. The bad items = negative valence. The good items = positive valence. Right hemisphere, left hemisphere—sugar water or quinine.

The negative valence items ("bad things") are processed by the right hemisphere and the positive items ("good things") are routed to the left side of the brain. To take it beyond the snow analogy, think of the neural circuits of this function as a simple traffic light—the good things go left once the green light switches on in the amygdala and the bad things turn right once the red light switches on. But what about the yellow light? That's the real secret: when the yellow light should go on—all the lights energize and the information gets processed by both sides of the brain. Aha!

The brain is incredibly efficient, and it requires very little energy to light up the green light and send good information to the left side, the valence shortcut. The amount of electrical energy required is very limited because the process has become so efficient. The more accustomed a person is to following this elementary good-bad evaluation system, the more often the neurons in the amygdala that label good connect to the left side of the brain. Because those neurons have been firing together since your parents started telling you right from wrong and good from bad, they are wired together like a wrist-thick cable holding up a pillar of the Golden Gate Bridge—so it will take some highly focused work to rewire them, and that's the goal of VETting.

Neurologically working this hard is inefficient, of course, but highly beneficial for your quality of decision making. More neurons fire, more waves vibrate, and we get more mental processing power. We're not just following the same old path in the snow; we're drawing an entirely new map. This is a map that was never seen by your tribe. Adaptation and evolution work by sticking to one tribe and working together to survive, but by definition we became incredibly judgmental. What we consider good or bad dictates how we *orient* ourselves to the rest of the world. To get great at anything requires your orientation to be as all encompassing and open as possible.

Orientation is the sum of all the options and possibilities we can think of. Michael Jordan famously dunked from the free throw line and played an explosive inside game. His original orientation was physical, dominant around the hoop. He changed his orientation. Learning to shoot from the perimeter, building an outside shot and looking at the problem (scoring) from a new orientation made him unstoppable and one of the greatest basketball players of all time. Limit your orientation to looking at the world from what everyone growing up put in your database and you peer at the world through a tiny keyhole. With the VETing process, you will unlock that keyhole first to a new window of possibilities and eventually to an entire glass house of unlimited potential.

Closed-minded is a phrase rooted in the science of what actually happens to judgmental people. Closing off half of our brain reduces fuel in the form of oxygen when we use valence shortcuts. The less you question things, the more efficiently and quickly you can make repeated, rote decisions. Sometimes shortcuts are good; you don't need to question pulling your seatbelt across your chest, pushing in the brake pedal, putting a hand on the steering wheel, and pressing the start button or turning a key. You can start your car without thinking about it. However, subconscious cookie-cutter actions limit creativity, problem solving, and ultimately success potential. Your goal should be to expand your orientation from that little keyhole all the way up to a glass house by being curious. This will build a much bigger database of prior beliefs and experiences in your subconscious mind and mathematically lower the possibility of excessive Free Energy. The challenge is that humans are, by design, closed-minded and energy efficient for survival. That's why it is so easy for us to be judgmental.

Judgments can be especially hurtful when we are critical of our own selves. Once you come to the realization that there is a deep ocean of hidden fears under the surface, you will begin to realize that you are making decisions and choices because of the influences of those fears. I'll keep hammering on my core message: decisions made out of fear almost always lead to regret. You want to be open to taking risks and living for happiness and make your choices out of opportunity. Realization of your hidden fears and their influence enables you to identify the defense mechanisms that protect against your hidden fears. You can take accountability for everything you do, which doesn't mean being self-critical, but rather understating what you can control and what you can't and accepting everything.

Imagine having a guest from Bahrain over for a traditional New England Thanksgiving dinner. After knocking back her second slice of apple pie, she rattles the windows with a belch that comes from way down in her diaphragm. Across her face rolls a gratified, benevolent smile. At the other end of the table your eighty-year-old grandfather is peeling the tennis ball off his walker to hurl at her for being so rude. His orientation is about to change when you explain that in Bahrain a belch means that you ate a satisfying meal and you are complimenting the host. But in the United States, we're taught that burping is rude and you'd never do it at the dinner table. The two guests had different perspectives on the same action. Luckily you were there to keep Grandpa's fastball at bay, but if he were practicing VETing he wouldn't have considered it rude; he would have wondered why we thinking burping is rude—and eventually why we make rules of behaving called manners. Rules passed down through the ages are always easy material to be questioned; after all, does it really hurt anyone if your elbows are on the table during dinner?

Humankind's differences are what define our orientation and also create judgment and fear. People who find Valence Elimination Training very difficult are those who have trouble letting go of their orientation—understandably so; we are used to judging everything we see. Those paths are hard-wired, and it takes effort to change

THE HIGH PRICE OF ASSUMPTIONS

Have you heard the old adage, "never assume because it makes an ass out of you and me"? Not only can it embarrass you; more painfully, it can cause suffering.

A lack of curiosity drives assumptions that you know the "truth" or that you are "right" when in fact your hypothesis might be nowhere near the truth for everyone. We often make assumptions because we don't have the courage to ask questions and challenge our beliefs or because we had rules put into our subconscious hard drive that we never questioned; these rules hold us back.

Assumptions born from fear constrain us rather than fuel us. Often the fear comes from wanting to be right or appear smart, to avoid the pain of being ridiculed or looking inferior. If we appeared smarter and stronger, we would have had a better chance of finding a mate, so ancient man would do whatever it took to win that battle and procreate. Today, however, it's like fear of snakes—a prehistoric behavior that has stuck with us. If you fear looking stupid by asking "Why?" "How?" "What?" or "Who?" you're missing out on big opportunities to learn. Trying to stay unemotional and saying, "I'm not sure" or "I don't know" will engage an entirely new part of your brain. While assuming will make you dumber, curiosity can make you smarter. Believing an assumption is erroneous and being curious about other possibilities will make you smarter in the long run because curiosity has been shown to increase memory and the processing capacity of the mind, according to a 2015 study by UCLA psychologist Dr. Shannon McGillivray and colleagues.[1]

Note

1. Shannon McGillivray, Kou Murayama, and Alan Castel, "Thirst for Knowledge: The Effects of Curiosity and Interest on Memory in Younger and Older Adults," *Psychology and Aging* 30, no. 4 (December 2015): 835–41.

them. We judge even before we have time to think about it because we have become so efficient.

One reason you spent an entire chapter finding your fear tells and another one on your face of fear is to create an awareness of amygdala activation and then your defense mechanisms that try to get you back to a state of zero free energy. We expect the world to be a certain way, and when it's not we act very quickly to fix whatever has made us uncertain by changing our predictions or updating our database. Seeing the destructive process that a two-million-year-old piece of software has on your life is the only way to keep your survival brain from holding you back. You must catch yourself making judgments and wiring negative circuits about yourself, too. It's easy for us to think a negative thought such as: "I'm a shy person" and then project a fear event based on that belief (fear of being alone or fear of being abandoned) to a moment in the future: "I'll never meet anyone and be alone the rest of my life."

If we feel our fear tells when those negative thoughts arise, we can recognize physiological changes in our body and see it as a moment of negative valence or a pattern of judgment created by an amygdala activation. That's when we can say "Stop." Getting increasingly aware of your fear tells and feeling the changes in your body day to day is the key to opening your mind and using your volition, or ability to choose.

Knowing your personality, knowing your face of fear, and understanding how you react in response to an amygdala activation will guide your growth. If you've followed the work in *Fear Is Fuel*, you sense when your hidden fears are making you act because you feel your tells; you know when you stop using the PFC to make choices and your Fear Frontier has been crossed so you can employ BASE to get you optimized. Next you're going to permanently rewrite the way you subconsciously respond to the world. This is the path to becoming more courageous, happier, healthier, and more successful. See how this is all coming together?

Rewriting your subconscious response changes your view on everything.

Rewriting the Script

If you are that shy person, your current fear-based script might now read like this:

I am a quiet and shy woman who is never going to meet the love of my life, the partner to share my passion for travel and intellectual challenges. I *know* I am destined to be a spinster missing out on finding my soulmate and building a family because I'm so terribly shy or afraid of rejection.

Or if you are not shy maybe you are judging others quickly and missing opportunities to grow. You might think this about someone on your team:

He's an average guy, living an average life. You can't expect much from him; he went to community college, his parents were factory workers, and he grew up living most of the time with his grandparents because his parents didn't want him. The boss doesn't event respect him, why should I want him on my team for the most important project of my career?

Those are two strong negative narratives rooted in your subconscious database. The first is a self-judgment that you are shy or worthless and shyness is a negative quality. The second example is a characterization based on another person's history and your assumptions. Both are destructive and both can be rewritten to help you and the people around you.

The first step in the valence elimination process and getting rid of your shortcuts is to frame your key characteristics as strengths and reaffirm them in your own database.

You reframe your perspective anytime you have a negative judgment about yourself or someone else. First you must realize your assumption. It doesn't matter if you are talking about yourself, your life partner, your best friend, or a sworn enemy; simply the act of rewriting the script is going to engage a part of your brain that has been dormant, and that will allow you to rewrite the script of your own reality. This is what Sarah Silverman did with the Twitter troll. The outcome might be equally as surprising to you as it was to Silverman.

The first exercise in VETing is to reframe the story, to change the script. To rewrite the script, you need to follow a three-step reversal:

1. Fear Frontier Tell:

| **2. Current Judgment** | **Underlying Cause** | **Future Strength** |

3. Turn Fear into Fuel:

For self-judgment like the shy person, the process of VETing requires that you define the state you are in today and the cause. Then you explore how to change your behavior into a strength and then how you'd use fear as fuel to get you to a new place. It could look something like this:

1. Fear Frontier Tell:
I hold my breath and feel my throat close up when I think about a boyfriend, a relationship, or having a family. My body feels weak. I'm going to be alone, never be loved, and I'll die a spinster, unhappy and old.

2. Current Judgment	**Underlying Cause**	**Future Strength**
Guys don't like me, don't want to be with me, or think I'm boring.	I'm shy and that's unattractive.	I'm cautious, I don't need drama or the limelight to be happy.

3. Turn Fear into Fuel:
I'm smart and intelligent and deserve love in my life. My fear of being alone will give me extra fuel when I meet someone I like, to engage him. I'll ask myself if that person would love having someone analytical, organized, and supportive in his life. Someone who makes him feel special just by having the courage to talk to him. When I can see how that is possible, I'll feel the energy and fuel that fear is offering me and use it to make a connection. When I feel that excitement, I might offer my phone number, suggest we get a coffee, or ask to see him again. *I know that the worst thing that could happen is for him or her to say no, or laugh at me. If I feel hot or rejected, I know that brief moment of embarrassment is better than the painful future of being alone forever.*

To reexamine the premise of other people, in the same way that Sarah Silverman did, it would look like this:

1. Fear Frontier Tell: I feel hot, and my jaw is clenched at the idea of having Donald on my team. He didn't go to business school and doesn't understand the consulting methods I learned at McKinsey. I get sick thinking the project will be ruined and delivered late if he's on the team.

2. Current Judgment	Underlying Cause	Future Strength
That guy isn't as smart or as valuable to the team because he didn't go to business school and comes from a blue-collar background.	He's dumb and not well educated, from a poor family.	Many of our clients didn't go to college and come from a similar background; he'll understand their needs better.

3. Turn Fear into Fuel: I value diversity and honesty. When Donald is critical and I feel my palms get sweaty, I ask myself if he might be right, can we do better? Could he really be helping me to push us to do something better and more empathetically than I otherwise would? Because he only went to community college and has a blue-collar background, he brings a different and valuable perspective to our team. His honesty is not meant to be hateful or punitive; he wants us to win. Am I being too polite and not helping people reach their potential by worrying about their feelings; should I be more like Donald?

Simply saying "STOP!" aloud or in your head, when you catch yourself in a moment of judgment (of yourself or of someone else) is the first simple step. Then using a positive affirmation (how you will use fear as fuel), starting by reminding yourself about a core value that is positive and important to you. This is basically what Ray Dalio did that turned him into one of the richest men in the world.

Recognize when your orientation—your background, your beliefs, your perspective—is causing you to believe something that may not necessarily be the truth. Your subconscious mind cannot rationalize or argue; it can only bring up emotions and events. If data was fed into your subconscious mind that airplanes are deadly because you witnessed a crash as a child, the only thing that will happen is that you will feel terror when you see an airplane. Not until you put a different story into your hard drive will that emotion change. Remembering that we can create excess Free Energy ourselves means that we can eliminate free energy as well. Simply asking "how do you know that to be the case?" is a very effective way of using your prefrontal cortex to think of different layers of possibility. Asking how you know you are right works equally well with a team that you might be leading. Getting them in the habit of asking how the opposite of their view could be true is a great exercise in open-mindedness.

Working with teams to be more creative, innovative, and flexible often starts with helping them realize they have a lot to offer. Start your meetings or strategy sessions with a positive reminder about one of their qualities. When I am on a project with a team, I will go around the table and have each person remind us of their strengths. "Hi, I'm Patrick and I am really good at seeing the big picture." This will literally prewire everyone's brain to deal better with threats.[9] Psychologically, this will teach you to be more curious and inquisitive, but neurologically you will actually start to wire your brain differently. The rewiring of the circuits will help you become more creative, more innovative, and a more tolerant and effective leader; you'll also be happier in your job as you view setbacks and roadblocks as positive learning opportunities.

Fearful moments pop up unexpectedly like a sniper that nails you on your best game of Fortnite. One of the key components to putting fear to work is not being afraid of admitting when you're surprised by something scary or dreadful. Being radically honest with yourself and those around you is what will enable you to use fear as fuel.

VETing is the ultimate way to ensure one of the most important rules we lived by at all of my start-ups—the no-asshole rule. Assholes don't try to look at the other side of the story; they don't try to override the fight response, especially when their own opinion or ego is at stake—they have to be right. VETing is the path to searching out the good in everyone and changing the world.

Dishonesty leads to a toxic culture that I've seen repeatedly. If you are leading a team at work and you are afraid you are in over your head, or fearful that you're a fraud, you have to rewrite the script to show that there is a completely different side to that story. If your hidden fear is that you are an imposter, or that you will be called out for being a fraud because you don't have all the answers or you're unsure, you may try to defend that belief. You must realize why you might be defensive and do your best to explore that thought. Your defense mechanism underlying that hidden fear might be to demand that your way is right because you're an expert or you're the boss, and you don't want to appear weak so you pull rank over better ideas. That shows that you are committed to fearful behavior. Ask yourself how much more powerful you'll be if you consider other ideas, and then weigh your decisions based on data, expertise, and authenticity. Doesn't a better project align with what is important to your success more than appearing smart? Weigh the choice based on *how* you know something is right. Using fear as fuel means you don't react to defend your authority or title, but rather that you are courageous enough to think of other perspectives, strong enough to let others give their opinion and use the power of diversity in decision making.

Just imagine how someone like Mark Zuckerberg's parents must have felt when he said he was dropping out of Harvard.

"You're doing what? Don't you realize how hard we worked to get you there . . . if you can't finish Harvard how will you ever accomplish anything?"

Imagine what his parents, and his parent's friends, and even his own friends must have thought. Yeah, I know what you're saying: but he's different. . . . No, he's not! The big difference between people who don't use fear as fuel and Mark Zuckerberg is that he had a huge belief, a belief he could do something truly astounding without needing a Harvard degree. One traditional belief entered in most kids' subconscious database (at least in the United States) is that to be successful you must graduate from college. If you want to change your database, you have to populate it with different messages.

An Hour of Judgment

The second exercise to do in Valence Elimination Training is to dedicate an entire hour of your day for a full week tracking the judgments that you make.

It might sound easy, but it's not.

The more active and outside you are, the easier and the more effective this exercise will be. As a thought crosses into your mind, or a new picture comes into your head, ask yourself what you think about the image when you first see or hear about it. If you walked into Starbucks and heard a gravelly voice rapping in French over the speakers when you were expecting a melodic Miles Davis riff, what was your gut reaction? Count it as one judgment. Where did you file that judgment—left side (good) or right side (bad), good or bad? If the woman at the counter has a jet-black Emo-style haircut, what is your reaction to that? Count it. When the barista puts whipped cream on your drink by mistake, what is your thought? In the course of an hour you will be amazed at how many judgments we make.

Each judgment you make without curiosity is another nail in your coffin of creativity, innovation, problem solving, and growth. Curiosity is what will feed the happiness of your soul.

An Hour of Judgment—The Case of the Three Whys

Try this exercise every day at lunch. It takes real focused effort; that's why you should start with an hour a day, but once you've counted your judgments and are aware of them it's time to start wiring some new neurons. You most likely have years and years of judgmental behavior to overcome; the good news is that the upside is huge when you start thinking with your whole brain; the bad news is that the years of practice judging and using valence shortcuts will take a lot of work to undo.

When you take your lunch hour, make the conscious decision that you will look at everything with wonder, curiosity, and openness, so that you don't rely on valence. Pretend you are Sherlock Holmes trying to answer a series of questions. If you find yourself starting to judge someone, say to yourself "Stop" and replace the judgment with three "Whys." If the receptionist didn't say good-bye when you walked out, don't judge her and think to yourself, "She's such a bitch." Instead wonder is she shy, do you intimidate her, can she be so focused on her work that she doesn't notice when you walk out? Then wonder why you had that initial feeling you had; why do you care whether she says good-bye? How come you let it get you upset? So why her and why me? Third, wonder why you came up with the orientation you did after contemplating the first two whys—did something happen when you were young; can you remember any specific memories? Next, as you wait in line at Starbucks for your half-caf, triple mocha and a barista who looks like the victim of a drive-by piercing asks you what you want, your first reaction shouldn't be to think "that freak looks like he went bobbing for bait in my tacklebox!" but rather to see the world through his eyes, to wonder what you can learn from both him and the reaction you initially had. Consider how your story of him being a freak with anti-authority issues could be 180 degrees wrong. Replace the thought with a story of envy: here's a person who has let go of his fears of fitting in, doesn't care what other people think, and obviously has a high threshold for pain. How did he cultivate those qualities? I can't even remove a splinter without a shot of Jägermeister! Why did I think he was a freak?

Every time you spend an hour fostering curiosity intention in action is another chip away at those deep grooves that are hiding the authentic you. Just like the swings of the hammer from a sculptor, each moment you can catch yourself judging, stop, and then replace your thoughts with inquisitiveness. That is a sound investment in your courage.

Replacing judgment with curiosity will bring you back from lunch with a new view of the world and make you more open to gratitude, which in turn drives a continued state of happiness. As you get closer to living an authentic life of courage, you'll also notice that the way people react to you will begin to change. In the past that barista might have been defensive and short with you; now, just because you are curious as to how he raised his threshold of pain and you ask him with curious intention, "didn't that hurt like hell?" he will sense your curiosity and respect, rather than sensing through micro expressions in your face feelings of disgust or fear. Within an authentic curiosity and respect, other people like him will react differently than if they sensed judgment or threat.

Dogma, rules, and unquestioned beliefs have created tragic loss of life and happiness from generation to generation. One of the biggest detriments to a peaceful society is judgment without questioning; it is also possibly the greatest opportunity for leaders everywhere. The neurobiology of forcing yourself to be radically curious opens the electrical connections in your mind and requires more oxygen to the brain to supply energy, so your blood-brain barrier opens and creates more circulation. Take the time to avoid a snap decision and think of all the possibilities first and your brain will come up with new and exciting revelations every day. A healthy brain and a deep self-awareness can even get you help in unexpected ways, as you'll find out in the next chapters. In the end, the best decision you'll never make, however, is the decision to let fear dictate your actions.

11

 ~

Blueprint for Bravery

Courage is resistance to fear, mastery of fear, not absence of fear.

—Mark Twain

This far into the book you've seen amazing examples of courage, growth, and empowerment. You now have an understanding of the Wright brothers' success, you felt the pain of Olympic failures, you've been surprised by smiling snake handlers, dissected the mind of a decapitator, and figured out how Greek philosophers three hundred years before Christ were able to influence Caesar's sworn enemy. When just one person finds courage, it can change the course of the entire world.

Imagine if you find the courage to be the person whom the people who love and depend on you need you to be. Imagine how your entire life will change. We all find courage in a different way, but there are some common threads we can weave together that will work for almost anyone.

Acting with confidence and courage is the fastest way to eliminate suffering, both yours and others'. One of the finest examples of a life well lived, as unconventional as can be imagined, was Beryl Markham, the pilot you met earlier. She was the first woman to fly a trans-Atlantic solo going east to west. Defying convention at a time when women were not expected to be adventurers or innovators inspired countless others. She had the courage and confidence to produce her own narrative on her terms, and not let rules or expectations influence her. Her father and those around her never set upper limits on what Beryl could do, so she never felt she would be rejected for failure, for bucking convention, for being her authentic self. How she got to that point of courage is an investigation we can all learn from.

When you were growing up what was your narrative? Did you believe that if you worked hard and got into a good college, you could achieve tremendous things? Did your family expect you to become a doctor or a lawyer? Or were you like me, of immigrant roots and simply owning a house and having kids was all you were taught to expect? Or maybe you don't even know your parents, and all you ever wanted was a stable relationship. What rules did people ingrain into you without explanation? There are many limits imposed on individuals that put a lid on potential happiness. You must have the courage to remove those limits.

If you reflect on your life right now, what components and areas are you really happy with? Your career, your family, your finances, your body or health? If you look at one area of your life that you feel really happy and proud about, why are you happy with it?

Write down your answer to this sentence in a journal or on your computer:

I'm really happy with _____ and the reason I'm happy with that part of my life is _____ _____.

Happiness and courage come from areas of your life that are aligned with your Prior Beliefs (PB). If you recall from chapter 4, PB are created by everything that has gone into your subconscious hard drive since you were born. The larger you can make that hard drive, the more courage you'll find because you produce less free energy moments. Happiness also comes when you have minimal disconnect between what you thought the future would be and what the current personal reality is. Happiness and courage come if you limit free energy. If things are better than you imagined, you will be exceedingly happy and have the courage to deal with areas that cause you to suffer.

If you have a PB that is vastly different from the current situation you are in, it's going to make you suffer. You might be sad, disappointed, and angry. You may also feel like not even dealing with life. If this disconnect between what you expected and where you are came suddenly, you can have a great deal of fear as well. No matter how you look at it, there is suffering involved. Time to eliminate that suffering in you, and those you touch as well. First identify where you are hurting by completing this:

I'm really sad or angry with _____ and the reason I'm suffering with that part of my life is _____

_____.

Your success and your suffering will set the stage for the high and low point of your current reality. The goal of this chapter is to raise both to a new level.

The lessons we can take away from the amazing people you've read about in this book, whether they're Beryl Markham, Wilbur and Orville, Chappie, or anyone else is clear: your background does not dictate your future. Even in countries still heavily steeped in a caste system or with strong religious constraints you can still change the world. Look at seventeen-year-old Malala Yousafzai, who stood up in a school bus against the Taliban and was shot in the head at point-blank range. She lived. Rather than let a bullet to the head terrify her into silence, it fueled her to courageous activism. She fought for women everywhere. Her work earned her the distinction of being the youngest person to ever win a Nobel Peace Prize. If a teenage girl in Pakistan can stand up to the Taliban, you can change your life, too. You can stand up to a tyrannical boss or take a risk to start your own company. It's never too early or too late to eliminate your upper limits, accept courage, and welcome fear as fuel.

You have to increase your Prior Belief (PB) to limit your free energy, increase your hypothesis of possible outcomes (good and bad) and make a choice to exercise the pathways related to the sgACC, the courage network, constantly. Like Beryl Markham or Tom Brady or Alex Honnold, soon you'll be able to control the amygdala and stop it from hijacking your body. Once you've trained it, you'll see that courageous people literally send signals from their PFC to sgACC and mute the connection to the amygdala. That's the key to the neuroscience we've learned so far in *Fear Is Fuel*—recognize when the amygdala tries to take over, understand how you learned to deal with your Fear Frontier, and shift the feeling of fear to fuel and excitement.

THE MAKING OF A LEGEND

Beryl Markham didn't plan her growth in a step-by-step manner for others to follow; however, a look at her life allows us to take away the key factors that led her to an extraordinary existence. I've high-lighted seven brave behaviors that contributed to her long-lasting, slow courage, increasing her beliefs and creating more hypotheses of how events could unfold. These seven behaviors can be the hab-its that guide your path to the virtue of bravery and close the gap between your current state and your perceived reality. If you want to end your anguish you can change your personal reality or get out of your current state—both take courage. The seven steps from Markham's life can be a game-changer if you think about applying them to your journey. During her life in Africa, Markham:

1. Grew confidence in her own abilities
2. Sought out high-quality training
3. Had a sense of control over herself and the situation
4. Wrote down her feelings
5. Never let her teammates down
6. Modeled the courageous behavior of others
7. Learned about big challenges she would face alone

Markham explains in her autobiography that she had not yet even scratched the surface of the place she called a photographer's paradise, a hunter's Valhalla, and an escapist's utopia when her father offered to take her away to Peru for a new opportunity. Like her father, her first love was horses. She had helped her dad deliver a stallion into the world and her father rewarded her by giving her the horse. At seventeen she decided to take the opportunity first with her horse and become a professional trainer in Kenya, rather than move away with her father. One year later she became the first woman in Kenya to be awarded a trainer's license and her decision, born out of opportunity, began paying off.

After her father left, they wrote to each other often. If she had succumbed to the fear of the unknown, she would have relished the safety, comfort, and protection of being with a parent, but she didn't. She looked for opportunity. Beryl was scared as she rode her horse Pegasus away from their old farm to the higher land of the north, but she used the fear of failure, fear of loneliness to drive her to perform. She was using fear as fuel by driving herself daily from dawn until the wee hours of the night learning everything she could about training and horses. Soon horse owners began to take notice and hired her. But it wasn't all roses; she had a major setback that had her, like many other great people in history, questioning her decision.

Markham was dealt a major blow when one of her clients took her best horse, named Wrack, from her just before the start of the racing season. The owner decided to bring the horse to a well-known, experienced trainer, believing that an eighteen-year-old girl would not be up to the task of creating a championship horse. She had spent the previous year turning Wrack into a potential champion who was poised to win the biggest race in Kenya that season.

Like anyone in this situation she questioned her identity, wondered whether she was really a fraud, and suffered greatly. It wasn't long, however, before the lessons from her upbringing kicked in and helped her accept this event as a challenge rather than a defeat. She saw the obstacle as the opportunity to really shine. She fought the demons whispering in her ear that her career was over and she would never amount to anything as a trainer, and put fear aside once again. She looked for opportunity and rose to the challenge by finding a horse (which she had helped deliver two years earlier) that was plagued with tendon injuries from an overly aggressive trainer. Markham asked the owner if he'd let her rehab the mare before the race and get her in racing form. It was risky to see if the tendons could handle training at a high level. The goal was to take on Wrack in the championship. Her childhood friend from the Murani tribe who came to work with her as an adult told her the filly, Wise Child, was going to win if they trained her together. Beryl laughed at the prediction, to which Arab Ruta, her friend, her warrior, her right hand, told her, "it is only that I have the power to make truths of my beliefs."[1] They started three months of intensive training together that would challenge her every day.

Race day arrived sooner than they wished. Standing alongside the moist brown soil of the track, the scent of fresh cut grass, African dirt, and equine sweat swirled together. Beryl's hands shook in the face of an amygdala hijacking, but she was no stranger to the sensation and leaned into feeling the fear. She focused on the positive work they had done and the opportunity to prove that she was as good as any other trainer. As for many before her doing something daring, doubt tried to creep in. She put it in a mental compartment and tried to set it aside in her mind. She knew that she had done everything she could to prepare the filly against her old pupil, the large stallion who was the favorite in the bookmakers' minds. As the horses lined up at the starting tape, the other entrants didn't even come into Beryl's thoughts—just her Wise Child and the old pupil Wrack. After a nerve-wracking false start, Wrack jumped to the lead. Beryl let the five thousand screaming voices roll over her unnoticed like a fog, she was so focused on her filly—using her intense senses and increased awareness fueled by fear so that she was not just watching the event unfold; she was reading the strategy of the race. She was watching the courage and intelligence of horse and jockey, absorbing every nuance. A minute into the race as the crowd's roar seemed to reach a crescendo for Wrack, the favorite, Wise Child slipped by like a leopard hunting in the night, to steal the lead. It was a bold move that catapulted her ahead but cost the horse dearly. Despite her massive heart the filly's weak tendons gave out and the six-length lead she had built around the final turn vanished as quickly as she found it. Beryl slumped on the rail, heartbroken. Astonishingly, Wise Child wouldn't let go. Her heart, not her legs, pushed past the big stallion one last time and she drove five more excruciating strides, crossing the finish line ahead of Wrack by a nose. In the last race of her career Wise Child set a track record.

After establishing herself as a successful horse trainer Markham embarked on a new adventure after she met a man who flew a plane into her life. She learned one of her great lessons in life, what "every dreaming child needs to know; that no horizon is so far that you cannot get above it or beyond it."[2]

Thinking it over for a few days, she announced to her loyal sidekick Arab Ruta, her partner in the horse training business, that she was going to leave the equine world to fly. There was no hesitation in her choice; it was driven by opportunity. He replied equally bravely, "If it is to be that we must fly, Memsahib, then we will fly. At what hour of the morning do we begin?"[3]

Markham learned in a DH Gipsy Moth, the first plane owned by Wilson Airways of Kenya, taught by Tom Black, the chief pilot who flew into her life on a blustery, dusty day in 1929. Eighteen months later Markham had her B license—the equivalent of a commercial pilot's license—and was delivering mail, picking up wounded hunters, and flying just about anywhere someone would pay her to go.

Beryl cultivated numerous relationships and mentors through her curiosity, willingness to learn, and confidence. Through hard work and self-reliance, she was gifted with courage, inspiration, and a knowledge of life that resulted in a style of transcendence, a courageous enlightenment, that led her to be the first woman to fly trans-Atlantic from London to Newfoundland in September 1936. She did what others had died trying, and accomplished a much more difficult feat than even the celebrated Amelia Earhart (who flew with the prevailing winds from west to east). She did so without sponsors; she used her life savings and fulfilled her wish on a shoestring budget. She always believed, like Arab Ruta, that if she believed it, she could make it so.

Beryl believed that courage must be cultivated every day. In her autobiography she reminds us that "if a man has any greatness in him, it comes to light, not in one flamboyant hour, but in the ledger of his daily work."[4]

I have tried to deconstruct Markham's life, the way an architect might try to create a plan from a masterpiece like Monticello. This is a blueprint for a brave life. She exemplified a life of courage, starting every day happy where she was and ready for anything. This is how she cultivated it. She

1. *Grew confidence in her own abilities*—From an early age Markham was exposed to new things, and never worried about failure. Her father encouraged her to learn how to ride and train horses, play the piano, and speak other languages. Her outside influences encouraged experimentation as well. Arab Ruta, the young Murani boy whose father worked on their farm, became Beryl's constant companion. As a young warrior he was being trained in hunting, tracking, and killing skills. He had to constantly practice throwing his spear, moving quickly and silently and finding prey. Beryl went along with him, because she was curious and fascinated. She learned to throw the spear with him. Soon she was good enough to hunt with the elders. Every time she learned new skills or got better, her confidence grew, she was happy to learn from her failures. She didn't let her identity become her failures—a white girl from England in a black indigenous African tribe is as out of place as anyone can be. Instead she felt just the opposite; she wanted to learn from these incredibly talented tribesmen and understand how they live. Failure was always tolerated by her mentors; there were no high-pressure private school recitals or Ivy League college test embarrassments. She learned that persistence and practice led to proficiency. She also learned that inside every failure comes a lesson that builds confidence and courage. She added to her confidence by bouncing back from failures. She also learned early on that she could do more than she thought she could. She was once attacked by a baboon who had his teeth dug in her arm and she took a cane and beat it to death

with her other arm. Surviving a baboon attack makes a college entrance exam seem paltry.

Build Your Courage: Getting out of your comfort zone, one step at a time, will eventually lead to a consistent courageous mindset. Try doing something you've thought of but never tried, like riding a horse, flying a plane, playing an instrument, speaking in front of hundreds of people, or even owning a snake. Set a goal to acquire a new skill that you know will have many failures before you can get good at it. Then plan the stages to get to proficient and every stride closer you get, focus on developing baby steps of confidence. Give yourself an extra commendation every time you fail, knowing that your skills are growing.

2. *Sought out high-quality training*—Learning from the best helps you meet and even exceed their skills. Air travel was only twenty years old when Markham decided she'd apprentice among the group of African bush pilots at Wilson Air. Having an instructor who was trained by the Royal Air Force along with a brand-new plane further built her personal confidence. She felt there was no place Tom Black couldn't fly in his confident and calculated manner. He sat like a statue on the way home from one of their early flight lessons as Beryl attempted to gain altitude and navigate over an eight-thousand-foot high plateau. Despite more power and more aileron, the plane was not rising. As the branches on the trees became visible and she could at last make out fist-size rocks, Tom finally grabbed the controls and did a steep one-hundred-eighty-degree retreat. "'Now you know what down-draft is,' said Tom. 'You get it near mountains, and in Africa it's common as rain. I could have warned you—but you shouldn't be robbed of your right to make mistakes.'"[5] Powerful neurochemicals like oxytocin and adrenocorticotropin were released as part of her fear cocktail, which intensified her focus and perception, at the same time strengthening the social connection between her and Tom when she was under stress. She got close enough to see the individual leaves before Tom took the controls. Using the fear cocktail to a successful outcome increased trust and wired the path to her courage network for brave behavior. Those chemicals, combined with that training, made Beryl the only woman among a group of a dozen or so men who were African pilots at the time. It is also what likely led to her and her flight instructor, Tom, becoming lovers. The close group around her, not the idea of being the next Charles Lindbergh, is what gave her motivation. Being in a state of flow, of feeling timelessness and doing something really well that

took no effort at all are by-products of turning fear into fuel. It is very true that bliss is on the other side of fear.

A 1982 study found that after graduating from training, UK army bomb disposal crews during the Irish troubles had a 95 percent success rate carrying out the courageous task of disarming a bomb. Almost all the graduates could disarm the bombs, despite huge variance in psychological profile testing, personality type, upbringing, and education. Slow courage is trainable no matter what your background; the more and better training you have the more courageous you become.

Build Your Courage: Find a group of experts you can join that will help you train under real-world stress, but in a way that you have a sense of protection and a feeling of trust. Joining an organization like Toastmasters to learn public speaking, signing up for a month of group lessons at your local climbing gym with a certified instructor and the latest equipment, planning a night out once a week ballroom dancing at an Arthur Murray Studio, all are ways you can put your body and mind under stress and learn to perform, but do it with a group of confidence-building mentors. You'll feel the butterflies of fear, but you'll be able to get them flying in the same direction with the help of professionals.

3. *Had a sense of control over herself and the situation*—When Beryl was just seventeen, her father gave her the choice of staying by herself in Africa or going with him to Peru. She chose to stay; she was in control of her future.

The more in control we feel, the less fear we will experience. Even fighter pilots in World War II, who had a 48 percent fatality rate, showed the highest level of courage in the entire war; part of that extreme level of bravery was a trust in their equipment and part was a feeling of control by having their hand on the stick and being in charge of their plane. Those pilots could also imagine the worst that could happen and did everything to prepare for that. Premeditating the evil is always a great way to evaluate what you are in control of and what you are not. Believing you can handle anything that comes your way is the key. Beryl saved a life by taking off in the darkest hours of the night to pick up a wounded hunter, flying on a simple compass course, heading over unforgiving terrain hours away, because she had confidence in her plane to keep flying and in her ability to navigate.

Build Your Courage: Take the time to determine what you can control and what you can't. When you do things that are courageous, remind yourself that you are in control. If you have a fear of being outdoors, remind yourself that you can always go back inside if things get intolerable; if you are afraid of failure in starting a new company, remind yourself that you can always go back to working for your old company, or in the same industry; if you are afraid to cold-call for fear of rejection, set a number of calls you need to hit in a day. Do not waste time, energy, or effort on worrying about things out of your control. Never adopt the mindset that someone else can make you scared, embarrassed, upset, angry, and so on. People can only affect how you feel if you give them permission. Only you have the power to determine how you feel. You are not a victim of circumstances; you are a creator of reality.

4. *Wrote down her feelings*—Markham's willingness to openly share her feelings is evident in the letters to her father, and later to her family and lovers. She shared the fact that she was unable to even talk about the boredom of being alive until she went to London for a year and hung out with a society group who had no adventure and lived their lives poisoned by a constant fear of others' judgments. It was in writing about our past failures that neuroscience has proven an amazing effect of attenuating fears in the present and future. Professor Brynne DiMenichi from Rutgers University and her colleagues showed that writing about past failures increased quality of performance in present high-risk activities.[6]

Build Your Courage: The Stoics all considered journaling the best way to keep themselves accountable. Marcus Aurelius used to scribe in the morning and determine what he wanted to master in that day, whereas Seneca used to review the day's events and explore his behavior and actions after his wife had gone to bed. The timing doesn't matter, but taking a few minutes to write about your thoughts and look as an observer on your behavior makes a huge difference, especially before big events or high-pressure activities. According to Matthew Lieberman, director of UCLA's Social Cognitive Neuroscience Laboratory, writing or talking about our fears makes them easier to deal with and takes away the feeling of paralysis. "This is ancient wisdom, but now we can verify it with brain mapping," Lieberman said. "Putting our feelings into words helps us heal better. If a friend is sad and we can get them to talk about it, that probably will make them feel better."[7] Thinking about an event and planning your behavior not only releases powerful neurotransmitters but continues to wire your courage network and the sgACC for courage and teaches you how to shut down the amygdala. That's why it helps us attain peak performance.

5. *Never let her teammates down, and could feel their pain*—Markham believed that the Golden Rule, treat your neighbor as you'd treat yourself, isn't just a way of being virtuous, but growing up in undeveloped Africa it was a means of survival in such an austere environment. Being brought up with the idea of getting back what you give and trying to understand what others were feeling is what let her move effortlessly in many socioeconomic circles. The Murani welcomed her into their tribe (literally) and taught her on the long hunts how to be a true team player. She never wanted to let people down; be they her horse-training clients, injured Murani tribesmen, or a tourist wishing to fly into a hunting camp, her sense of duty was always put ahead of her feeling of fear, and understanding how others felt in the moment gave her the courage to put herself in a bit of suffering to relieve it in others.

Build Your Courage: Become part of a team or group that would need to rely on you. In college when I started rowing, I was in both eights and fours; after college I was often in team boats. Belonging to these groups made practice easy in any conditions, and was much more fun than rowing alone. I always knew there were other men waiting on me, counting on me, and I'd never want to let them down. When I started rowing the single scull it was just me, so if it were forty degrees and pouring rain, I could stay in bed and tell myself I'd go out later if I wanted to. It's much tougher going at it alone. When you have others counting on you, others who sacrifice and work hard, you understand what they are feeling and you are compelled to reciprocate. The higher the stakes, the higher your indebtedness to them—so much so that many people have given their lives in acts of courage for their friends. Joining a community playhouse production, trying out for a recreational sports team, volunteering at an event are all simple ways to join a group that would count on you and that could push you out of your comfort zone as well.

6. *Modeled courageous behavior of others*—Beryl walked calmly, just two powerful bounds, in front of a lion, not once in her life, but twice. Both times the lions attacked; once it pounced on her and the other time it attacked the chief of the Murani tribe. Both times Markham watched

others with her and used self-talk to remind herself to do what the bravest warriors would do, or were doing, in the same situation. Witnessing someone act with courage and being encouraged to do the same is another prime way to learn slow courage. Modeling behavior, as psychologists call it, can further hard wire the connections to courage.

Build Your Courage: Courage is contagious—the problem is that so is cowardice. If you go bungee jumping and everyone in line in front of you jumps, then you are more likely to jump than if two or three people back out. That's because modeling behavior is what we are wired for as a species. Make sure you find mentors who are courageous, people who not only push you out of your comfort zone but push themselves as well. If you are starting a new division in your company, put together your own personal board of advisers—people who have done it before—and ask them to meet with you regularly. Reading biographies of great people like Beryl, Bill Clinton, the Wright brothers—anyone that you want to emulate—will usually show that great people can come from meager backgrounds. You don't need special training; you aren't constrained by money. Great leaders and innovators need only courage. Sometimes it takes some careful planning to know and take into account when you'll lack courage. After I recovered from leukemia, I started adventure racing and doing endurance challenges that had never been done before. Some of those races were multi-day events without sleep. If it was at the halfway point and I needed to sleep, I would never do it at a dedicated checkpoint. The checkpoints had volunteers, food, warm drinks, and heated rooms usually—and most importantly, it had quitters. People who dropped out had to go to the checkpoint to be extracted. I never wanted to be influenced by any of them so I'd get a twenty- or thirty-minute nap either before I hit a checkpoint or a ways after.

7. *Learned about big challenges she would face alone*—As soon as Beryl was able to ride a horse, her father took advantage of having another light rider to ride out and exercise the horses he trained. This one didn't cost him anything but room and board. Initially, she was on calm and predictable mares, but as her skills grew she graduated to more feisty mounts with the guidance of some of the more experienced jockeys and trainers on the farm. When her father gave her a young colt that she delivered at birth he knew she'd have to be ready to ride an unpredictable stallion before long, so he sent her out first

on the track with other riders, and eventually on her own on other stallions. It built a confidence in young Beryl's mind that she could handle everything that came at her. Later in life when snakes and lions spooked her stallion, she was ready for it and her calm control saved both her and the horse.

Build Your Courage: Practice doesn't make perfect; perfect practice does. You need to replicate what you will face in the real world to perform at your peak, and not choke. You also need to put yourself in the real-world situation if you have any anxiety or dread over something. Virtual Reality can help with some of this, but real-world replication has the biggest impact. If you are going to be speaking in front of a huge audience you need practice at the mic in front of live people; you need to get on the actual stage before the event to get familiar. Try to break your terror down into component parts and address each one at a time. Similarly, if you have a fear of flying then break it down into the physics, the equipment, and the pilots. First learn the basics of why and how planes fly—study a little physics online and learn that even if the engines stop working the plane can glide for quite a while (as Sully did to land on the Hudson River), look up the statistics for the type of plane you are likely to fly in or the number of passengers each year (four billion people flew in 2018), then go to the airport and talk to some pilots and ask them questions, or go to your local flight school and learn from them.

Markham turned fear into fuel. She built a long-term courage that was undeniable. Her purpose was adventure and living the best life possible, and she got the courage longevity benefit as well—she lived to the ripe old age of eighty-four at a time in Kenya when the life expectancy wasn't even sixty years. If you practice and become confident enough in a new mindset, the chemistry inside your brain changes with that new mindset. The fear cocktail of norepinephrine, cortisol, DHEA, and other enzymes that sharpens your focus and increases your performance can transition to a super drug. If you clear your working memory, you can produce pleasure-inducing compounds like oxytocin, anandamide, dopamine, endorphins, and serotonin. Then you have the best of both worlds: using the survival response for performance and the pleasure drugs for happiness, you get the courage high!

It's true that Beryl Markham lived an extraordinary life; it started that way because her father seeded a life of adventure and curiosity that germinated in Africa. However, the chances she was given are not unique to her; there were many other young English girls in Africa at the time who lived in fear. Even her own mother fled the country. My own story as a child of first-generation Irish immigrants who never went to college, who worked multiple jobs just to get by, is not a rarity. The Wright brothers were sons of a preacher. Richard Branson's father was a lawyer and his mom was a stewardess. To become the richest man in the world you should find a mother who would give birth to

COUNT YOUR COURAGE

Take a tip from the world-class leaders at West Point, the US Military Academy. Colonel Patrick J. Sweeney (call it a coincidence if you want—I don't think so!) and his colleagues found that a key courage trait was openness to new ideas and experiences. In the Free Energy Principle that's called expanding your Prior Beliefs.

A good way to remind yourself to be open to new ideas and experiences is to choose a path of opportunity and write about it. Every time you make a meaningful decision based on opportunity, it takes courage. To turn your courageous connections into a habit and actually grow your neural network, you should reward yourself. Counting courage is an easy way to stay courageous and remind yourself of your achievements.

Our survival brain defaults to fear-based decisions. It takes effort to choose opportunity, because you're fighting survival instincts. Our default action is to simply survive, not thrive. There is nothing wired in our survival brain that cares about living big, being happy, or changing the world. That's where mental rewriting of our brain's hard drive comes into play. Every time you make a decision based on opportunity—"I'm going to ask Acme Anvils to expand their contract with us and it will be a win for both of us"—that's a courage-based decision; most people default to "I shouldn't rock the boat with Acme; they've been a loyal customer for five years. I don't want to lose that gravy train, there goes the country club membership if I do." Classic fear-based thinking. Choose courage and keep score.

Every time you are faced with a big decision, STOP! Recognize fear-based alternatives and opportunity-based options. Write them down in a journal like Appendix A and put a star next to every courage-based decision you make. As the stars add up, so will your long-lasting courage.

you at sixteen and have a dad who was working in a retail store for $2.75 an hour, because that's how Jeff Bezos came into this world. The list of ordinary lives that turned extraordinary fills a vast ocean, making waves of change throughout history. Sadly, the number of wilting lives that make up the barren desert of humanity that never reached their potential is much easier to inhabit. Know that no matter where you started in life, or even where you are now, you have within you the power to create a wave of change, a legacy of leadership, an instant of innovation; it only requires courage and persistence.

APPENDIX A

Counting Courage Journal

Every day you are faced with dozens of choices, with many moments of reflection. To live a braver life, to be the fulfillment of everything you can be, you must trust that the universe is a very friendly place. You have to make the intention to use fear as fuel and approach everything as a challenge, not as a threat. Learning to act courageously will provide rewards beyond what you can imagine. Not only that—simply setting the right example can be the ultimate act of courage for those around you. Track every major choice you make and notice whether you are making it out of fear (fear of failure, fear of loss, fear of embarrassment, etc.); if fear drives your decisions you know you have not yet reached your potential. If you make a decision out of courage, give yourself a star; as the stars build up so will your courage network and sgACC—the part of your brain that makes you brave. In the world of bravery the legendary Roman politician and wealthy patron Seneca the Younger would examine every day, not passing a detail by to see if he were acting with courage and virtue. Journaling was his primary action of self-reflection. It can be yours too.

12

❧

Creating a Culture
of Courage at Work

Courage is the first of human qualities because it's the quality that guarantees the others.

—Aristotle

It was 1997; I was exercising my brain, transitioning from full-time athlete to twelve-hour-a-day student. The world's hardest-working graduate business school was filling my head up fast with everything from Black-Scholes models to Stakeholder Theory. This was the University of Virginia, and everyone here was world-class. Personal courage was still a long way away for me, but an incredible summer internship was about to pass on a lesson in cultural courage firsthand from a well-loved CEO.

"There are no secrets here. It's simple; I want everyone to do what they think is right, that's what I do," the middle-aged, six-foot-tall, handsome Texan drawled out while I looked across the top floor of this Dallas high-rise. Dozens of desks floated orderly across this wide-open expanse like islands in a sea of brown carpet. "We don't have walls because we want to know the good, the bad, and the ugly. I want people to see us all getting more excited about the possibilities and less hung up on the letdowns."[1]

Walking briskly with a slight stoop, the tanned fifty-year-old resembled Tip O'Neil more than his hero, Ronald Reagan. He explained the open floor layout at Trammell Crow's headquarters in Dallas, Texas. The founder's son, Harlan Crow, had taken over the real estate empire and family investment office several years earlier. His dad, and the company's namesake, Trammell, retired a billionaire years ago.

The previous eight months, my first year of MBA schooling, was chock full of the latest business theory. I worked hard enough to get my choice of internships for the summer between first and second year and put theory to practice. After much deliberation I took an internship with Crow. I soon found out that Harlan's reputation for confronting fear and using it to fuel peak performance was legendary. I was the opposite; just the thought of facing fear at that point in my life sent chills of panic through me. Before my trip to the headquarters in Dallas I had heard some of the more shocking stories about Harlan from the guys in Washington, DC. He had a presence and confidence that only comes with an intimate relationship with fear. Crow knew courage firsthand, and it seemed like failure never made it onto his radar. The more fearful I became, the more in awe of someone like Harlan I was.

I was in Dallas for my internship orientation with a group of other MBA students. The legend everyone wanted to verify was about a deal negotiation several years earlier. Imagine one of those impossibly long, regal conference tables often seen in movies. Opposing negotiators perch at opposite ends of the table like hockey goalies defending their respective nets. A court of minions ready to do financial battle flanked both sides, slinging formulas and data back and forth at each other to get the best deal. Harlan was the one at the far end of the table, his back to the massive window overlooking the Dallas skyline. When he and his adversary finally agreed on terms, Crow was so excited that rather than navigate around the crowded sides of the table, he jumped up on top, bounded across the shiny mahogany in his cowboy boots to the other end to seal the deal with a grasp of hands. Could you see yourself ever doing that? When I asked him if he walked across the table, his answer was a proud, "Hell yeah!"

Back to my meeting with Harlan. My mind raced and I struggled to differentiate fear, excitement, or intimidation created by this CEO taking a few minutes to share some company legend with a new intern. The message he spread throughout the organization was clear: focus on the upside and the success of the deal and become excited about the possibilities. Do everything you can to limit the risk, but never fixate on the possibility of failure. Risk comes with the territory.

THINK YOU'VE GOT A BIG SET?

Size does matter! That's what Dr. Joe Kable from the University of Pennsylvania told me about his latest research. By "set" of course I mean your two almond-shaped glands that I've talked so much about—the amygdalae. It turns out that the size helps people take risks. People willing to take more financial risks have more grey matter in the amygdala. Size matters, and so does the connection strength. Kable found three neurological attributes that predict a person's appetite for risk:

1. The structural connections
2. The functional connections
3. The volume of amygdala

Just by looking at these features of your brain, neuroscientists could have a reasonable idea whether you are someone who will take risks.

Kable was the first ever to use multiple types of the latest technology to show that people with the biggest amygdala take the biggest risks and, most importantly, reap the biggest rewards.

He also noticed that the same risk-tolerant subjects had fewer connections to the medial prefrontal cortex. But even though they had fewer links, the energy between these two regions was more coordinated—a measure called functional connectivity—compared with those who would rather play it safe. It means they have fewer bad connections and more really powerful ones that get used often. Risk taking creates a more efficient brain.

Risk tolerance is a key attribute of top-performing CEOs, according to the *Wall Street Journal*. The good news is that because of neuroplasticity anyone can increase the size of the amygdala and increase risk tolerance, simply by practicing using fear as fuel and doing things you would have shied away from in the past. Get out of your comfort zone as often as you can and you'll grow a bigger set!

The experience of meeting Harlan helped me to realize that this was the kind of place where I wanted to work. The leaders took everyone seriously and they did everything to be the best in the industry, even if it meant taking big risks; they wanted to win. For Trammell Crow Company it wasn't about the security of appearance or protecting the status quo. Harlan, and the entire company, fully expected even an intern to try new things, go out on a limb, and add value, not just pick up lunch and follow executives around hoping to catch a lesson here or bit of wisdom there. This company was a lot different from some of the big consulting firms I had interviewed with for my summer internship. That summer I had my first inkling of corporate courage. The difference I felt started at the top with the company's leader, but really it started nearly fifty years earlier with his father, the founder of the company, who was able to master the three kinds of courage needed to make a company dominant in its industry and create an icon.

I was lucky to have chosen Trammell Crow for my internship; it didn't pay the most or have the biggest brand name so it was a bit illogical, but I had a friend who worked there and that made a big difference.

Trammell Crow has a cultural acronym called RISE—Respect, Integrity, Service, Excellence. The CEO believed in spending time with an intern because everyone coming onboard has to believe in the vision to "Uphold, nurture, and promote an entrepreneurial and rewarding work environment." It takes courage to truly live in that kind of radically transparent and performance-based environment, but when you can build it, the results are unparalleled. If you want to find that same unshakable inner confidence and create that culture throughout your organization, you need to find these three kinds of courage:

1. *Personal Courage*—Being comfortable as the authentic you. That means acting no differently in your organization than you do when you're at home, with your best friend, or alone. Knowing when to make big decisions out of opportunity and never out of fear. Understanding what you can and can't control, focusing on the things you can control, and creating the best opportunity to fulfill your life's purpose.
2. *Corporate Courage*—Creating a culture where people feel safe making an argument against anyone in the organization, where the best ideas come forward and the people with the most information and experience are given the most weight, no matter their title or tenure. The ability to be completely transparent and open with the team. When you obtain this level of corporate courage the organization spits out people who don't fit within the structure.

3. *Transcendent Courage*—The courage for a leader to transform an industry or change the world by making huge, audacious bets that will not just forever alter the makeup of a company but revolutionize an entire industry. Having the courage to take these risks also means having the courage to put it all on the line with no turning back, the ability to "burn the boats."

In 1948, not long after the end of World War II, a young navy accountant left the service to return to his native Dallas, Texas. It took only a short time before his work with a moving and logistics company presented him with an opportunity to become part of the growing city he called home. Ray-O-Vac battery company had been asking around about any possible warehouses for lease in the area. They weren't the only ones looking, either. The young commander, now a tough-as-leather entrepreneur, was named Trammell Crow. He saw an opportunity if he were willing to take a risk, so he scratched and saved to amass $500, which he put on the line building a warehouse before he had a single tenant to pay him rent. At the time speculative real estate development was virtually unheard-of, yet Trammell was confident in his idea. He leased enough of that first spec warehouse to Ray-O-Vac to cover his costs, and had more space left over, which led to a handsome profit when he leased that remainder. Crow didn't go buy a big house or fancy cars with the proceeds; he took his profit and principal and built another warehouse to double down again. And again. And again. Trammell built the $500 into a multibillion-dollar real estate empire, bigger than Donald Trump's or any other American developer. Trammell exemplified a billionaire's decision-making process—he made bets based on opportunity, never on fear; he built a corporate culture of courage, and he transcended fear to change an industry. He was willing to take risks, which, combined with his courageous openness, taught others the value of mentorship, trust, generosity, sharing, and a focus on the positive.

Almost fifty years after he founded the company, Trammell's third son, Harlan, was running the show when I arrived as a summer intern. Harlan failed out of Emory College and had to come home to Dallas with his tail between his legs. But his dad never thought less of him, or worried about a single failure ruining his son. Instead, Trammell made him go back and try it again by enrolling in the University of Texas to finish a degree and prove his grit. The kid who was once a big failure in the eyes of the old-school Dallas elite because he couldn't get through Emory was now running the world's biggest real estate empire. This part of Harlan's past gave me hope and inspiration. He didn't just accept mistakes; he embraced them as a way of learning and honestly believed anyone could rise to the top if they worked hard and took calculated risks. Every leader in this company thought big, and every member in the company shares in success. It was not a culture of wondering if a partner would get a 5 percent raise for turning in a good report. These men and women expected a million-dollar bonus for changing the company or developing the next game-changing project.

Trammell had a secret sauce for being the best—he believed in hiring the best people and building a culture of courage and transparency from the top down. It wasn't always comfortable, but using fear seldom is. Having a structure where there is radical transparency and the decisions are opportunity-based on merit, not on title or tenure, allowed the company to take big risks with confidence. He knew which choices were bet-the-company and he knew the ones that were run-of-the-mill and worked to make sure each employee knew the difference as well. Merit-based decisions are what motivated a lowly intern like me to think I could actually have input from day one.

Crow's recipe was to create a culture of courage that encouraged risk taking and enabled an evidenced-based meritocracy. Trammell's financial formula was always to offset profit by loading up properties with debt; that way they would not have taxes to pay on profit. He timed it so that the company would own the building after fifteen years; then they would refinance and take out cash tax-free. It was risky to have a lot of debt, but it worked because no one was keeping secrets when things went bad. There were seldom surprises. A courageous culture takes great bravery and commitment. It's easy to do when it's a handful of employees and you are starting the company; it's tougher to do when you run a massive organization.

Harlan's commitment to the culture and the people were why the CEO sat at an open desk surrounded by his team. Good decisions were made based on merit and believability.

Trammell Crow grew to be the largest real estate developer in the United States. When I was interviewing, they were just expanding a high-tech practice and they wanted someone passionate about technology to set up an East Coast division. A summer internship was the first step, so we could each test-drive the relationship. I was still afraid of what I didn't know, afraid of failing, afraid of not being significant; but around the men and women at Trammell Crow Company I felt a collective confidence and equality that I had only felt in a rowing shell. I believed that if I failed and was able to learn something it might actually be OK, and I should focus on the upside, not on the failure. Both the CEO and the multimillionaire leader of the DC office had their desks right in the middle of everyone else; that was different. The more I listened to people at the desks around me the more I overheard conversations about opportunity, about taking risk, but never about the fear of failure. I never heard whispers of fear or complaints of unfair bosses.

The internship worked out so well, I stayed on as part of the DC team during my last year of grad school and was about to dive in full-time after graduation, when another event put that start temporarily on hold. I had to face a milestone that I had been putting off for several years already because of yet another fear; the fear of commitment. I was about to get married.

I had a gorgeous and supportive fiancée named Christen. We had been dating for five years. Christen was from Annapolis, Maryland, and like me, went to UVA. She was tall and blonde with an infectious laugh; we hit it off right from the start. In a few years, with my athletic career over, my graduate sheepskin in hand, and a job locked in, my quiver of excuses had finally run out. We marched down the aisle at Saint Mary's Church in Annapolis just a week after graduation.

Initially, I was in the politically driven enclave of Georgetown, just a walk down the road from the White House. What a contrast the Trammell Crow culture of courage and openness was compared to the many government wonks I met trying to get up the "GS" pay scale. After about six months in DC, it became clear that the technology sector was exploding in northern Virginia. I moved out to Trammell Crow's newest office in Tyson's Corner, Virginia, to dive into the deep end of the internet boom.

During my time at Crow we had been responsible for over six million square feet of data center space just as the internet was wiring its way into the machinery of global business. There was more internet traffic flowing through Tysons's Corner, Virginia, than anywhere else in the world at the time. It took more than twenty-five years for the internet to diversify enough to where the exchange in northern Virginia didn't transmit the bulk of the traffic.

HAPPILY MARRIED TO YOUR CAREER?

Having transparency and truthfulness in an organization means there will be conflict.

If you are making decisions based on merit, then heated arguments will boil up as people express their opinions. This is healthy conflict; this is part of a high-performing organization that requires people to face an uncomfortable situation and make decisions based on data, knowledge, or experience—not emotions. Looking at the data value of each decision is what it takes to fuel peak performance. Intel became the dominant chip company in the world based on a cultural strategy of constructive conflict.

The times in my career (and as an angel investor) when I've seen truly exceptional talents fail is when they do not welcome conflict or opposing views to fuel radical transparency. They avoid conflict and criticism. If you feel that urge to flee and avoid it, STOP! Observe the context, and then use your fear to make you stronger and move forward, making your case. If your heart is in the right place and you are doing something to achieve excellence or industry dominance, your opinion should be highly valued. Conversely, hiding your opinion and succumbing to the fear of conflict and protecting your opinion or ego will eat away at your own integrity and actions.

Learning constructive conflict is also great for romantic relationships since the number one predictor of failed marriages (according to the Gottman Institute) is not dealing positively with conflict, but instead holding your spouse in contempt or blame.

It takes practice but let your team (or your spouse) know you want to learn how to share your observations and ideas openly without blame or shame.

Back to 1999 and the dot-com mania in full swing. I had helped several big companies innovate and grow and adopted the mindset the leaders at Crow had taught me: that I was expected to think big and take risks. The corporate culture of risk-taking was clear. One of my clients was an early Internet Service Provider (ISP) called Digital Nation or DN. I negotiated leases and eventually helped the owner, Bruce Waldack, buy and build a state-of-the-art data center. We even started developing plans for a museum of the history of the internet (the museum would never come to fruition but is still a great idea today). I became close friends with the founder, who sold the company to Verio and NTT for one hundred million dollars in cash. He owned over 90 percent of the stock at the time of the sale. My first thought on hearing the details of the acquisition was, "I could do that." Seeing someone else take that big a risk and succeed helped me believe it was possible for me to do it as well.

A few years later when I started my first big tech company, ServerVault, I replayed the conversation I had had with Harlan in Dallas. Nobel Prize–winning researchers Daniel Kahneman and Amos Tversky had just published a paper about loss aversion and how most people put twice as much emphasis on the fear of loss than on the possibility of gain. It gave me concrete data on how to look at the world, which increased my confidence and encouraged risk taking like the Crow family did. The problem was that I was often angry, or self-critical, and had a constant anxiety that was actually becoming addictive. I was always worried about other people's opinions and other things I couldn't control. I was never sure I could handle all the different situations I might face. My challenges still seemed like threats that other people were pitting against me, like villains in my own soap opera. I hadn't found the kind of courage that it takes to really be successful and happy, I never thought I was good enough and that addictive anxiety was eating away at me and at my relationships. I was about to build the world's most advanced and secure state-of-the-art data center and I had some radical ideas that no one else had thought of, but I was terrified to leave Crow. I felt that if I didn't go for it, I would regret it for the rest of my life. The Crow lesson about building a culture of courage wasn't radical, but it would end up saving the company I was about to launch three years later.

Imagine the tension you'd feel realizing there's a chance you could build a wealth-creating, game-changing company and finally prove your significance and self-worth as a person but you had a loyalty and affinity for a group of executives who took a chance on you before you even finished graduate school. Some people might define it as stress and anxiety but what I was feeling was the Hulk against Ironman playing tug-of-war over my conscience as if I were a Stretch-Armstrong figurine. My fear of leaving the remarkable team at Trammell Crow was palpable; they helped me learn the nuances of real estate and become a budding authority in the data center industry. I lost count of the number of nights when I shot bolt upright out of a fitful sleep, second-guessing the idea of quitting, afraid of all the things that could go wrong if I started my own company, afraid I'd never get a chance like the one I had, afraid I wasn't good enough—afraid and wanting to avoid that feeling of fear. I learned a lot at Crow, but I still hadn't learned how to use fear as fuel. I learned how to recognize courage, but not how to find it.

Pushed by my friend Waldack, who had just pocketed ninety-seven million dollars and believed in me more than I believed in myself, I finally got the courage to start putting together my business plan and idea. I had decided in grad school that if I was going to amount to anything I needed to get rich. Money would be my fear antidote. I would make a fortune of forty million dollars by the time I was forty years old. If I wanted to meet this "forty by forty" goal I decided I had better start doing something about it, and Crow had helped me think like a billionaire. As Bruce put it when we were talking about my forty-by-forty goal: "Aren't you setting your sights a little low?"

Fortunately, I wasn't so self-critical and anxiety ridden that I couldn't hear my heart. Love helped shape some of my decisions too. Christen was working at a software company and bringing in a good salary and despite massive graduate school debt, on paper we looked financially stable. I didn't want to leave my hard-working wife without some stability if I were going to jump off an entrepreneurial cliff. We needed a rock to anchor our future on and create a safe haven. We both wanted to escape the temporary confines of apartment dwelling and buy our first house. Of course, we needed to get a mortgage. It all came together; and the day we signed on the mortgage was the day I quit my job; it just wasn't as easy as it sounds.

When I gave my notice to three of my mentors, their first question was "What can we do to make you stay?" The second question was "Where are you going?" When I told them it wasn't a competitor, but rather I was taking the plunge into entrepreneurship their reaction both surprised and flattered me: "Can we invest?"

I'm still good friends with them twenty years later. Great leadership creates positive, loving, and successful long-term relationships. It takes courage to have those kinds of relationships, but they are the only kind worth having. The executives at Crow all had a demonstrable ability to take risks. I didn't know the neuroscience at the time, but those three guys, and the entire Trammell Crow team, were helping me rewrite the subconscious database in my mind. It seemed that it was tough at the top, but a lot of fun. I saw a group of leaders who were comfortable with the uncomfortable; that is the foundation of great leadership.

Great companies have all three levels of courage, personal, corporate, and transcendent. Courage and using your fear as fuel is what will allow you to speak your mind, even if that means running across the top of a conference table. (If you said no way when I asked if you could do that, ask yourself now, Why not? And think about what type of fear might be holding you back.) Your own personal level of courage and always making decisions based on opportunity is the first step to reaching that transcendent level of courage. You must master that self-confidence to choose in the face of fear. The other side of fear in your decision making is the courage that will change your entire life. Personal courage is a choice; meditating and doing some of the courage exercises are what will help get confident quickly. A personal commitment to courage will keep you from becoming sucked into the toxicity of office politics or poisoned by the shadows of gossip, both of which are by-products of fear.

If you are always acting in integrity, always being your authentic self, no matter what other people think, do, or say, you will find that you're the combination of your passion married with your vocation. It is what Diana Chapman from the Conscious Leadership Group calls living in your genius. You'll also end up in the perfect spot for you; it just may take some time for you to get there.

I combined lessons from Trammell Crow, values from my Olympic days, and some training from business school to create the perfect work environment for me. However, I was still a long way from embracing fear as fuel and being truly courageous. I still hadn't discovered my authentic self. That would take the ultimate loss to find.

TESTING THE STRENGTH OF A CULTURE

Most companies have a culture of fear and blame. They don't start out that way; they evolve blindly with leaders who decide using a brain designed for survival. If you don't know how to find fear and use it to power peak performance, then when you feel your tells you will react. When you react, it's going to be with a fight, flight, or freeze response and you'll do something you'll regret.

One of the toughest challenges of starting my own company was convincing people I really, truly wanted all employees to speak their minds and defend what they believed was the truth or the best answer. Many of our new hires were afraid of speaking their minds because they were punished for it at past companies. It was one of the reasons I avoided titles at ServerVault. I always thought titles were more harmful to a culture than helpful, because they gave ideas credibility based not on merit or value but on title. I wanted to do everything I could to promote a culture of courage.

ServerVault was the first big company I founded. I took the idea of a data center and made it as bad-ass as possible. I created a home for the most sensitive electronic information in the world. We built the company around logical security, physical security, and operational security. Governments, banks, insurance companies could all feel safe hosting their data with us—we were the first real Cloud back when clouds were only where rain came from. We created a safe, courageous environment that would end up saving the company more than once during the tumultuous years after the dot-com bust.

I bought prime real estate next to the world's largest ISP at the time, America Online (AOL). It was an exciting experience hiring the nation's top internet architects to build something that had never been done before. I had a vision of a place that was ultra-secure, conveyed our mission with its presence, and would be the coolest place to work in the mid-Atlantic region. We had one of the plank owners (founders) of SEAL Team Six as our facilities security expert, and we began revolutionizing the data center of the future. In addition to the facility being ultra-secure from hackers, terrorists, and potential threats such as fires and earthquakes, it was an incredibly safe place to work emotionally because we fostered a culture of courage starting with the design of our headquarters, which was all open office with no separate offices for higher-level executives.

ServerVault was my first big CEO role, and I could have had any office I wanted. I could have put up a gold-leaf door with soundproofing and flashing lights, but I didn't because of the lessons I learned at Crow. Anyone could walk up to Harlan and give their thoughts or ideas. I wanted the ServerVault team to feel that same level of safety and trust in me. The facility was an extension of that philosophy. It clearly conveyed the strategy that no one person's ideas or value was higher than another's; we just wanted the best solutions. We were all valuable team members. We carried this trust into day-to-day operations. I believed what Andy Grove, Intel's CEO, was constantly driving toward—constructive conflict. People passionately presented their points of view; then decisions were made based on the likelihood of success.

Everyone at ServerVault had to withstand a US Department of Defense–level background check. That meant at the lowest level fingerprinting and financial history. Everyone was enrolled in our biometric access system to all areas of the Vault. Once you were part of the team you were fully part of the team. Some CEOs I interacted with at the time were shocked that any one person had the capability to shut down the entire data center; I didn't understand their thinking. If I were hiring people to be part of our team I had to trust them completely. I had to know they shared our same belief in the values and principles that ServerVault stood for. If they didn't align with our vision of "Securing the Internet," they didn't belong on the team. Our core ideologies were:

- Hire only the best
- Constantly innovate
- Act with the utmost integrity
- Create supremely satisfied clients

The facility, the values, and our actions created a culture of courage that saved the company from ruin and turned it into a case study for entrepreneurship. We wanted free thinkers and creative innovators. People believed our commitment to these ideals beyond a statement on the wall. Everyone had the mandate to constantly innovate; if they weren't focused on that they didn't fit. I once asked a system administrator what he was thinking by doing a project the way he did; he told me because that's how it had always been done. The first time he answered me that way I told him to find a better, more innovative way. He did the same thing about a week later and again I asked him why. The second time he gave me the same answer "because that's how it's always been done," I fired him.

Having the best people constantly enforcing a culture of courage made for a very safe place, emotionally, to work. Problems were discussed openly not as good or bad, but as challenges. Tactics were constantly questioned to find more innovation and efficiency. We expected a lot from every single person, whether an intern or a C-level executive. In return, as at Crow we were generous with stock options and an ability to share in our success. The open, often uncomfortable conflict always felt much better than hiding our feelings or thoughts and bottling things up. It was the possibility of losing this courageous culture and my lack of personal courage that almost killed us as a company.

As a first-time CEO I had made a bunch of mistakes, but the biggest one was choosing the wrong financial partners. Greed got in the way of long-term vision and integrity. Remember there are just two ways to make decisions—out of fear or out of opportunity. I chose our venture capitalist (VC) partners out of fear. That always leads to regret and it certainly did in this instance. When we needed our next round of financing we were in a very good spot; the internet bubble was still filling up without so much as a strain on the seams. We had a unique plan to meet a real market need and a world-class team to execute it. Because of this combination we had four or five different venture capitalists interested in financing our growth. I had taken a trip over to Ireland to look at data center space in Dublin when I was seduced by my fears. The press was calling Europe's hotbed of technology the Celtic Tiger. I was involved with a charity called the American Ireland Fund that was helping to promote the peace process in Ireland. As a dual citizen of Ireland and the United States I had deep roots to the Auld Sod. In Dublin I met a venture capitalist who loved the idea of our company. He told me I shouldn't wait around for the stogy old US-based venture firms. He would wire a million dollars to our bank account on a handshake as a bridge loan to the entire round. I was flattered and jumped at the chance because we might never get money anywhere else; I was afraid of failure. His higher pre-money valuation meant that for the ten million dollars we were raising I thought (spoiler alert) we would keep more of the company. I wasn't experienced enough at the time to know about things like liquidation preferences, participating preferred shares, and other mechanisms that venture capital firms leverage to get higher returns and take more of a company. I eventually learned those intricacies the hard way. I also learned the value of having partners and employees who were fully transparent and radically honest. And the cost of those who were not.

After September 11, 2001, the dot-com bubble was spinning around the room hissing out air. Companies that were buying our services stopped spending money. We failed to meet our revenue projections and our group of first-time venture capitalists got scared. I was worried all the time, so anxiety and dread were nothing new to me. I was afraid we'd miss our numbers constantly, and when we finally did the VC decided it was because of me and made me "Chief Strategy Officer." That's how venture capitalists push out a founder with as little fanfare as possible, so things look to outsiders as if everything is A-OK. It wasn't long before the new interim CEO and the venture capitalist realized that finding new customers was really tough, and it would require a bigger infusion of cash to get us through these tough times. Our technology was groundbreaking; we had designed a system to stack in more than five times the density of a normal data center so our fixed costs were a lot lower, our brilliant technology team automated the security systems on each server, basically the electronic equivalent of having someone walk around and make sure all the doors and windows were locked in a giant hotel, and our uptime was the industry's best at 99.99987 percent. These innovations were unheard-of at the time. When the new CEO realized that we were going to need more money and the VC firms that made up our financing group didn't have the money to put in, they tried to take our proprietary security technology with the idea of starting a new software security company. Our chief technology officer was the one who discovered this underhanded behavior, and he came to me and our Chief Financial Officer (CFO) to figure out a plan.

We went to our legal team at Cooley Godward and laid out the entire story, which was shaping up like a John Grisham novel. (Did I mention the mafia death threat yet?)

The investors were in effect trying to steal intellectual property. Our legal team suggested that we get them to clearly articulate their intentions so there would be no misunderstanding. While I was petrified of what might happen if we did, I had the steady guidance of one of the highest-integrity partners I could wish for: our CFO, Jim Zinn, to give me courage.

A former Ernst & Young accountant, Jim was the first CFO of the Capital One credit card company and was at the financial helm when they went public, then decided he wanted to be part of the dot-com excitement. Jim's gray-hair presence painted a stabilizing picture of his years of experience at Ernst & Young as an accountant and then as a public company CFO. We planned to face the situation head-on at the next board meeting. Anguish made sure I slept no more than a few hours each night leading up to that day.

The board meeting was a week away and we started planning our strategy. When the time rolled around and the meeting started, the VC acted surprised that we had figured out what was going on. We clearly caught them off guard, so they wanted to reschedule the meeting while they "looked into it." We were running on fumes at the time, and the venture capitalists were providing the pre-promised financing in tranches—never fully funding the amount they had committed to but rather trickle feeding us. In a karma-like twist of fate, we got an email from one of our board members that allowed us to save the company. The trust and transparency we had built with employees ensured that the company didn't implode, as many companies did at the time. We were scared for sure, but we were using that fear as fuel.

Bizarrely, one of our board members broke a fiduciary commitment by sending us an email asking to be paid off ahead of everyone else. Our lawyers suggested we find another financing alternative to satisfy the secured and unsecured creditors (who had priority) and take back control of the company. I was in shock at this crazy turn of events but realized that we might be able not only to save the company but take back control and turn our dream into a success after all.

As someone who was afraid of everything, the whole idea terrified me, but with Zinn and our brilliant CTO John Broome's support I started to use that fear as fuel to save ServerVault. Over the course of sixty days, we went to more than one hundred private equity firms all over the East Coast. About halfway through our search for new funders, we ran out of money. The fifty or so team members working at the Vault were humming away keeping our remaining customers satisfied while we were on the road, but no new revenue was coming in. It was Thanksgiving and the holidays were just around the corner; that's when the safety of our founding strategy saved the company. It was a culture of courage that kept us alive.

My hands were sweaty and shaking when we called an all-hands meeting of the company. I had the same nausea that I felt during the 1992 Olympic Trials; it was miserable. I had apparently only found courage on the racecourse because I was petrified. Acting with the utmost integrity meant that, as Harlan had said, I shared the good, the bad, and the ugly with the team. In this instance I had a vision of all of them walking out the door, and our dream company withering away and dehydrating to death like a pilot crash landing in the middle of the Sahara Desert. I began the meeting with hands trembling and butterflies in my stomach. My voice cracked and my eyes were moist. I explained every detail of what happened and that with the VC no longer funding us, we were out of cash. There were dozens of faces with mouths agape, slack-jawed in disbelief. What the news meant was that no one would receive a paycheck for the foreseeable future and no one would get an end-of-the-year bonus. I told the team it was their choice to stay without pay. Many had families, mortgages, college tuition bills, and other obligations and they could vote with their feet.

In one of my proudest moments as an entrepreneur, everyone stayed. I drove home that night with tears in my eyes thinking about how trusting, loyal, and committed everyone on that team was. By building a culture of courage, a safe place where people felt they could be themselves and could share their fears and doubts while working toward a common goal, we had created something beyond a job. We were committed to a mission.

One of my professors in graduate school was Jim Collins, who wrote *Good to Great*.[2] He is famous for advising leaders to think of your company as a bus; every single seat was valuable and had to be taken up by the perfect person. I always thought of my companies as an eight-man rowing shell—each seat had tremendous value and in addition you needed to find the perfect person to be rowing in the same direction as hard as they could in synchronicity with everyone else. We had done that at ServerVault.

In mid-January of 2002 as companies all around Silicon Valley, Boston, and Washington, DC, were imploding, our 101st financing pitch meeting brought success. We found a private equity firm in Cincinnati that funded us and helped us put together a restructuring plan that Jim and I worked hard to get all our creditors to agree to. We executed the plan and took back the company. Later, we sold it for five times what these new financing partners had put into it, and then it was sold a couple years after that after merging with another company for over three hundred million dollars. The culture of courage was threatened at times, but the core team enabled innovation and execution, which helped a lot of companies. Creating a culture of courage is easier to do when you start from the ground up—it's much more difficult if you have to change a big company, as you'll find out in the next chapter.

13

❡

The Big Squeeze

I might have been given a bad break, but I've got an awful lot to live for.

—Lou Gehrig

Dunedin is a sleepy enclave of snowbirds escaping the Northeast's harsh winters. However, each year the town wakes up with a flurry the first week of February. The difference between Dunedin and similar retirement communities in Florida is the thirty-year-old baseball stadium just a few blocks off Main Street. The manicured grass, 10,000 seats, and oversized parking lot seem out of place, like a concrete UFO that landed among new condominiums, single-family homes, and a scattering of brewpubs and never left. On a sunny, seventy-degree February day I strolled down Main Street toward the stadium, surrounded by fans with baseball gloves in their hands, wearing Toronto Blue Jays shirts, adding an interrogatory "Eh?" to the end of each sentence. Canadians had come south for spring training.

At the stadium's main entrance I flashed my ID. A heavyset, tan woman with an explosion of white hair sent me up the elevator to the manager's box at the top of the stadium. After a cursory wrap at the door I walked in to find Mark Shapiro alone inside the ten-by-fifteen-foot grey room, a platter of fresh fruit untouched on the hightop table in the center of the box. He was sitting on the far side at a waist-level bar facing the baseball diamond. Five empty chairs lined up next to him all faced expectantly out the open box to the field and crowd below. Shapiro tapped a pen on the bar, then scribbled a note. He popped up to give me a hearty greeting and welcome, then launched into details of the guy up at bat. It was legendary Red Sox and Yankees pitcher Roger Clemens's son, Kacy. The stats and figures rattled out of Shapiro like bullets out of a machine gun. In seconds I had a better take on Clemens's spring training than if I spent a week scouring the web. Statistics and data painted a picture in Shapiro's mind of the young man's chances of earning a seat on the bus in Shapiro's effort to turn this team from good to great. To look at his quick smile and healthy complexion, I could never have imagined how scary this new challenge was for Shapiro. The irony is that he had gone looking for fear at a time when he was safest in his career—that's what makes him a great leader and a person from whom we can all learn. I was there to ask him why and how he was going to create his same level of courage throughout a new four-hundred-person organization.

Moneyball is the classic Michael Lewis baseball book turned into a blockbuster movie.[1] Lewis chronicles a season with Billy Beane, the general manager of the Oakland A's who hired a Harvard-trained data scientist to help build his team. It was an entirely new approach

Hug or Handshake

We are programmed to be community animals that love social interaction. One of the easiest ways to see the value of this contact is in tough times—we turn to friends, family, and loved ones for support. There is science behind why and how this works. Oxytocin, the cuddle hormone that makes us feel loving after sex and warms our heart when we get a hug, reduces feelings of anxiety, pain, and fear.

Basketball, baseball, rugby, even cricket team members often hug each other or share complicated handshakes to celebrate and support each other on the sidelines. The fear of failure or fear of losing doesn't go away; however, relaxed teams that feel supported and connected can better use their fear as fuel for their best performances ever. If you're faced with a workplace crisis or a daunting physical challenge, having friends by your side can make all the difference between success and failure. Before your next big presentation, or when you're getting ready for a test, bring your favorite coworker with you for support, at least get a hug, or teach him or her your own champion's handshake. It will add fuel to your competitive fire.

to selecting players. Almost everyone in the league rejected the Ivy League quant-jock who knew nothing about baseball. Their old-boy attitude was a classic example of making a fear-based decision; scouts saw computers taking their jobs, managers carried superstition of changing the status quo, owners didn't want to be blamed for breaking an organization that had been built up over decades. Everyone in baseball except Billy Beane was missing the chance at an opportunity-based action. Everyone but another rising baseball executive named Mark Shapiro.

Shapiro is a Baltimore-bred sports genius who got into baseball in his twenties, starting out with the Cleveland Indians. His dad was the agent for all-stars like Cal Ripken and Kirby Puckett, so baseball was in his blood. It wasn't long before Shapiro climbed the ranks to become the Cleveland Indians' assistant general manager. The Indians were perpetual cellar-dwellers in Major League Baseball's most competitive division—the American League East. Normally, big paychecks bring in big talent. The New York Yankees and the Boston Red Sox feed the fattest payrolls in baseball. Those are the two teams most often in the playoffs, perpetually battling for a chance at a World Series trophy.

When Shapiro started as a mid-level executive with the Indians in 1991, they were in what fans called a "thirty-three-year slump." It took a while, but eventually his analytical approach to decision making earned him the spot of general manager in 2001. The Indians' total payroll in his first full year as GM (2002) was $78.9 million. The Yankees were spending 63 percent more—over $125 million a year and the Red Sox were at $108 million. Most of baseball believed that to get the best players you had to buy them—pay big salaries for proven all-stars. Shapiro knew he could never compete on salary. Other team GMs feared the new system of analytics that they didn't know; consequently they acted based on fear and didn't use the statistical approach. They were regretting that action now. Shapiro acted on opportunity. Instead of fearing that he'd never have the budget to build a championship team he took it as a challenge. Shapiro hated to lose. He took the long view and built a player development program based on statistical analysis that would become the envy of Major League Baseball. Soon the Indians' owners saw the change in the organization and they made Shapiro president of the entire team. He was winning more and more. With the analytic approach the "Tribe," as they are known, became contenders for the

American League championship for the first time in decades. The Indians won an American League division title in 2007 by beating the Yankees when the Tribe's payroll was just $61 million compared to the Yankees' $190 million. Not surprisingly, *Sporting News* named Shapiro sports executive of the year. He took a seemingly impossible threat and turned it into an award-winning challenge.

After twenty-four years with the Indians, Shapiro was as beloved in Cleveland as LeBron James. He was at the top of his game. His system was not only working; it was leading in a world where each year the press and fans bring the highest expectations and scrutiny to the results. The problem was that Mark knew himself and knew when he was not growing. He recognized that he needed a fresh challenge. He spent a career pushing out of his comfort zone and embracing fear as fuel, and he becomes restless when it feels as if nothing is at stake. What he became afraid of was complacency.

Every time I talk with Shapiro it's clear that he never looks at issues as threats, only challenges and opportunities of which to take advantage. He knew he had built an elite system and structure with the Indians. Because of the leaders he had empowered, the team could survive without him putting in much effort. By hiring an incredible staff, from his perspective, he had built the team into a sustainable machine on cruise control. He didn't like the feeling. For a longtime athlete like Shapiro (he played football at Princeton and still works out daily) it was as if someone was lifting weights for him while he sat on the couch watching them sweat. His mind, body, and soul were not getting the fresh challenge he knew they needed to be happy and at their peak. He needed a growth opportunity. It was time for a change. He was deciding out of opportunity and this is what transcendent courage is all about.

Shapiro wanted to stay in the top of the top, the most competitive division in baseball; that meant finding an opportunity with one of the five teams that make up the American League East. When one of those teams, the Toronto Blue Jays, began looking for a new leader, he jumped at the chance. The move was "unsettling, but that was actually part of the attraction. Viewing challenge as opportunities to grow and staying growth focused was so important to me," Shapiro told me as I sat next to him in the owner's box.[2]

Shapiro's focus on talent, culture, and constant improvement drove an underfunded, also-ran club into a contender in professional baseball's toughest division. Transforming the Indians also earned him one of the most respected reputations in professional sports. He built a player development system (minor league teams) producing some of the best players in the league and still driving Cleveland's regular contention for a playoff berth even after his departure. The Toronto opportunity was Shapiro's chance to prove that his management system and philosophy worked anywhere.

While it doesn't always seem that way, Toronto is in a different country and has a different culture from Cleveland, Ohio; its baseball team represents an entire country, not just a city. Mark was from Baltimore and didn't walk, talk, or act like a Canadian; he wasn't taught the national anthem at twelve and never played hockey. He had a wife and kids (who had spent their whole lives in one place) to think about and he was stepping into a marketplace where the owners, former president, and former manager were beloved Canadians. When he heard the job was open, he rationalized that since the team hadn't been in the playoffs in twenty years there was tremendous upside to coming in and turning things around; it was a perfect challenge. Then the upside vanished and the job got exponentially more difficult.

After Shapiro decided to take the job in mid-2015, Toronto's outgoing GM and CEO made their biggest push ever to make the playoffs. Paul Beeston, the outgoing CEO, was the Jays' first official employee and a big fan favorite; for five years he had served as the president of Major League Baseball. He was Canadian sports royalty. The Blue Jays had not been in the playoffs for almost twenty years and Beeston believed the fans deserved a winning season. The only currency they had to bring in great players was their future prospects. Beeston and his staff traded more than a dozen of their key future prospects to fuel a play-off run. Miraculously, they made it. They had the best second half of the season in the team's history and finished by winning the American League East. An electrified fan base created greater interest in Canadian baseball than ever. Winning in 2015 catapulted the team from mildly popular to the darlings of not just Toronto, but an entire nation. That created a much brighter spotlight on Shapiro because the coming years without those future prospects and not much of a budget would be nearly impossible to manage. Now Shapiro had two immediate challenges: he had to figure out how to bounce back from a short-term success to create a long-term sustainable machine like he had in Cleveland, and he had to completely change the way the organization made decisions and looked at data. Time to get to work.

The team's anomalous winning season created tremendous internal headwind against cultural change because the employees had tasted success. Winning seemed, to everyone from ushers to scouts, like progress. Shapiro was no longer coming in as a savior. The entertainment and public-facing stakeholders soon filled with animosity toward Mark. After three months of winning capped by taking the Americana League East title, many internal employees did not want to rock the boat. They hoped that even without the future prospects traded away they could keep winning in the AL East. Almost overnight the situation changed radically for Mark (and his family). No longer was he the talented baseball executive who could come in and set up a system for the Blue Jays and help them become long-term contenders. Now he was the outsider poised to come in and ruin this winning organization. Shapiro, well aware of the vilification he was facing in the press, was fearful of the abuse his kids were going to take at school, he was fearful that his wife would have trouble settling into their new environment, he was naturally also concerned about how he could build a culture for the long term. He would always have the challenge of the American League East and a new challenge dealing with a different currency and exchange rate. But like all great leaders, fear fueled him to push forward.

Shapiro knew the only way to deal with what had gone from a great upside to a difficult situation was to be his authentic self. He focused on being confident and consistent and controlling what he could control. Shapiro knew that if he trusted in himself and was self-assured over time, his virtues would resonate. He focused on the job of building the organization into something great. His strategy was to first articulate his essential values for success. Mark launched three changes from the start:

1. Focus on the business reality—the Blue Jays were in the American League East—a money-rich marketplace; that meant, with a much lower budget than the Yankees and Red Sox, they would always be a third- or fourth-place team based on ability to buy talent. They also had the Canadian Exchange Rate to compete against. If they wanted to outperform their fiscal constraints, they needed a plan. The strategy was to build a championship culture on collective intelligence, tapping into everyone's expertise, and let the best ideas win. This was a huge departure from the existing hierarchical model. Employees harbored anxiety and fear because they didn't believe they were allowed to fail and still keep their jobs. They didn't feel

empowered. But it would take Shapiro's management philosophy, which he calls compression, to make this strategy a reality. You'll hear about that soon.

2. Decide with data—The team had to move from anecdotal decision making by a single person to data-driven informed choices with input from many. Shapiro's job was to give employees the resources to find and distill the data. He immediately set up a new group focused on collecting and disseminating information. He wanted the organization to make choices based on the opportunity of upside and improvement, not being afraid of changing the status quo.

3. Make choices by committee—Shapiro set up strategic teams of people to collaborate on big initiatives. He didn't want one person to dictate the strategy. Groups worked closely together to make recommendations and present their choices in front of what they call the BLT—business leadership team. The only acceptable result was a well-researched and thoughtful recommendation based on as much data as possible. These committees decide on make-or-break actions for the club—everything from how to optimize ticket pricing to offering new corporate services to changing spring training budgets. There were no VPs to steer the outcomes; the committees were populated by low- and mid-level executives only.

Coming in at the top Shapiro knew he could also hire a team of senior executives in the front office who believed in him and his philosophy; but how could he change a four-hundred-person organization as quickly as possible? Shapiro came up with a strategy he calls compression. This is an effective way of changing any large organization to a culture of courage and excellence.

Compression starts at the top with courageous and transparent leadership. Shapiro and his top leaders clearly defined the team's values and mission statement. When they got together for their first off-site, Shapiro was digging for an easy-to-understand mission statement that encompassed their philosophy. He needed a simple jewel that could liberate the Blue Jays from their perpetual island of mediocre performance. Like all great leaders, Shapiro has a loyal following, so key members of his Cleveland team followed him to Toronto. Eric Wedge rejoined Mark to run the player development organization— the lifeblood of upcoming talent that would build long-term success for the Jays. Ross Atkins left to become Shapiro's general manager.

At the first big team off-site meeting, Atkins said that if they want to be champions, they have to get better every day. Simple, growth minded, and courageous, that line hit home. "Getting Better Every Day" became the mission statement. As you walk through the Jays' spring training facility, you see the phrase embossed on notebooks the coaches carry, painted on walls, and permeating the entire organization. That simple phrase at the top says it all. No matter what the new CEO says in a company, there are still some people who refuse to change and the Jays had people who didn't want to get better every day. That's where compression comes in.

The point of compression is to push the values and mission down unrelentingly from the top and then hire and empower ambitious young people climbing up from the bottom with a belief in the mission and the courage to push the philosophy upward. To steal a baseball phrase, the squeeze play of compression starts at the top and then takes root at the bottom of the organization. Baseball teams are in a constant state of hiring; as young rising talent looks for upward mobility, they often leave holes at the bottom of a team's organization. Shapiro told me that he puts more effort into hiring interns than many Fortune 500 companies put into hiring at the VP level and above. To find the smartest, most ambitious talent at the bottom, he has to provide a safe environment from the top. He has to deploy "air cover" for young executives to come in and shake things up. The top-bottom combination will compress mid-level executives who may not be aligned with the team's vision and mission. This makes it tougher for average performers to hide in a maze of mid-level executives who otherwise could coast along doing things "the way they have always been done," echoing the dying defense of stagnant uninspired employees everywhere. Shapiro demands that people who are afraid to take risks, afraid to try something new, afraid to fail, afraid of changing the status quo, get pushed out of his organization. Compression is the most effective method of clearing the middle, but Shapiro had to prove to skeptical employees that he meant what he said in those early days.

In the old days the Blue Jays had three or four executives who communicated to the other 396 employees. Shapiro wanted to be more inclusive; he hosts regular town hall meetings now with many presenters. He recalls the first meeting after he had been working for a while with the strategic internal committees they set up. He found a mid-level manager who believed wholeheartedly in the Shapiro strategy of taking responsibility, putting a championship effort together every day, and being growth oriented. This guy was getting better every day, and Shapiro noticed it. He had this young manager present to the whole organization at the town hall meeting. He remembers proudly that "all these other people were so excited for him and so excited to see this young guy named Eric Cowell, a ticket operations manager, a mid-level manager, make a presentation and guide us about a major decision, and it was a major decision. They started to believe in empowerment and opportunity."[3]

From the perspective of the hundreds of people at the Blue Jays organization, it was a scary time. Saying good-bye to the Blue Jays' first employee, the CEO who had become royalty in the Canadian sports world, meant a lot of uncertainty. There were big changes in the wind. What many existing employees didn't realize was that they had a leader who understood their perspective and sent a clear message through the organization that if they performed like champions every day, they would have a fun, rewarding place to work. He could sympathize with their feelings but didn't have empathy for those afraid to grow. Shapiro believes that fear is a good thing for employees to experience because they can learn to understand fear, and realize that fear is a natural feeling, it's proof that we're still alive. "It's part of knowing that you are in a worthwhile situation because it means there is something at stake and there's an opportunity to grow, develop, and learn. When you're in that situation you have to focus on what you can control and let all the other stuff go."[4]

A challenge of compression, Shapiro says, is dealing with replacing people who don't buy into the mission. Mark and I both believe that the only way to win in a competitive and chaotic marketplace like technology or sports is hiring people who can handle ambiguity and disarray, who think creatively, and who bring confident, honest opinions to the table. Courage and excellence are two other virtues we both look for. At ServerVault and then ODIN, I did my best to build a culture where we would have a sense of body-part rejection if we made a bad hire. Our culture was so strong that if our values and mission didn't align with what a person believed they would realize it, or their peers would sense it, and everyone would be painfully uncomfortable. This would help us eliminate the hiring mistake and act as fast as possible to get them out.

However, there's one place where Shapiro and I differ: I fired as quickly as possible even if that left a hole in the organization. Shapiro believes that the Blue Jays don't have the luxury of firing a key employee without first finding a world-class replacement. We both agreed on one critical area of leadership and one that requires the most courage—we had to not just tolerate mistakes but embrace them as learning opportunities. Failure is expected, and for compression to work you have to go so far as to celebrate failure. This holds true for start-ups as well as large organizations. Many of the best opportunities in start-ups come from the early failures.

Technology is similar to baseball in the sense that everything is measureable. In the early days running my first big start-up, Server-Vault, no one in the industry was promising 99.9 percent uptime for websites they were hosting. We decided to go all in to differentiate ourselves and promised our clients 99.999 percent—"five nines" of uptime. To put that in perspective, "three nines" means your website or portal can be offline for almost nine hours a year (that's a full work day for some people); contrast that with just five minutes a year of downtime if you are promising five nines. Uptime percentage is the baseball equivalent of on-base-percentage: the higher the better.

One day at the start of ServerVault's second year our entire network went down. As you can imagine it was chaos, with all hands on deck. Every engineer in the company scrambled to troubleshoot and diagnose the issue. In the end, it turned out that while we had two bandwidth providers at the time they shared the same fiber optic loop, within the same pipe, that came into our data center. Construction a mile away had split the pipe and caused far-reaching connectivity outages. It cost us thousands of dollars in penalties, but it might have saved us millions in the coming years. Within a month, we found another pipe via a different underground route and created a redundancy contingency that became a positive marketing message. Soon this method became standard practice in the hosting industry. The original mistake turned into a competitive advantage for a while because we embraced mistakes as learning opportunities. Shapiro believes that for compression to work you must authentically live in a culture of courage.

The foundations to build a culture of courage are:

- Help individuals cultivate personal courage. Put systems and programs in place to help employees find their authentic selves, have time for self-reflection, even do internal programs like meditation training or physical training.
- Teach employees to embrace their fear, feed it, and use it as fuel for peak performance.

- Help employees focus on what they can control and accept what they can't control.
- Reward and promote team members who put curiosity ahead of ego—looking good should never be more important than performing at a championship level.
- Put as much effort into hiring entry level as you put into hiring at the C-level.
- Articulate your vision and values and make sure everyone in the organization believes in the philosophy and principles.
- Make it everyone's job to improve the organization; constantly improving must be an expectation. This creates a growth mindset and not a toxic fixed mindset.
- Embrace radical honesty and integrity; expect and embrace criticism and conflict but make sure it's never personal.
- Drive strategy and resolve conflicts with as much data as possible.
- Create a safe environment so decisions can be made with healthy conflict.
- Explain that criticism shouldn't be taken personally but should only be given with the idea of making things better.

If you recognize your personal fears and shortcomings, you can act with courage and confidence. Mentoring others to also explore deep self-awareness and feel when their amygdala activates is the only way to help them learn how to clear their working memory of the fight, flight, or freeze response. This sets the stage for a radically transparent culture that grows optimally. Occasionally there's a big fat angry animal that impedes progress and compression; that's when you need to use even more force.

COMPRESSING THE HIPPO

"I filled out the survey, but I didn't give truthful answers; they say it's anonymous, but I know they have my IP address."

"Why are you afraid of answering truthfully?" I asked.

What would your answer be to the question I asked the director of product management in Palo Alto—"why don't the surveys reflect what all the employees *really* think?"

One of the top internet companies in the world had hired me to help develop their future leaders. Twenty years ago it was a poster child for dot-com success. A lot had changed in the past two decades, and their new CEO wanted to get the old mojo back and one of his top initiatives was to create a culture of courage.

Did the CEO know how bad it was within the ranks? Probably not; without a transparent culture of courage it's tough to get to the truth. Without dedicated, empowered, and ambitious people the goals of the CEO would never come to fruition. In a stagnant fear-based organization most people want to tell the boss what they think he or she wants to hear. Employees were so afraid of saying what was in their hearts that they lied and lived each day working in fear. Shining a light of authenticity on the root cause wasn't going to be easy. Finding out more about the culture would require more interviews, so I pressed several employees about the dynamics of their product development meetings—the lifeblood of their innovation. I was curious as to what happened when they worked in these small agile teams (they sounded like the committees Shapiro had put together at the Blue Jays to empower the rank and file) and if they could trust each other to make great decisions. The answer shocked me:

"It comes down to the HIPPO."

"Hippo? Who is that?"

"It's the highest paid person's opinion."

Jaw drop moment.

In the 1960s there was a famous experiment in which an actor playing a doctor, complete with white lab coat, told volunteers to keep administering a shock to other volunteers (who were secretly also actors). Most of the volunteers kept giving the actors in the next room a shock despite hearing them scream and believing they were really suffering. This experiment created a new term called *authority bias*.

When there is no data to guide a choice, teams often default to an authority bias, even if there are subject matter experts available. In fact, it's this authority bias that enables lower-level managers to have more successful projects than senior managers on average. In a study from Rotterdam University, senior leaders created failing projects more often than their lower-ranking counterparts because the junior managers welcomed and received extensive critiques to their project plans. They got honest feedback from different perspectives. Bringing in other orientations and observations and being open to improvement created a more successful project. The same talented employees in these hierarchical organizations didn't have the courage or feel safe giving critical feedback to high-status leaders; that's because a HIPPO is sucking up any chance of empowerment and living off ego.

WHO LET THE HIPPO IN?

HIPPOs are most often found in fast-growth companies. As a company explodes in size, there isn't time for succession planning, so simply knowing one or two pieces of critical information makes certain employees indispensable, long after their skill set has been maximized. With only a single piece of key knowledge, they keep getting promoted and people are hired below them to fill out a team. Therefore, a new leader coming in needs to adopt Shapiro's strategy of compression, and that's where the CEO of this internet darling failed.

If your organization is making decisions based on the HIPPO, based on rank or seniority, or even worse just based on some loose consensus, you are missing the opportunity to leverage the collective intelligence and orientation of your team. Every member of the team has to embrace a culture of courage, and they have to believe they are empowered to do so. If they can't act when they are fearful and make a decision out of opportunity, they will make a decision out of fear. Just cultivating team members who believe in both themselves and the strategy or mechanisms in place will give many people the confidence to present a completely unfiltered opinion. Compression only works when there is relentless pressure from the top and bottom, like Vince Vaughn sitting on a whoopie pie.

Compression requires choices that are made based on opportunity—looking for that competitive advantage. The first step in making decisions based on opportunity is that you and your team members all feel safe being authentic and confident taking risks. You have to make sure that you have a radically transparent and nonjudgmental environment. Then you need to have dedication to a feedback loop where you can learn and grow and reevaluate after every action.

One way to help kill the HIPPO mentality and create a transparent and open workplace is to follow Shapiro's town hall meeting idea. Google does this every Thursday afternoon with their TGIF town hall meetings, too. Every Thursday, senior Google executives (usually with at least one C-Level person) host a meeting where everyone is updated on the latest news and updates; an extensive

Q&A session is held. Anyone can ask a question from anywhere in the world; employees vote on questions to be answered right on the spot and the management team makes it clear nothing is off limits. One of the Google TGIF town halls that was posted on YouTube even has Google's CEO Sundar Pichai saying, "there is a lot of fear inside Google . . . and we must trust and fall back on our values."[5] He was speaking about outside forces but was confident and open enough to acknowledge, like Shapiro, that fear is a part of life and something we must learn to face.

Google leadership made it clear all the employees leave their rank, title, and pay grade outside the meeting. Everyone is equal during the TGIF meetings and that's critical to creating a safe environment and building confidence. Everyone is equal in Shapiro's town hall as well; that's why a young ticket executive can tell billionaire owners what to do with their main revenue stream.

If you are at the same stage in your career as Eric Cowell was, who fortunately was with the Toronto Blue Jays when Shapiro took over, then you need to make sure you are in a winning workplace as well. You need to find a home that has a culture of courage so you can be the best version of you, and do work that is fun and meaningful. You spend a third or more of your life at work; make it count.

If you are thinking of joining a company, you should spend at least half a day onsite trying to get the real picture of the culture and leadership values. If you are a senior executive, you are more likely to have to implement Shapiro's compression strategy, and you'll want to make sure you've got support as well. Seeing any of these five signs is a dead giveaway of a fear-based culture:

1. Titles, Status, and Hierarchy Matter to Management

Corner offices, reserved parking spaces, and benefits that visibly separate classes of people are a classic indication that image is more important than performance. When this happens, you often have high-level executives with a sense of entitlement, who fear failure or rejection and are afraid to look stupid. They would rather appear smart than be challenged by smarter people to brainstorm and reach optimal outcomes. This is common in highly protected or regulated industries—because anywhere else these hyper-competitive cultures just wouldn't survive. Contrast that with Mark Shapiro's philosophy that everyone throughout the whole organization has to

put forth a championship effort, take responsibility, and lead excep-
tionally regardless of role. When I asked him who a person was, he
told me Eric; I asked his title and Mark said, "Patrick, I don't know
anyone's title, that doesn't mean anything to me."[6]

2. The Offices Are Quiet

I speak to thirty to forty companies and associations each year. I
always try to do a bit of early research before an event and talk with
employees to get the pulse of the organization. The tension and fear
is palpable in some companies where I walk the halls and people
are locked away in their offices, treating each other formally and not
engaging the way you would with friends and family. You can't be
two different people and always be your authentic self. If there is no
laughter, no people sharing and having fun, why would you want
to spend a third of your life there? If everyone is saying I can't wait
until Friday, it's because the environment is toxic.

3. People Spend Days Preparing for Meetings

I've used this as a barometer for years. I've invested in more than
thirty start-ups and sometimes when I perform due diligence I'll
ask about board meetings and how a company prepares for them. If
people are afraid to look foolish, or scared to act curious, I want no
part of them. If someone spends precious days to create the perfect
presentation, the perfect argument, rather than engage the collective intelligence of what should be the most impactful group (the
board) to solve problems, they are living in fear. I've seen panic in
many board meetings where the CEO is so afraid to be challenged
or to appear weak, that he or she comes in and restates everything
in the board book. This is a classic waste of everyone's time, rather
than asking the board to help him or her with big strategic decisions.

4. People Say "That's the Way We've Always Done It" and "Those Are the Rules"

People are hiding behind tradition and history and are terrified of
change and innovation. Often this is driven by fear of loss. I once
fired a sysadmin at ServerVault for giving me that answer, twice. The
first time, I told him that that thinking doesn't lead to breakthrough,

innovation, or improvement. The second time, I told him, "You're fired." Mid-level execs in these cultures would rather keep a low profile and not rock the boat, sticking to the status quo, than take a risk and do something extraordinary. It's career cowardice. This is especially prevalent after acquisitions; often the acquirer doesn't want to rock the boat, and it ends up creating two opposing factions in what should be a single organization. A classic example is the United Airlines–Continental merger. It took place in 2010, yet nine years later flight attendants are still calling themselves "Continental crew based out of . . ." over the PA. An organization that is growth focused will have employees who wake up every day trying to make improvement, trying to do things better than they were done yesterday, and in that challenge comes fulfillment.

5. No High-Fives and Hell Yeahs!

Celebrating wins makes everyone feel better. Victories, no matter how small, are great ways to bring joy and camaraderie into the office. A sense of community and shared mission drives a culture that is open, accessible, and merit based. If it's a toxic, fear-based culture, people won't feel safe joking about things or calling out a solution for fear of looking stupid or silly. They'll be afraid to look for a high-five or give a big hug.

BONUS—Everyone Knows What a HIPPO Is

How are decisions made when there is a lack of analytical data or lack of credible experts? In fear-based cultures teams will default to the Highest Paid Person's Opinion (HIPPO). According to an Erasmus University study in 2016,[7] this creates more failed projects because lower-level employees fear questioning and pushing high-level managers to make their proposal better. Look for cultures that give weight to the expert on the subject and the data supporting the choice.

Joining or creating a culture that takes the long view, has a growth mindset, and employees who come in every day with a championship attitude will eventually pay off. And as Mark Shapiro puts it, "We'll have a really fun place to work, we'll enjoy our work, we'll develop as people and executives and always be challenging ourselves to get better."[8]

Conclusion:
The Value of Courage

Courage is the first of human qualities because it guarantees all the others.

—Winston Churchill

Everyone's journey with fear begins at birth. Life is a constant battle to bring expectations and reality into balance and avoid surprise. Humans who choose to create that balance are called courageous or fearless. My journey to courageousness didn't start until I checked into Johns Hopkins Oncology Center in 2004. My journey to courage wasn't really by choice. Circumstances forced me to make a choice. At the time I thought my life was going to end. I thought I had missed my one chance. As you now know, that day created a whole new beginning. I am one of the luckiest men in the world to have been given a second chance. I'm making the most of it every day and I discovered that courage was my super-power.

After I left Hopkins with an IV in my arm, a mask on my face, and orders to keep any strangers out of our house for two months while my immune system recovered, I yearned for insight and knowledge about how other people, the finite few hundred people in the world who had the same disease, dealt with the close proximity of death. What should I do knowing the grim reaper is pressing a razor-edged scythe just sharply enough against my Adam's apple to draw a drop of blood? So close to being at the edge of reality's end. Dr. Tom Loughran[1] shared with me the story of the first patient he diagnosed with the disease who was, at the time, eighty-six years old; that gave me great hope and inspiration. Loughran also gave me the online chat room for patients like me, or so I thought.

I logged on eagerly to the chat room when I got home, like a newly incarcerated convict looking for a safe haven before the first shower. What I found was what inspired me to the most amazing life imaginable; what I read was the catalyst for committing to living big the rest of my life.

When I made the choice to live big, to choose courage, to make my life an amazing experience vastly different from the first thirty-plus years of my existence, my education about life hit warp speed. I learned much new information about myself and the world every day. I realized what life could be like. It was nothing like what I had thought, or even what my parents taught me.

Some days I was literally struck dumb with awe. I wasn't doing anything crazy or super-daring; I was doing things I had done time and again. I rode my horse across our farm and it was like being in a foreign land. I held my daughter through the night, sitting up just looking at her sleep and it was like a riveting movie to me. Expressing what those first few flight lessons were like goes beyond my literary capacity. I had no idea that much potential excitement and passion had been hidden from me, untapped because of my prior beliefs or what other people had convinced me of.

In that moment of reverie and excitement, the childlike joy of discovery seemed (and has stayed) limitless. That's when I wanted to share the magic of life with the rest of the world. My heart sank (and still sinks) when I saw people letting the grip of fear ruin their lives—whether that meant not visiting friends and relatives because they were afraid to fly, treating another human being like a terrorist because they looked different, or letting the election of an official cast a cloud over their day-to-day life and change how they acted with people they loved.

Searching for greatness reveals the courage of great leaders in every walk of life. I was fortunate to spend five years just searching out the brightest, most courageous minds. All over the world I saw people regulating their primal fear response, literally controlling the messages their nervous system sends so they could create the ultimate life that they desired. I witnessed new and emerging science that proved "Transformational leaders not only regulated their own nervous systems better than most; they also regulated other people's"[2] to create cultures of courage. I saw people questioning rules and traditions that no longer served them.

Yet, seeing suffering is what drove me to embody the change I wanted to see in the world. Another single choice, to be the change, infected me with a bug of curiosity. Once bitten, I flew all over the world to talk to neuroscientists and psychologists, see the research firsthand, and look inside our minds. I wanted to share the excitement, the fun, the magic of life with you. I want to help you to eliminate your suffering and find courage.

So what was it that I saw on the chat room that made me get out and learn to live really big? What inspired me to move to a foreign country, explore adventure races, rock climb the sheerest faces, set crazy world firsts, invest in risky companies, or fly planes upside-down?

I saw people who were satisfied with survival.

I saw people suffering because the thought of the scythe against their neck froze them in a state of permanent dread. I logged on to that site Loughran suggested and saw threads and threads of people who couldn't wait for the next doctor's visit, who had adoring nicknames for the toxic drugs they had to take. Patients—not at all like me—who were living to survive. Fuck that. I had another chance to live the life of my dreams I was going to thrive like that eighty-six-year-old guy who first gave me hope.

Everyone has fears. It's what we do with those fears that matters. Since fears are subjective, we don't know if you feel more fear than I feel, but we're getting closer to having technology to measure fear and courage. The more we learn about the human brain, the more we can change how we use that organ to make us happy, fulfilled, and able to reach our full potential. We all have unlimited potential but you cannot simultaneously reach your potential and be a coward. You must choose to be brave. You must take a risk.

If you made it through *Fear Is Fuel*, I sincerely hope your life will change for the better. Simply creating awareness of what happens and why is the first step to understanding fear. The next giant leap is making the commitment, choosing out of your own volition, to be courageous. (I hope you thought of one of the bravest men to walk on the face of the earth and the moon, Neil Armstrong, with that paraphrase.)

Crossing that line from the old you to the new you is scary. If you are committed to using fear as fuel, it will be both a challenging and wondrous first few months. My sincere hope is that you start to laugh at the number of times you catch yourself defaulting back to fear-based choices, or feeling like a victim, but you are self-aware enough to catch yourself in the act. I hope you see the amazement when you realize someone you thought was a jerk, or annoying, suddenly is revealed for what they are—scared. Or when your own fear of scarcity is replaced by wondering how to avoid getting fired, a promotion falling through or an investment failing may be the best thing that ever happened to you. I hope you build enough trust in the universe being a very friendly place so you begin to expect luck, happiness, and even miracles. I hope you begin to see obstacles as challenges to learn from and make your life better.

If your life transforms the way mine has changed over the past fifteen years, you'll find your courage will have as much, if not more, impact on the ones who love you and count on you, as it has on you. Continue your journey; be brave, be courageous, and welcome fear every day. Never shy away from it, even when it's difficult. Push out your Fear Frontier little by little. Continue to take risks even after you've exceeded your goals. You can find more fear and learn from it. Don't do it just for yourself; be brave for everyone who loves you, and who depends on you. Use fear as fuel and inspire all the people you don't even know who someday may hear your story and change their lives, too.

Acknowledgments

The research, writing, and creation of what peaked at more than 120,000 words of prose and was carved down to the book you now hold in your hands was only possible with copious help from all over the world. My family was incredibly patient as I spent hours upon hours planted on the couch listening to interviews repeatedly to get the essence of some esoteric neuroscience theory or research and then trying over and over to translate it to what I hope is easily understandable language. My Young President's Organization forum of friends, who convinced me to search inside myself for my true genius and encouraged me to pursue what I love and feel passionate about are at the top of my list of people to thank as well. Al, Ann, Gerry, Jim, Mark, Mark, Nat, and Rosa were a great source of motivation and each one provided invaluable feedback and inspiration. Nat's creativeness inspired the name Fear Frontier for the concept I was trying to convey, Al's questioning my presentation and logic was especially helpful in boiling my concepts down to their essence, and Jim and Rosa did a great job of making sure I kept it fun and readable. My wise counselor Diana challenged me constantly and laid the groundwork almost a decade ago for us to find our genius.

Big thanks to everyone who contributed to the book with their time, wisdom, and energy. Shout out to the Olympic Training Center docs like Shane Murphy, mentalists and supporters like Warren Negri, Bill McGillicuddy, Bob Bullock, and Will Maney, who taught me how to change my own body and mind and supported me when I needed it most. I'm sad that Coach Allen Rosenberg didn't get to see the final copy; I think he'd be proud. Thanks as well to father Eddie Hathaway and Father Joe Clarke, who kept me in touch with God as well, without getting caught up in dogma.

I wrote one of my best chapters, and refined several more, while sequestered in a Jack Nicholson, *Shining*-like state at the Lambert's Cover Inn on Martha's Vineyard during the winter of 2018–2019, when the hotel was closed and deserted for renovation. Thanks to everyone there for the great support.

Thanks to Daniel Pink for clarifying his curiosity about courage.

There were so many helpful and engaging neuroscientists, neurobiologists, and psychologists I spoke with that it would be tough to name them all, but the ones I spent the most time with, or was particularly influenced by, include:

Professor Sian Belliott; Anna Beyeler, PhD; Alia Crum, PhD; Professor Karl Friston, MD; Dan Gilbert, PhD; Professor Werner Helsen; Joseph LeDoux; Abigail Marsh, PhD; Mo Milad; Earl K. Miller, PhD; Shane O'Mara, PhD; Scott Orr, PhD; Elizabeth Phelps, PhD; Professor Karl Pillemer, PhD; Maxwell Ramstead, PhD; John J. Ratey, MD; Thomas Ryan, PhD; Kay Tye, PhD, Bessel Van Der Kolk, MD; and Linda Van de Voogd, PhD.

Now, if you've read this far into the details, I feel that I should let you in on a little secret. Several times in the book I purposely use the phrase "face everything and accept responsibility." If you notice, the acronym that forms is FEAR, although I never call that out in the text.

Notes

INTRODUCTION

1. George W. Melville, "The Engineer and the Problem of Aerial Navigation," *North American Review*, December 1901, 820–83.
2. David McCullough, *The Wright Brothers* (New York: Simon & Schuster, 2015), 18.
3. McCullough, *Wright Brothers*, 116.
4. McCullough, *Wright Brothers*, 134.
5. McCullough, *Wright Brothers*, 66.
6. Octave Chanute to Wilbur Wright, September 5, 1901, in *The Papers of Wilbur and Orville Wright*, vol. 1, ed. Marvin McFarland (New York: McGraw-Hill, 1953), 93; McCullough, *Wright Brothers*, 277.
7. "Flying Machine Fiasco," *New York Times*, October 8, 1903, 1.
8. Leland D. Case, "Orville Wright: First Man to Fly," *Rotarian*, April 1948, 100.

CHAPTER 1. FEAR FLUENCY

1. Author's interview with Dr. Mo Milad, Harvard University/Massachusetts General Hospital/Charlestown Navy Yard facility, June 30, 2017.
2. Borwin Bandelow and Sophie Michaelis, "Epidemiology of Anxiety Disorders in the 21st Century," *Dialogues in Clinical Neuroscience* 17, no. 3 (2015): 327–35.
3. Author's interview with Dr. Scott Orr, February 7, 2017, Massachusetts General Hospital, Charlestown, MA.

CHAPTER 2. FORGET WHAT YOU THINK

1. Will Ferrell, "The 134th Commencement Speech," University of Southern California–Los Angeles, May 12, 2017.

2. WENN, "Ferrell's Stage Fright," IMDB, July 21, 2008, https://www.imdb.com/news/ni0264624.

3. History.com Editors, "Theodore Roosevelt's Wife and Mother Die," A&E Network, April 7, 2019, https://www.history.com/this-day-in-history/theodore-roosevelts-wife-and-mother-die.

4. Theodore Roosevelt, "Citizenship in a Republic," speech, Sorbonne University, Paris, April 23, 1910.

5. Author's personal conversation, September 2015, Fontainebleau Hotel, Miami, FL.

6. Rebecca Traister, "The Truth about Carly," *Salon*, October 19, 2006.

7. Frank Bruni, "Carly Fiorina Means Business," *New York Times Magazine*, June 2, 2010.

CHAPTER 3. FEAR TELLS YOU ABOUT YOU

1. Joe Navarro, *Phil Hellmuth Presents Read 'Em and Reap* (New York: HarperCollins, 2006), loc. 1833.

2. Christof Koch, "Pupil Dilation Marks Decision Making," *Caltech Matters Magazine*, February 12, 2008.

CHAPTER 4. THE ROOT OF ALL FEARS

1. Author's telephone interview with Paul Badcock, March 20, 2019.

2. Elise Payzan-LeNestour, Simon Dunne, Peter Bossaerts, and John P. O'Doherty, "The Neural Representation of Unexpected Uncertainty During Value-Based Decision Making," *Neuron* 79, no. 1 (2013): 191–201.

3. Author's interview with Karl Friston, February 17, 2019.

CHAPTER 5. THE FACES OF FEAR

1. Calvin Coffey and Michael Stains were awarded a silver medal for the pair with coxswain at the 1976 Olympics, losing to an East German crew who later admitted to doping during their training, leaving Coffey and Stains with the knowledge that they were the true Olympic champions.

2. Author comment: I've known Commander Laurie Coffey and her family for more than twenty years. When the idea for this book began to take root, I knew right away that she (and her parents' influences) would

be a fascinating profile. I've had countless interviews and discussions with her and additionally offered her the first draft of this chapter to correct and comment on.

3. In case you were wondering about the other tests I took over the years: I'm an ENTP on Myers Briggs and an 8-7-3 Enneagram type, which are a couple of systems that resemble my analysis here. Taking the time to learn about the different systems is fun and beneficial in building confidence and curiosity, and as a strategy for my own personal growth.

CHAPTER 6. SCARE YOURSELF

1. Sculling is using two oars, and can be done with one, two, or four people. Sweep rowing, or crew, is done with one oar per person and is done in two-, four-, or eight-person boats, sometimes with a coxswain steering and not rowing, sometimes just the rowers. The eight-person boat always has a coxswain.

CHAPTER 7. THE BASE METHOD

1. Tara L. Kraft, "The Role of Positive Facial Feedback in the Stress Response," *KU Scholar Works*, April 1, 2011.

2. Margarita Tartakovsky, "Using EMDR Therapy to Heal Your Past," *Psych Central*, October 8, 2018.

3. Luca Ostacoli et al., "Comparison of Eye Movement Desensitization Reprocessing and Cognitive Behavioral Therapy as Adjunctive Treatments for Recurrent Depression," *Frontiers in Psychology* 13 (2018): 74.

4. Judy L. Van Raalte, "Self-Talk Interventions for Athletes: A Theoretical Grounded Approach," *Journal of Sports Psychology in Action* 8, no. 3 (2017): 141–51.

5. U. Herwig et al., "Training Emotion Regulation Through Real-Time fMRI Neurofeedback of Amygdala Activity," *NeuroImage* 184 (2019): 687–96, https://www.sciencedirect.com/science/article/pii/S1053811918319402.

6. R. Shibata, "Adiponectin and Cardiovascular Disease," *Circulation Journal* 73, no. 4 (2009): 608–14.

7. J. A. Mattison et al., "Caloric Restriction Improves Health and Survival of Rhesus Monkeys," *Nature Communications* 8 (2017): 14063.

CHAPTER 8. THE COURAGE CONUNDRUM

1. Christopher J. Keller, "Courage, Psychological Well-Being, and Somatic Symptoms" (PhD diss., Seattle Pacific University, 2016).

2. Abdonas Tamosiunas, Laura Sapranaviciute-Zabazlajeva, Dalia Luksiene, Dalia Virviciute, and Anne Peasey, "Psychological Well-Being and Mortality: Longevity Findings from Lithuanian Middle-Age and Older Adults Study," *Social Psychiatry and Psychiatric Epidemiology* (January 2019).

3. Author's interview, Georgetown Campus, July 12, 2018.

4. Some people have suggested that babies are born fearless. This is only true of two sides of the Terror Triangle, the physical and emotional fears. The instinctual fears are there at birth and wired into our DNA.

5. An algorithm is just a set of steps our brain (or a computer) follows to solve a problem. In this case the algorithm is deciding whether to act courageously or not.

6. Abigail A. Marsh, Sarah A. Stoycos, Kristin M. Brethel-Haurwitz, Paul Robinson, John W. VanMeter, and Elise M. Cardinale, "Neural and Cognitive Characteristics of Extraordinary Altruists," *Proceedings of the National Academy of Sciences of the United States of America* 111, no. 42 (2014): 15036–41.

7. Michael S. Gaffrey et al., "Subgenual Cingulate Connectivity in Children with a History of Preschool-Depression," *Neuroreport* 21, no. 18 (December 29, 2010): 1182–88.

8. Uri Nili, Hagar Goldberg, Abraham Weizman, and Yadin Dudai, "Fear Thou Not: Activity of Frontal and Temporal Circuits in Moments of Real-Life Courage," *Neuron* 66, no. 6 (2010): 949–62.

9. Angela Duckworth, *Grit: The Power of Passion and Perseverance* (New York: Scribner, 2016).

10. Beryl Markham, *West with the Night: A Memoir* (New York: Open Road, 2012).

CHAPTER 9. SHARE TOGETHER OR FEAR APART

1. Joseph Addison, *Cato: A Tragedy and Selected Essays*, Act V, Scene IV, Line 55, https://oll.libertyfund.org/titles/1229#Addison_0714_2836.

2. Author's interview at Picower Institute, MIT, March 6, 2019.

3. Bradley Peterson et al., "Less is More: Exposure to Stimuli for Overcoming Phobia," *Science Daily*, February 6, 2017.

4. Miller interview, March 6, 2019.

5. Plato, *Phaedo*, 58e, https://chs.harvard.edu/CHS/article/display/5305.

6. Mona Simpson, "A Sister's Eulogy for Steve Jobs," *New York Times*, October 30, 2011, https://www.nytimes.com/2011/10/30/opinion/mona-simpsons-eulogy-for-steve-jobs.html.

CHAPTER 10. THE BEST DECISION YOU'LL NEVER MAKE

1. Abdonas Tamosiunas, Laura Sapranaviciute-Zabazlajeva, Dalia Luksiene, Dalia Virviciute, and Anne Peasey, "Psychological Well-Being and Mortality: Longevity Findings from Lithuanian Middle-Age and Older Adults Study," *Social Psychiatry and Psychiatric Epidemiology* (January 2019).
2. Yulia Akbergenova, Karen L. Cunningham, Yao V. Zhang, Shirley Weiss, and J. Troy Littleton, "Characterization of Developmental and Molecular Factors Underlying Release Heterogeneity at *Drosophila* Synapses," *eLife Journal* (July 10, 2018): e38268.
3. Stacey Leasca, "A Guy Viciously Trolled Sarah Silverman on Twitter—and Then She Turned His Life Around," *Men's Health*, January 2, 2018.
4. @SarahKSilverman, Twitter feed, December 29, 2017.
5. Leasca, "Guy Viciously Trolled Sarah Silverman."
6. Maeve Duggan, "Online Harassment," Pew Research Center, October 22, 2014, http://www.pewinternet.org/2014/10/22/online-harassment/.
7. Ray Dalio, "How to Build a Company Where the Best Ideas Win," TED video, 16:34, April 2018, https://www.ted.com/speakers/ray_dalio.
8. Dalio, "How to Build a Company."
9. Anna J. Finley, Adrienne L. Crowell, and Brandon J. Schmeichel, "Self-Affirmation Enhances Processing of Negative Stimuli among Threat-Prone Individuals," *Social Cognitive Affective Neuroscience* 13, no. 6 (2018): 569–77.

CHAPTER 11. BLUEPRINT FOR BRAVERY

1. Beryl Markham, *West with the Night: A Memoir* (New York: Open Road, 2012), loc. 2111, Kindle.
2. Markham, *West with the Night*, loc. 2371.
3. Markham, *West with the Night*, loc. 2358.
4. Markham, *West with the Night*, loc. 1984.
5. Markham, *West with the Night*, loc. 2424.
6. Brynne C. DiMenichi, Karolina M. Lempert, Christina Bejjani, and Elizabeth Tricomi, "Writing About Past Failures Attenuates Cortisol Responses and Sustained Attention Deficits Following Psychosocial Stress," *Frontiers of Behavioral Neuroscience* 12 (March 23, 2018): 45.
7. Matthew Lieberman, *UCLA Newsroom*, March 18, 2010.

CHAPTER 12. CREATING A
CULTURE OF COURAGE AT WORK

1. Author's personal conversation with Harlan Crow, Dallas, TX, June 1997.

2. James Collins, *Good to Great: Why Some Companies Make the Leap . . . And Others Don't* (New York: HarperBusiness, 2011).

CHAPTER 13. THE BIG SQUEEZE

1. Michael Lewis, *Moneyball: The Art of Winning an Unfair Game* (New York: Norton, 2003).

2. Author's interview with Mark Shapiro, Dunedin, FL, February 2018.

3. Author's interview with Mark Shapiro, March 23, 2018.

4. Shapiro interview, March 23, 2018.

5. Al Bokhari, "Leaked Video: Google Leadership Dismayed Reaction to Trump Election," Breitbart.com, September 12, 2018, https://www.breitbart.com/tech/2018/09/12/leaked-video-google-leaderships-dismayed-reaction-to-trump-election/.

6. Shapiro interview, March 23, 2018.

7. Balazs Szatmari, "We Are (all) the Champions: The Effect of Status in the Implementation of Innovations," ERIM Ph.D. Series: Research in Management, Erasmus University, Rotterdam, 2016, http://hdl.handle.net/1765/94633.

8. Shapiro interview, March 23, 2018.

CONCLUSION. THE VALUE OF COURAGE

1. Loughran, who is a teaching doc at UVA now, was the man who, along with Dr. McDevitt, were part of the team that saved my life.

2. Steven Kotler and Jamie Wheal, *Stealing Fire: How Silicon Valley, the Navy SEALs, and Maverick Scientists Are Revolutionizing the Way We Live and Work* (New York: Dey Street Books, 2017), 105, Kindle.

Index

About the Author

Patrick J. Sweeney II has been dubbed the "Fear Guru" for his work with more than five hundred global CEOs, actors, professional athletes, Navy SEALs, and corporations. He inspires tens of thousands of people each year through keynote speeches and seminars teaching tools to live the biggest, most fulfilling life possible. In addition to founding the Fear Institute for executive seminars and research, he also lectures at leading universities from Harvard Business School to the University of Virginia. He was the founder and CEO of four technology companies, holds seven patents, produced award-winning adventure documentary films, and is an angel investor in more than thirty start-ups. Before earning his MBA from the Darden School at the University of Virginia, he placed second in the Olympic Trials in rowing the single scull, and is the only person to ever summit and then ride down from Mt. Elbrus, Mt. Kilimanjaro, and Mt. Everest Base Camp by bicycle. In 2018 he won the Race Across America in a four-person team. He was the chair of the Young Presidents Organization Sports & Entertainment Network and has been a member for more than ten years. Sweeney has appeared on CNBC, CNN, *Good Morning America*, Fox News, and the *Today Show*. He sits on the Business School Advisory board of Trinity College Dublin. He is a licensed commercial pilot and competes in competitive aerobatics. Sweeney was graduated from the University of New Hampshire. He lives in Boston, Massachusetts, and Chamonix, France, with his wife, three children, and two dogs.